SAFEGUARDING CHILDREN AND YOUNG PEOPLE

This is a book for anyone who wants to work with children or who needs to improve their knowledge of current policy and practice aimed at safeguarding children and young people. In this valuable addition to the Social Work Skills Series, Corinne May-Chahal and Stella Coleman bring together their considerable teaching and practice experience to provide a reliable and practical guide to child protection work.

Safeguarding Children and Young People covers the range of practice issues raised by child maltreatment that will confront frontline workers in child care and related fields. These include:

- maltreatment assessment and risk management
- achieving inclusive anti-discriminatory practice
- working therapeutically with children
- working together with parents
- legal requirements and going to court.

Sources of support are highlighted and practical suggestions are made throughout the book for practitioner survival and development.

This core text takes an evidence-based approach to child protection and makes use of contemporary research policy and case studies. It is also a practical aid to learning, providing readers with extensive exercises to evaluate their progress.

Corinne May-Chahal is Professor of Applied Social Science at Lancaster University and **Stella Coleman** is Senior Lecturer in Social Work at the University of Central Lancashire.

the social work skills series

published in association with *Community Care*

series editor: Terry Philpot

the social work skills series

- builds practice skills step by step

- places practice in its policy context

- relates practice to relevant research

- provides a secure base for professional development

This new, skills-based series has been developed by Routledge and *Community Care* working together in partnership to meet the changing needs of today's students and practitioners in the broad field of social care. Written by experienced practitioners and teachers with a commitment to passing on their knowledge to the next generation, each text in the series features: *learning objectives; case examples; activities to test knowledge and understanding; summaries of key learning points; key references; suggestions for further reading.*

Also available in the series:

Managing Aggression
Ray Braithwaite
Consultant and trainer in managing aggression at work. Lead trainer and speaker in the 'No Fear' campaign.

Commissioning and Purchasing
Terry Bamford
Former Chair of the British Association of Social Workers and Executive Director of Housing and Social Services, Royal Borough of Kensington and Chelsea.

Tackling Social Exclusion
John Pierson
Senior Lecturer at the Institute of Social Work and Applied Social Studies at the University of Staffordshire.

SAFEGUARDING CHILDREN AND YOUNG PEOPLE

Corinne May-Chahal and Stella Coleman

Routledge
Taylor & Francis Group

LONDON AND NEW YORK

communitycare

First published 2003 by Routledge
2 Park Square, Milton Park, Abingdon, Oxon OX14 4RN

Simultaneously published in the USA and Canada
by Routledge
270 Madison Ave, New York, NY 10016

Transferred to Digital Printing 2008

Routledge is an imprint of the Taylor & Francis Group, an informa business

© 2003 Corinne May-Chahal and Stella Coleman

Designed and typeset in Sabon and Futura
by Keystroke, Jacaranda Lodge, Wolverhampton
Printed and bound in Great Britain by
TJI Digital, Padstow, Cornwall

British Library Cataloguing in Publication Data
A catalogue record for this book is available from the British Library

Library of Congress Cataloging in Publication Data
A catalog record for this book has been requested

ISBN 10: 0-415-27547-4 (hbk)
ISBN 10: 0-415-27548-2 (pbk)
ISBN 13: 978-0-415-27547-7 (hbk)
ISBN 13: 978-0-415-27548-4 (pbk)

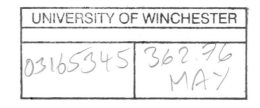

CONTENTS

FIGURES

TABLES

GUIDANCE

DEVELOPMENT ACTIVITIES

SNAPSHOTS

ABOUT THE AUTHORS

Corinne May-Chahal (previously Wattam)
Professor of Applied Social Science
BA Hons (Sociology), DASS, CQSW, PhD

Following seven years in practice as a social worker and three years as a research practitioner, Corinne became NSPCC Research Fellow at Lancaster University, continuing research for policy development in relation to child care and protection. Early work concerned the nature of evidence in cases of offences against children and membership of the Home Office Steering Group that drafted the Memorandum of Good Practice for Interviewing Children in Criminal Proceedings. Subsequently, she became Co-ordinator of the Concerted Action on the Prevention of Child Abuse in Europe (CAPCAE). Corinne joined the University of Central Lancashire in 1998 as Professor of Child Care. Since then she has managed or participated in further EU-based projects including the Control and Use of Personal Information on Child Sex Offenders (CUPICSO), Social Inclusion and Family Support (SIFS) and PANDORA, a comparative project on the use of confidentiality in relation to reporting child maltreatment. As a result of this work Corinne was invited to be a temporary task adviser to WHO European and World consultations on child abuse. She has published widely on the subject of child protection.

Stella Coleman

Stella Coleman has worked with children and their families for thirty years in a range of contexts and settings. She is currently a senior lecturer in social work at the University of Central Lancashire, a PQ assessor and an Independent Family Group Conference Co-ordinator. Previous roles include community development; women's refuge worker, senior social worker in a child protection unit and a children and families fieldwork team manager. She has a long-standing commitment to effective inter-disciplinary working and has developed and delivered joint training to social workers, police, teachers and nurses.

ACKNOWLEDGEMENTS

With grateful thanks for the help of service users and colleagues in practice and teaching and for enduring family support.

PREFACE
A note on child maltreatment terminology

We have attempted not to use the terms 'child abuse' or 'risk of child abuse' in this book and have substituted the terms 'child maltreatment', 'significant harm' and 'likelihood of significant harm' wherever possible. This is for three reasons that we consider are worth noting. The first is owing to European colleagues who pointed out that the term 'child abuse' is a relative newcomer to European languages. Most European countries have their own terms which translate more closely to 'maltreatment'. Abuse is generally reserved for sexual abuse alone. It is therefore confusing to use the term 'abuse' in anything other than an English-speaking context. The second related point is that (as some of our European colleagues suggest) 'child abuse' suggests there is a proper use of children. This notion of use is associated with concepts of ownership and possession – some of the very concepts that have been intrinsic to the continued perpetration of child harm and injury. A third issue concerns debates in the English-speaking world about the value and meaning of the term 'child abuse' at a more political level. In the English-speaking world child abuse has come to incorporate a range of different harms and injuries, the threat of harm, and also behaviours that may result (for some children) in no harm at all. We consider that it is important, particularly in an evidence-based practice environment, to be clear about the terms we refer to and their meaning. Equally, we aim to direct practitioners to respond to harm rather than inflate fears of risk of abuse that have done so much in the past to unbalance the safeguarding system (though possibly not in the ways that were identified through Messages from Research (Department of Health 1995) – for further clarification see Wattam 1996a and 1996b). This substitution has sometimes been difficult because others, whose work we are citing, have used the term and also because old habits die hard.

REFERENCES

Department of Health (1995) *Child Protection: Messages from research* London: The Stationery Office

Wattam C. (1996a) Can filtering processes be rationalised? In N Parton, *Child Protection and Family Support: Tensions, contradictions and possibilities* London: Routledge

Wattam C. (1996b) The social construction of child abuse for practical policy purposes – A review of Child Protection: Messages from Research *Child and Family Law Quarterly* 8, 3: 189–200

CHAPTER 1

UNDERSTANDING CHILD MALTREATMENT

LEARNING OBJECTIVES

By the end of this chapter you will understand:

- The importance of the 'rediscovery' of child abuse

- That notions of child maltreatment and child protection are historically and culturally specific and change over time, within and across cultures

- That opinions as to what causes child maltreatment depend on how child abuse is defined and constructed

- Dominant definitions and theories of maltreatment

- Cross-cultural issues in relation to defining maltreatment

- The rights of children in relation to significant harm.

Children, like adults, are victims of violence in all countries of the world and it has always been so. This violence can take many forms: physical, sexual, emotional or psychological. It can be perpetrated by a range of different people, individually and collectively, and can result in a wide spectrum of initial and long-term harms and injuries. Yet not all violence to children is thought of as child maltreatment. For example, definitions generally exclude violence outside the family by peers (bullying and gang or youth violence), war and organised violence. Children are also dependent on adults to have their needs met. This varies according to age and ability, but all infants begin life as dependants. Fundamental needs of shelter, warmth, clothing, food, access to health care and social relationships are the right of all children (UN CRC 1989) yet not all of these are available to all children. Even when they are not, this is not always thought of as neglect or maltreatment. Excluded from maltreatment definitions are children who die of starvation because of their region or country's circumstances, such as famine or war; children who die of AIDS who have been denied access to health care; and children who are homeless and live on the streets.

From these fundamental starting points it becomes evident that child maltreatment is very difficult to define. Though most can agree that it happens and that it is a bad thing, there is debate across the world about what are acceptable and unacceptable treatments of children, who is responsible, what is a crime against children, what should be a crime and what is morally unacceptable. In all countries there are debates about what should correctly be identified as maltreatment.

Childhood itself is socially defined (James and Prout 1997) and the definition of what a child is varies across the world. For example, the age of consent to sexual relationships is generally seen as an indicator of ability to make adult decisions. Yet across European countries this ranges from 12 to 17. In Malta and the Netherlands the age of consent is 12. In Spain it is 13; in Croatia, Hungary, Austria, Portugal, Germany and Iceland it is 14; in Poland and France it is 15; in Finland, the UK, Cyprus, Norway, Czech Republic, Switzerland and Uzbekistan it is 16; and in Ireland it is 17.

THE REDISCOVERY OF CHILD 'ABUSE'

Actions that would now be included under the definition of child maltreatment, such as leaving babies to die, throwing them in rivers to see if they survive and beating children until they were seriously injured, have all been acceptable at some point in the history of civilisation (De Mause 1976). However, our understanding that certain harmful practices towards children constitute abuse depends on more recent history.

It is broadly accepted by large numbers of health and welfare professionals that the Western world's rediscovery of child abuse is attributed to Kempe et al. (1962). These two paediatricians identified, with the help of paediatric radiologists (Caffey 1946), a new syndrome, known as 'battered baby syndrome', which later broadened out to include child physical, sexual and emotional abuse and neglect. From a non-American perspective, there is some debate as to the authenticity of claims to the discovery, or even rediscovery of child abuse by the Kempes. For example, Wolf (1997) suggests that interest in child abuse was certainly a characteristic of National Socialism and Nazi Germany. As a consequence it contributed to a deep scepticism of the right of the state to intrude into family life in Germany even today. Child-saving movements emerged across Europe in the late 1800s leading to the establishment of several societies for the prevention of cruelty to children, including the National Society for the Prevention of Cruelty to Children in England in 1887 (Ferguson 1990). However, whether it was recognised in the same way or not, what is certainly the case is that the rediscovery of child 'abuse' brought renewed attention, new laws and an investment by governments and children's organisations in various countries designed to better protect children.

DEFINING CHILD MALTREATMENT IN THE TWENTY-FIRST CENTURY

Definitions of what is harmful to children are subject to cultural variation and personal value judgements (Giovannoni and Becerra 1979, Korbin 1997). All practitioners working with children must be aware of their own values and opinions and must ensure that these are compatible with child-care work. It is therefore important to know how you personally define child maltreatment. Child-care practitioners can find they are confronted with a lot of 'grey areas' where they must decide whether or not something is, or isn't, child maltreatment. Though there are procedures and official definitions (see below and Chapter 2), these must be put into practice by individuals. As part of the UK's first national prevalence study on child maltreatment, a randomly selected sample of 18–24 year olds (N = 2,869) were asked what they considered to be acceptable and unacceptable ways of treating children. Because definitions of maltreatment change over time and across cultures (Department of Health 1995), one aim of this study was to find out what the general public considered to be child maltreatment in the United Kingdom at the beginning of the twenty-first century. Their responses are given in Development Activity 1.1. As a beginning activity to find out where you stand on the definition of child maltreatment you might consider what your response would be.

Views about what are acceptable and unacceptable child-rearing practices will be influenced by personal experience. If physical punishment is seen as an important part of being a good parent within a given cultural group, then it may be considered abusive not to discipline children in this way. We also know from research that people who have received physical punishment, sometimes involving severe physical violence, are less likely to view this as wrong or abusive (Kelder *et al.* 1991; Bower and Knutson 1996). It may be helpful to think about the influence of your own experiences of childrearing when you work on Development Activity 1.1.

Globally, definitions of child maltreatment reflect levels of awareness, beginning with physical abuse and neglect and expanding to incorporate emotional abuse, sexual abuse and commercial exploitation. Most definitions include an identifiable harm and responsibility for care in their criteria (Gough 1996). For example, an early definition by the Council of Europe defined children who were maltreated as:

> Those subjected to physical injury and those who are victims of neglect, deprivation of affection or mental cruelty likely to jeopardise their physical, intellectual and emotional development, where the abuse is caused by acts or omissions on the part of persons responsible for the child's care or others having temporary or permanent control over him [sic].
>
> (Council of Europe, Recommendation No R (79) 17)

This definition refers primarily to physical abuse and neglect. As awareness has grown of sexual abuse and commercial exploitation, including child prostitution and child labour, these have been given their own definitions. A widely accepted definition of child sexual abuse was that offered by Schecter and Roberge (1976):

> The involvement of dependent, developmentally immature children and adolescents in sexually abusive activities they do not fully comprehend, to which they are unable to give informed consent or which violate social taboos of family roles.

DEVELOPMENT ACTIVITY 1.1: UNACCEPTABLE WAYS OF TREATING CHILDREN

Ways of treating children	NSPCC Childrearing Study (Cawson *et al.* 2000)	Your opinion	Your experience
Warning about fear figures (e.g. 'bogey man')	41% Occasionally justified 44% Never justified		
Slapping with an open hand	52% Occasionally justified 37% Never justified		
Isolation (e.g. sending/locking child in room)	41% Occasionally justified 50% Never justified		
Silence (not speaking to a child)	32% Occasionally justified 61% Never justified		
Verbal threats of beating or similar (not acted upon)	27% Occasionally justified 67% Never justified		
Making the child miss a meal/part of a meal	26% Occasionally justified 70% Never justified		
Embarrassing or humiliating a child	20% Occasionally justified 77% Never justified		
Slapping with a soft implement (e.g. a belt)	10% Occasionally justified 88% Never justified		
Slapping with a hard implement (e.g. a stick)	3% Occasionally justified 95% Never justified		
Hitting with a closed fist	2% Occasionally justified 96% Never justified		

This definition does not define what 'sexually abusive activities' might be and places too much focus within families for a present-day context that must also recognise maltreatment and commercial exploitation outside families. Some definitions are very broad. For example, the National Commission of Inquiry on the Prevention of Child Abuse reached a definition through consulting professionals and those with direct personal experience. They concluded that:

> Child abuse consists of anything which individuals, institutions, or processes do or fail to do which directly or indirectly harms children or damages their prospects of safe and healthy development into adulthood.
>
> (NCIPCA 1996: 2)

THE EVIDENCE BASE

Empirical data has been collected in many countries of the world on the prevalence of child maltreatment. This research has focused on physical and sexual abuse and less is known about the prevalence of neglect, emotional abuse and other forms of maltreatment.

The most commonly used technique for measuring the prevalence of physical maltreatment has been the Conflict Tactics Scale (CTS) (Straus 1979, Straus *et al.* 1996, 1998). The scale was developed through the application of conflict theory, which proposes that all human relations involve some degree of conflict, which can be both positive and negative. The issue becomes one of how conflict is resolved. The original scale was based on three areas of conflict resolution: rational discussion (the 'reasoning scale'), the use of verbal and non-verbal acts which symbolically hurt the other (the 'verbal aggression' scale) and the use of physical force (the 'violence scale'). The advantage of the CTS is that it measures behaviour rather than attitudes and opinions. It also has demonstrated validity and reliability. It has been applied in more than twenty countries and, so long as the questions are asked in the same way, the scale accurately measures the incidence and prevalence of positive and negative conflict resolution behaviours. Child maltreatment is defined using the categories of 'Psychological Aggression', 'Physical Assault' (a distinction is made between minor and major assault) and 'Neglect' (see Figure 1.1). Sexual abuse is not measured by this scale.

Difficulties in comparison between prevalence studies on physical maltreatment and sexual abuse occur because different sample populations and methods of data collection have been used. In summary, research reported over the past decade shows rates for physical maltreatment ranging from 7.5 per cent (Finkelhor *et al.* 1994, USA) using the definition of completed family assault and 26.9 per cent (Enzmann *et al.* 1998, Germany) using a translated version of the CTS. A prevalence rate for physical maltreatment (defined by using the CTS) in the UK is 21 per cent, including 7 per cent of the population experiencing severe violence at the hands of their parents or caretakers (Cawson *et al.* 2000).

Prevalence rates for sexual abuse also vary according to definitions and methods used in the study. In early research, people were given a definition of sexual abuse and asked whether they had that experience (Baker and Duncan 1985, Creighton and Russell

---

Scale and Items

Non-violent Discipline

A.   Explained why something was wrong
E.   Gave him/her something else to do instead of what he/she was doing
Q.   Took away privileges or grounded him/her
B.   Put in 'timeout' (or sent to room)

Psychological Aggression

F.   Shouted, yelled, or screamed at him/her
N.   Threatened to spank or hit but did not actually do it
J.   Swore or cursed at him/her
U.   Called him/her dumb or lazy or some other name like that
L.   Said you would send him/her away or kicked him/her out of the house

Physical Assault

Minor Assault (Corporal Punishment)

H.   Spanked him/her on the bottom with your bare hand
D.   Hit him/her on the bottom with a hard object
P.   Slapped him/her on the hand, arm or leg
R.   Pinched him/her
C.   Shook him/her: Child aged 2 or older

Severe Assault (Physical Abuse)

V.   Slapped on the face, head or ears
O.   Hit some other part of the body besides the bottom with a hard object
T.   Threw or knocked down
G.   Hit with a fist or kicked hard

Very Severe Assault (Severe Physical Abuse)

K.   Beat up, that is you hit him/her over and over as hard as you could
I.   Grabbed around neck and choked
M.   Burned or scalded on purpose
S.   Threatened with a knife or gun
C.   Shook him/her: Child under age 2

Neglect

NA.   Had to leave your child home alone, even when you thought some adult should be with him/her
NC.   Were not able to make sure your child got the food he/she needed
NE.   Were so drunk or high that you had a problem taking care of your child
ND.   Were not able to make sure your child got to a doctor or hospital when he/she needed it
NB.   Were so caught up with problems that you were not able to show or tell your child that you loved him/her

---

FIGURE 1.1   Conflict Tactics Scale

Source: Straus *et al.* 1996, 1998

1995). Over the past decade studies have adopted a similar approach to the CTS, asking people if they have experienced specific behaviours. For example, in the most recent UK study 18–24 year olds were asked about the behaviours shown in Figure 1.2. Respondents were then asked who did it, how often, how old they were and whether they suffered any lasting effects.

Before you were 16 did someone:

Hug or kiss you in a sexual way, whether you agreed to it or not

Touch or fondle your sex organs or other private parts of your body

Get you to touch their sex organs or sexually arouse them with your hand

Attempt oral sex on you

Attempt sexual intercourse with you

Attempt anal intercourse with you

Have full sexual intercourse with you

Have anal intercourse with you

Have oral sex with you

Put their finger, tongue or an object into your vagina or anus

---

FIGURE 1.2   Examples of behaviours used to measure child sexual abuse
Source: Cawson *et al.* 2000

Many teenagers experience some sexual behaviour. Much of this is illegal because the age of consent in the UK is set at 16. In the NSPCC prevalence study, sexual abuse was defined where the person experiencing it was under 16 and it was against their wishes, or the perpetrator was five or more years older and they were under 12, or the perpetrator was a parent, carer or relative (Cawson *et al.* 2000). Thus, some illegal behaviour was not necessarily defined as abusive since sexual relations between consenting teenagers would not fall into any of these categories.

Two rigorous research reviews of sexual abuse prevalence studies in the United States have been conducted in recent years. The first by Gorey and Leslie (1997) analysed 16 studies and proposed a prevalence rate of between 12 to 17 per cent for girls and 5 to 8 per cent for males. The second by Bolen and Scannapieco (1999) found a prevalence rate of 30–40 per cent for females and 3–13 per cent for males. In a review that included 21 studies conducted outside the US, Finkelhor (1994) proposed that an estimated prevalence rate of 20 per cent for females and 10 per cent for males was realistic. In the UK it is estimated that 16 per cent of the child population will experience some form of sexual abuse before they are 16 (Cawson *et al.* 2000, Creighton and Russell 1995).

Some findings are consistent across countries. These include:

- a gender difference for victims of sexual abuse with males having lower rates than females. There is debate within the literature about the extent of sexual abuse of males and whether data collection methods are sensitive to this form of maltreatment. Most studies find that girls are two to three times at higher risk than boys.
- a gender difference for perpetrators of sexual abuse, with males comprising the majority for both female and male victims.
- there appears to be less of a gender difference for perpetrators of physical maltreatment, with mothers and fathers hitting in almost equal numbers. Some commentators argue that the rate for mothers is lower if the amount of time mothers spend with their children is compared to that of fathers.

THEORIES OF CHILD MALTREATMENT

SNAPSHOT 1.1: COULD THIS BE MALTREATMENT?

Carly is an 18-year-old single parent. She has nothing to do with her mother, her father lost contact with her when she was 3 and she has fallen out with her two sisters. She has a son, Nathan, who is now 3 years old. They are watching TV and eating in the children's area of a local burger bar. The programme is a cartoon about a gang of boys fighting with another gang. Nathan is excited, he's jumping on the seat and trying to stand on the table and spills his drink. Carly leans over and hits Nathan hard around the head, then she shouts 'You stupid little idiot, you're stupid stupid stupid. I can never go anywhere with you.' Nathan screams and hides under the table. Carly sits back down and kicks him with her boot. Nathan cowers on the floor. 'Stupid boy, stop whinging, you never do anything to help me,' she says. She looks up to see the woman at the next table looking at her. Carly turns and loudly says 'What are you staring at, you got nothing better to do?' The woman looks away. Carly gets up and drags Nathan from under the table. She pulls him roughly by the arm while he continues to cry, quickly pulling him out through the door. She can be heard shouting at him in the street as she moves away from the restaurant. The woman who has looked at Carly turns to another woman and they both shake their heads. A man behind them says 'Good on her, good to see someone's still giving out a bit of discipline these days.' The women carry on eating their burgers and drinking their coffee.

We have begun to raise the difficulty of defining child maltreatment and Snapshot 1.1 gives another example. Is Nathan being maltreated or not? There is no right or wrong answer to this question. Some would clearly maintain that he was, others would be more in sympathy with the male observer who interpreted Carly's behaviour as reasonable parental discipline. If Carly was doing this to Nathan regularly, most professionals would agree that Nathan was subject to inadequate parenting. At the very least he could be described as living in an environment of 'low warmth and high criticism' (Gibbons *et al.* 1995), which has been found to be damaging for children. Others would go further and classify this as physical maltreatment.

There are a number of theories as to why child maltreatment occurs, but much depends on how it is understood. One set of theories can be described as socio-cultural. Carly's treatment of Nathan can be understood as excessive discipline. Social values support the punishment of children and condone smacking and verbal discipline. Carly could be like this with Nathan because she has adopted these values and taken them a step further; in this sense she is trying to be a good parent. Violence in the media and local environment is commonplace and lends reinforcement to its acceptability (Straus and Gelles 1986). In not taking any action, Carly may interpret the non-response of other people in the restaurant as condoning her behaviour. Survivors of maltreatment often say that other people knew what was happening to them but no-one ever did anything to stop it even if they thought it was wrong (NCIPCA 1996). There are also expectations about how 18-year-olds ought to behave and what they should be doing. Carly could be feeling trapped by Nathan and resent the fact that he prevents her from going out with her friends, going to pubs and enjoying the early independence years that form the transition to adulthood. These socio-cultural theories (Table 1.1) help us to understand maltreatment as an integral part of the way in which society is organised.

Yet another way of understanding Carly's situation and her behaviour towards Nathan is to look at it in terms of power. Child-rearing is a gendered activity, which in Western society is largely expected of women. Carly, like her mother before her, is a woman on her own who has been left with the responsibility of child-rearing. The gendered nature of child care brings with it social values about how Carly should behave as a mother and she may be feeling constrained by them. There are expectations that females nurture and care for children and this may be part of Carly's expectation too. Contrary to these expectations, she is getting no help from her mother or sisters that can make feelings of isolation and lack of support more difficult to accept. Perhaps she feels she cannot escape the situation she finds herself in; she is ambivalent about working – women should look after children when they are young and it's not really worth losing benefits for the amount she would be able to earn in her home town. Carly, as an adult and as a parent, also has power over Nathan and she exercises that power through shouting at him and hitting him. Feminist theories of abuse encourage us to understand the problem in terms of the wider patriarchal relations that pervade society.

Alternatively, Carly's angry outburst could be understood as poor parenting arising from her experiences as a child. The reason for taking an excessive disciplinary approach to Nathan may be linked to Carly's own childhood and experience of child-rearing. She may have modelled her behaviour on her own mother (Bandura 1977). If she was herself physically and emotionally maltreated, she is likely to have developed ambivalent, avoidant or disorganised attachment behaviours which will apply to her adult relationships, including her parenting relationship with Nathan (Ainsworth 1980, Steele 1997). This combines with the frustration of trying to cope on her own as a teenage mother. When she had Nathan, Carly may have hoped she was getting someone to love her and now feels that the reverse is true. Nathan isn't behaving as she expected him too; in her eyes he is always being difficult. Her fantasy of being a parent is not matching up with the reality (Steele 1997). These psychodynamic approaches

TABLE 1.1 Socio-cultural theories

Theory	Exponents	Strengths and weaknesses
a) Child maltreatment is an extension of normative violence. For example, corporal punishment is an approved form of discipline and the state should not interfere with the privacy of family life	Goode 1971, Straus and Gelles 1986	(S): Suggests explanation for cases where punishment goes too far. Solutions focus on alternative forms of discipline
b) Stresses arise from social exclusion (financial, social and physical). These stresses lead some individuals to maltreat but the ultimate cause is political	Gil 1978, Parton 1985, Garbarino 1977	(W): Some physical maltreatment is not linked to punishment. Not all people living with social exclusion maltreat their children
c) Innocence, purity and virginity are valued sexual characteristics. These lead children to be perceived as sexual objects	Kitzinger 1997	(S): Explains how it is possible that sexual abuse occurs as an extension of normative sexual values
d) Males are socialised into assertive and controlling sex roles. Sexual abuse is an extension of patriarchal relations and a vehicle for men to control women and children	Herman 1991, Macleod and Saraga 1988, Kelly 1988, Driver and Droisen 1989	(W): Does not explain why a minority of women sexually abuse or why the majority of men do not

explain behaviour in terms of individual experiences and links between early childhood and later adult relationship patterns. In Development Activity 1.2 we have left the final column blank so that you can consider the strengths and weaknesses of the different theories.

Finally, maltreatment can be explained in biological terms. Carly has been left unsupported in what might be termed conditions of adversity. She may consider her own survival, over and above that of Nathan. If she forms a relationship with a new partner and has more children, Nathan may be seen as a threat. More recently, some exponents have suggested there may be a genetic link to maltreating behaviour. Carly's mother has not demonstrated nurturing behaviour and neither has Carly. This theory is controversial, as it fails to address the mediating effects of social and psychological influences and like many theories of maltreatment has not been proven (Macdonald 2001). Nevertheless, it is a theory for which scientists may seek an evidence base in the future.

Child maltreatment can take many different forms and, as Carly and Nathan's case demonstrates, can have competing and multiple explanations. There is no single theory

DEVELOPMENT ACTIVITY 1.2: PSYCHOLOGICAL THEORIES

Theory	Exponents	Strengths and weaknesses
a) Attachment: Poor attachment relationships (parent/child) can lead to anxiety, low self-esteem and inability to relate, make parents more likely to maltreat and children more likely to repeat the pattern	Crittendon and Ainsworth 1989, Frodi and Lamb 1980, De Zulueta 1993	
b) Psychodynamic: Parent misidentifies the child as the embodiment of his/her own bad self (acquired through frustrated ego development in parent's own childhood)	Steele and Pollock 1974, Steele 1997	
c) Learning theory: Parents learn dysfunctional child-rearing practices which they model and repeat on their own children	McAuley and McAuley 1977, Smith and Rachman 1984	
d) Cognitive: Parents interpret children's behaviour negatively, see children as an extension of themselves but lack the ability to empathise	Newberger and White 1989, Azar, 1997	

that explains all forms of child maltreatment, and no one form of child maltreatment is adequately explained by just one theory.

Much of the literature on child maltreatment states the importance of intergenerational transmission as a risk factor for future violence to children. Both psychological and biological theories (Table 1.2) include an element of intergenerational transmission as part of the explanatory framework. For example, if child maltreatment is modelled behaviour, it will be transmitted from one generation to the next unless new methods of child-rearing are learned. The evidence base for proving that child maltreatment is passed from one generation to the next is not conclusive (Macdonald 2001). It is known that not all children who are maltreated go on to harm their own children and also that people who do maltreat their children have not all been maltreated themselves. The relationship is complex and not inevitable, and reviews estimate a transmission rate of

TABLE 1.2 Biological theories

Theory	Exponents	Strengths and weaknesses
a) Animals are known to kill or neglect their young in conditions of environmental adversity and humans may have similarities in this respect. For example, in times of food scarcity the strongest offspring may be fed at the expense of the weakest. Males have a biological instinct to father their own offspring. Applied to humans this could mean that a non-biological father may see another man's child as a threat to his current, or potential, biological children	Riete 1987. For a review of socio-biological approaches see Gelles and Lancaster 1987	For example: (S): May help people to understand what feels like irrational behaviour (W): Does not explain the majority of maltreatment that occurs in non-environmentally extreme conditions
b) There may be genetic influences that predispose some individuals to care for their young better than others	Krugman 1998	

approximately 30 per cent (Kaufman and Zigler 1993, Egeland 1993). One reason for this may be that some factors cushion the effects and break the cycle (resilience factors); another would be that other factors particularly those identified in socio-cultural theories are more influential. Resilience factors which appear to prevent inter-generational transmission include stability in current relationships and the presence of a supportive parent when maltreated in childhood. Quite crucially from a socio-cultural perspective, a recognition of the violence or neglect as abuse and a determination not to repeat the same patterns is also important. In this way, child-rearing practices which were once viewed as inevitable are questioned and challenged.

THE ECOLOGICAL FRAMEWORK

The ecological model (Belsky 1980, Garbarino 1977) integrates many of the theories we have introduced. This framework proposes that the causes of child maltreatment operate at four levels: the individual child, carer or person in a relationship of trust; the family or immediate domestic environment of the child; the community in which the child lives; and the society, which includes social, economic and cultural factors (Table 1.3).

TABLE 1.3   Contributing factors to child maltreatment in an ecological framework

Factors	Source literature examples
Individual level factors: Perpetrator	
Witnessing, experiencing maltreatment in childhood	Boswell 1996, Bugental 1993, Cichetti and Carlson 1989, Crittenden 1993,
Experience of trauma in childhood	Edelson 1999, Falkov 1996, Fergusson *et*
Parental immaturity	*al.* 1996, Fleming *et al.* 1997, Harrington
Parental mental illness	*et al.* 1995, Herenkohl *et al.* 1984,
Parental physical illness	Merrill *et al.* 1996, Milner 1993, Monck
Parental alcohol/substance abuse	and New 1996, Mullen *et al.* 1993,
Unrealistic expectations of child	Paradise *et al.* 1994, Straus and Kantor
Cognitive distortions	1994
Relationship conflict/domestic violence	
Individual level factors: Child	
Young/small	Browne and Saqi 1987, Cawson *et al.* 2000,
Female (sexual abuse)	Fergusson and Mullen 1999, Lynch and
Premature/low birth weight	Roberts 1977, White *et al.* 1987
Disability	
Insecure attachment to carer	
Community factors	
Social isolation/lack of social capital	Coohey 1996, Crittenden 1985, Garbarino
Socio-economic/unemployment/housing	1997, Pelton 1994, Peterson and Brown
Emphasis on family as 'private'	1994
Societal/macro level factors	
Norms granting adults ownership of children	Kitzinger 1997, Straus and Gelles 1990,
Norms which equate sexual attractiveness with innocence, purity and youth	Straus *et al.* 1980, Parton 1985
Approval of corporal punishment of children	
Cultural ethos that accepts violence as a way of resolving conflict	
Tendency to individualise the problem	

CROSS-CULTURAL ISSUES

What is recognised as child maltreatment has changed over time and varies across cultures (Department of Health 1995). We must caution against adopting majority culture values as a yardstick to judge the child-rearing styles of minority groups. Thorpe (1994) demonstrates that Westernised child protection systems in Australia have a disproportionate percentage of aboriginal children referred to them. The child-rearing styles of aboriginal kinship groups, where child care is shared between adults and where children are accorded a degree of independence, may conflict with Eurocentric nuclear family parenting expectations. Under these conditions children may be defined as neglected when they are living within normal standards for their own communities. This raises the issue of cultural relativism. What is right for one culture may not be right for another. Cultural sensitivity is important when defining and practising in the area of child maltreatment. It is a difficult issue because some would argue that there are absolute values and that just because one culture accepts a certain practice, it is not necessarily beneficial. One example here would be female circumcision (sometimes referred to as female genital mutilation). Apart from the pain endured and the subsequent loss of sensation, girls who are circumcised often get infections from the dirty instruments used and can die from the practice. There is now agreement in international organisations such as UNICEF and WHO that female circumcision is an unacceptable practice and should be stopped. Nevertheless, it is still practised in many countries.

This chapter makes it clear that defining child maltreatment is complex even within one culture and depends on circumstances and contexts as well as actions and responsibilities. Defining maltreatment across cultures is no different in this respect and it will depend on the individual circumstances of each case. As a rule of thumb, Korbin (1997) suggests that actions that are not part of the cultural repertoire of child-rearing behaviours (i.e. are outside normal standards of child-rearing) for any given group, are an indication of potential maltreatment. She also argues for cultural competence in child protection work. This means understanding the child-rearing practices of different cultures and assessing each case on its merits. We will return to this point in Chapter 3. However, as the example of female circumcision demonstrates, a children's rights framework demands a degree of absolutism.

CHILDREN'S RIGHTS

The United Nations Convention on the Rights of the Child (CRC) defines a child as:

> Every human being below the age of 18 years unless under the law applicable to the child majority is attained earlier.

The CRC asserts the right of all children to be protected from maltreatment and contains articles that relate to this right. It sets down certain principles that should guide all activities carried out in respect of children, including attempts to prevent violence against and amongst children, and protecting them from violence. Children should be treated without discrimination (Article 2), and their best interests should be the primary concern (Article 3). Their views should be taken into account in a manner consistent with the maturity and evolving capacities of the child (Article 12). Article 19 sets out the obligation on States to protect children from all forms of violence and outlines some of the measures that might be taken in this regard. Other articles draw attention to groups of children who are at particular risk from violence, children who are sexually exploited (Article 34), or exploited through work (Article 31), children who misuse substances (Article 33), children in armed conflict (Article 38) and disabled children (Article 23). The convention also recognises the different actors who play a part in protecting children from violence, drawing attention to the responsibilities of parents (Article 5), and the vulnerability of children deprived of their parents (Article 9). It recognises that sometimes children may need to be cared for outside the family (Article 20), and sets down conditions for that care (Article 25). Article 39 sets out the importance for the child to have the opportunities to recover from violence and to be able to reintegrate into society in an environment that fosters the health, self-respect and dignity of the child. The convention forms a unifying strand in a contested area, indicating those aspects of the treatment of children that are almost universally condoned or, conversely, considered unacceptable.

SUMMARY

Definitions of child maltreatment vary in their scope from narrow specifications of behaviour to broad statements that include all avoidable harm to children. All definitions share the common aspects of harm and responsibility.

Research evidence suggests that physical maltreatment is experienced by 21 per cent of the UK child population (with 7 per cent in the severe category), psychological maltreatment by 7 per cent, serious absence of physical care by 6 per cent, serious absence of supervision 5 per cent and sexual abuse by 16 per cent (11 per cent with contact) (Cawson *et al.* 2000). There is some overlap between these groups and between 15 to 20 per cent of children and young people will experience some form of serious maltreatment during their childhood.

Theories of child maltreatment are not generally supported by empirical evidence and require further research. Theories can be grouped under three broad headings: socio-cultural theories which focus on the social and cultural context in which maltreatment occurs; psychological theories which focus on individual and family characteristics, relationships (attachment) and interpretations of behaviour (cognitive); and biological theories which focus on genetic factors and inherent biological characteristics.

There is no single theory that explains all forms of child maltreatment, and no one form of child maltreatment is adequately explained by just one theory. The ecological approach combines theories and views maltreatment as a multi-level problem which requires multi-level solutions.

Child maltreatment is culturally relative. Some behaviours that are viewed as normal in one culture may not be so regarded in another. Cultural relativism does not mean that 'anything goes', however. A bottom line is offered by the UN Convention on the Rights of the Child. Within the CRC there can be cultural variations and professionals working with children must develop culturally sensitive practice.

FURTHER READING

Bifulco, A. and Moran, A. (1998) *Wednesday's Child: Research into women's experience of neglect and abuse in childhood and adult depression* London: Routledge
Brown, G. R. and Anderson, B. (1995) Psychiatric morbidity in adult inpatients with childhood histories of sexual and physical abuse *American Journal of Psychiatry* 148: 55–61

Cawson, P., Wattam, C., Brooker, S. and Kelly, G. (2000) *Child Maltreatment in the United Kingdom: A study of the prevalence of child abuse and neglect*, London: NSPCC

Corby, B. (2000) *Child Abuse: Towards a knowledge base*, 2nd edn, Buckingham: Open University Press

Finkelhor, D. and Dziuba-Leatherman, J. (1994) Children as victims of violence: A national survey *Paediatrics* 94, 4: 413–420

Gelles, R. and Lancaster, J. (eds) (1987) *Child Abuse and Neglect: Biosocial dimensions* New York: Aldine de Gruyter

Kempe, C. H., Silverman, F. N., Steele, B. F., Droegemueller, W. and Silver, H. K. (1962) The battered child syndrome *JAMA* 181, 1:17–24

Macdonald, G. (2001) *Effective Interventions for Child Abuse and Neglect: An evidence-based approach to planning and evaluating interventions* Chichester: Wiley

Schecter, M. D. and Roberge, L. (1976) Sexual exploitation. In R. E. Helfer and C. H. Kempe (eds) *Child Abuse and Neglect: The family and the community* Cambridge, MA: Ballinger

Wattam, C. and Woodward, C. (1996) '[. . .] And did I abuse my children. NO! – Learning about prevention from people who have experienced child abuse. In *Childhood Matters: The Report of the National Commission of Inquiry into the Prevention of Child Abuse, Vol. 2, Background Papers* London: HMSO

REFERENCES

Ainsworth, M. D. S. (1980) Attachment and child abuse. In G. Gervner, C. J. Ross and E. Zigler (eds) *Child Abuse Reconsidered: An agenda for action* New York: Oxford University Press

Azar, S. T. (1997) A cognitive behavioural approach to understanding and treating parents who physically abuse their children. In D. A. Wofe, R. J. McMahon and R. DeV. Peters (eds) *Child Abuse: New directions in prevention and treatment across the lifespan* Thousand Oaks: Sage

Baker, A. W. and Duncan, S. P. (1985) Child sexual abuse: A study of prevalence in Great Britain *Child Abuse and Neglect* 9, 4: 457–467

Bandura, A. (1977) *Social Learning Theory* Engelwood Cliffs, NJ: Prentice Hall

Belsky, J. (1980) Child maltreatment: An ecological integration *American Psychologist* 35: 320–335

Bolen, R. and Scannapieco, M. (1999) Prevalence of child sexual abuse: A corrective metanalysis *Social Service Review* September: 281–313

Boswell, G. (1996) *Young and Dangerous* Aldershot, Hants: Avebury

Bower, M. E. and Knutson, J. F. (1996) Attitudes towards physical discipline as a function of disciplinary history and self-labelling as physical abuse *Child Abuse and Neglect* 20, 8: 689–699

Browne, K. and Saqi, S. (1987) Parent–child interaction in abusing families: Its possible causes and consequences. In P. Maher (ed.) *Child Abuse: The educational perspective* Oxford: Blackwell

Bugental, D. B. (1993) Communication in abusive relationships: Cognitive constructions of interpersonal power *American Behavioral Scientist* 36: 288–308

Caffey, J. (1946) Multiple fractures in the long bones of infants suffering from chronic subdural hematoma *American Journal of Roentgenology* 56: 163–167

Cawson, P., Wattam, C., Brooker, S. and Kelly, G. (2000) *Child Maltreatment in the United Kingdom: A study of the prevalence of child abuse and neglect* London: NSPCC

Cicchetti, D. and Carlson, V. (1989) *Child Maltreatment: Theory and research on the causes and consequences of child abuse and neglect* Cambridge: Cambridge University Press

Coohey, C. (1996) Child maltreatment: Testing the social isolation hypothesis *Child Abuse and Neglect* 20: 241–254

Creighton, S. and Russell, N. (1995) *Voices from Childhood: A survey of childhood experiences and attitudes to childrearing among adults in the United Kingdom* London: NSPCC

Crittenden, P. M. (1985) Social networks, quality of parenting, and child development *Child Development* 56: 1299–1313

Crittenden, P. M. (1993) An information processing perspective on the behavior of neglectful parents *Criminal Justice and Behavior* 20: 27–48

Crittenden, P. M. and Ainsworth, M. D. S. (1989) Child malteatment and attachment theory. In D. Cicchetti and V. Carlson (eds) *Child Maltreatment: Theory and research on the causes and consequences of child abuse and neglect* New York: Cambridge University Press

De Mause, L. (ed.) (1976) *The History of Childhood* London: Souvenir Press

Department of Health (1995) *Child Protection: Messages from research* London: The Stationery Office

De Zulueta, F. (1993) *From Pain to Violence: The traumatic roots of destructiveness* London: Whurr

Driver, E. and Droisen, A. (1989) *Child Sexual Abuse: Feminist perspectives* London: Macmillan

Edelson, J. (1999) The overlap between child maltreatment and women battering *Violence Against Women* 5, 2: 134–154

Egeland, B. (1993) A history of abuse is a major risk factor for abusing the next generation. In R. J. Gelles and D. R. Loseke *Current Controversies on Family Violence* Newbury Park: Sage

Enzmann, D., Pfeiffer, C. and Wetzels, P. (1998) *Youth Violence in Germany: A study of victimization and delinquency in four major cities* Hannover: Criminological Research Institute of Lower Saxony

Falkov, A. (1996) *Study of Working Together Part 8 Reports: Fatal child abuse and parental psychiatric disorder* London: Department of Health

Ferguson, H. (1990) Rethinking child protection practices: A case for history. In The Violence Against Children Study Group *Taking Child Abuse Seriously* London: Unwin Hyman

Fergusson, D. M., Horwood, L. J. and Lynskey, M. T. (1996) Childhood sexual abuse and psychiatric disorders in young adulthood. Part II: Psychiatric outcomes of sexual abuse *Journal of the American Academy of Child and Adolescent Psychiatry* 35: 1365–1374

Fergusson, D. M. and Mullen, P. E. (1999) *Childhood Sexual Abuse: An evidence-based perspective* Thousand Oaks, CA: Sage

Finkelhor, D. (1994) The international epidemiology of child sexual abuse *Child Abuse and Neglect* 18, 5: 409–417

Fleming, J., Mullen, P. E. and Bammer, G. (1997) A study of potential risk factors for sexual abuse in childhood *Child Abuse and Neglect* 21: 49–58

Frodi, A. and Lamb, M. (1980) Child abusers' response to infant smiles and cries *Child Development* 51: 238–241

Garbarino, J. (1977) The human ecology of child maltreatment: A conceptual model for research *Journal of Marriage and the Family* 39: 721–735

Garbarino, J. (1997) The role of economic deprivation in the social context of child maltreatment. In M. E. Helfer, R. S. Kempe and R. D. Krugman (eds) *The Battered Child*, 5th edn, Chicago: University of Chicago Press

Gibbons, J., Conroy, S. and Bell, C. (1995) *Operating the Child Protection System: A study of child protection practices in English local authorities* London: HMSO

Gil, D. (1978) Societal violence and violence in families. In J. Eekelaar and S. Katz (eds) *Family Violence* Toronto: Butterworth

Giovannoni, J. and Becerra, R. (1979) *Defining Child Abuse* New York: Free Press

Goode, W. (1971) Force and violence in the family *Journal of Marriage and the Family* 33: 624–636

Gorey, K. M. and Leslie, D. R. (1997) The prevalence of child sexual abuse: Integrative review and adjustment for potential response and measurement biases *Child Abuse and Neglect* 21, 4: 391–398

Gough, D. (1996) Defining the problem *Child Abuse and Neglect* 20, 11: 993–1102

Harrington, D., Dubowitz, H., Black, M. M. and Binder, A. (1995) Maternal substance use and neglectful parenting: Relations with children's development *Journal of Clinical Child Psychology* 24: 258–263

Herman, J. (1981) *Father–daughter Incest* Cambridge, MA: Harvard University Press

Herrenkohl, E. C., Herrenkohl, R. C., Toedter, L. and Yanushefski, A. M. (1984) Parent–child interactions in abusive and non-abusive families *Journal of the American Academy of Child Psychiatry* 23: 641–648

James, A. and Prout, A. (eds) (1997) *Constructing and Re-Constructing Childhood*, 2nd edn, London: Falmer Press

Kaufman, J. and Zigler, E. (1993) The intergenerational transmission of abuse is overstated. In R. J. Gelles and D. R. Loseke *Current Controversies on Family Violence* Newbury Park: Sage

Kelder, L. R., McNamara, J. R., Carlson, B. and Lynn, S. J. (1991) Perceptions of physical punishment *Journal of Interpersonal Violence* 6, 4: 432–445

Kelly, L. (1988) *Surviving Sexual Violence* Cambridge: Polity Press

Kitzinger, J. (1997) Who are you kidding? Children, power and the struggle against sexual abuse. In A. James and A. Prout (eds) *Constructing and Re-Constructing Childhood*, 2nd edn, London: Falmer

Korbin, J. E. (1997) Culture and child maltreatment. In M. E. Helfer, R. S. Kempe and R. D. Krugman *The Battered Child*, 5th edn, Chicago: University of Chicago Press

Krugman, R. D. (1998) Keynote address: It's time to broaden the agenda *Child Abuse and Neglect* 22: 475–479

Lynch, M. and Roberts, J. (1977) Predicting child abuse: Signs of bonding failure in the maternity hospital *British Medical Journal* 6061: 624–626

Macdonald, G. (2001) *Effective Interventions for Child Abuse and Neglect: An evidence-based approach to planning and evaluating interventions* Chichester: Wiley

Macleod, M. and Saraga, E. (1988) Challenging the orthodoxy: Towards a feminist theory and practice *Feminist Review* 28: 15–55

McAuley, R. and McAuley, P. (1977) *Child Behaviour Problems* Basingstoke: Macmillan

Merrill, L. L., Hervig, L. K. and Milner, J. S. (1996) Childhood parenting experience, intimate partner conflict resolution, and adult risk for child physical abuse *Child Abuse and Neglect* 20: 1049–1065

Milner, J. S. (1993) Social information processing and physical child abuse *Clinical Psychology Review* 13: 275–294

Monck, E. and New, M. (1996) *Report of a Study of Sexually Abused Children and Adolescents, and of Young Perpetrators of Sexual Abuse Who Were Treated in Voluntary Agency Community Facilities* London: HMSO

Mullen, P. E., Martin, J. L., Anderson, J. C., Romans, S. E. and Herbison, G. P. (1993) Childhood sexual abuse and mental health in adult life *British Journal of Psychiatry* 163: 721–732

NCIPCA (National Commission of Inquiry into the Prevention of Child Abuse) (1996) *Childhood Matters: Volume 1 The Report*. London: The Stationery Office

Newberger, C. and White, K. (1989) Cognitive foundations for parental care. In D. Cicchetti and V. Carlson (eds) *Child Maltreatment: Theory and research on the causes and consequences of child abuse and neglect* New York: Cambridge University Press

Paradise, J. E., Rose, L., Sleeper, L. A. and Nathanson, M. (1994) Behavior, family function, school performance and predictors of persistent disturbance in sexually abused children *Paediatrics* 93: 452–459

Parton, N. (1985) *The Politics of Child Abuse* Basingstoke: Macmillan

Pelton, L. H. (1994) The role of material factors in child abuse and neglect. In G. B. Melton and F. D. Barry (eds) *Protecting Children from Abuse and Neglect: Foundations for a new national strategy* New York: Guilford

Peterson, L. and Brown, D. (1994) Integrating child injury and abuse-neglect research: Common histories, etiologies, and solutions *Psychological Bulletin* 116: 293–315

Reite, M. (1987) Infant abuse and neglect: Lessons from the laboratory *Child Abuse and Neglect* 11: 347–355

Smith, J. E. and Rachman, S. J. (1984) Non-accidental injury to children II: A controlled evaluation of a behavioural mamagement programme *Behaviour Research and Therapy* 22: 349–366

Steele, B. F. (1997) Psychodynamic and biological factors in child maltreatment. In M. E. Helfer, R. S. Kempe and R. D. Krugman *The Battered Child*, 5th edn, Chicago: University of Chicago Press

Steele, B. and Pollock, C. (1974) A psychiatric study of parents who abuse infants and small children. In R. Helfer and C. Kempe (eds) *The Battered Child*, 2nd edn, Chicago: University of Chicago Press

Straus, M. A. (1979) Measuring intrafamily conflict and violence: The conflict tactics (CT) scales *Journal of Marriage and the Family* 41: 75–88

Straus, M. A. and Gelles, R. (1986) Societal change and change in family vilence from 1975 to 1985 as revealed by 2 national surveys *Journal of Marriage and the Family* 48: 465–479

Straus, M. A. and Gelles, R. J. (eds) (1990) *Physical Violence in American Families* New Brunswick, NJ: Transaction Books

Straus, M. A., Gelles, R. and Steinmentz, K. (1980) *Behind Closed Doors: Violence in the American family* New York: Anchor Press

Straus, M. A., Hamby, S. L., Boney-McCoy, S. and Sugarman, D. B. (1996) The revised conflict tactic scales (CTS2) *Journal of Family Issues* 17, 3: 283–316

Straus, M. A., Hamby, S. L., Finkelhor, D., Moore, D. W. and Runyan, D. (1998) Identification of child maltreatment with the parent–child conflict tactics scales: Development and psychometric data for a national sample of American parents *Child Abuse and Neglect* 22, 4: 249–270

Straus, M. A. and Kantor, G. K. (1994) Corporal punishment of adolescents by parents: A risk factor in the epidemiology of depression, suicide, alcohol abuse, child abuse and wife beating *Adolescence* 29: 543–561

Thorpe, D. (1994) *Evaluating Child Protection* Buckingham: Open University Press

UN Convention on the Rights of the Child (1989) UN General Assembly Resolution 44/25, November

White, K., Bendict, M., Wulff, L. and Kelley, M. (1987) Physical disabilities as risk factors for child maltreatment: A selected review *American Journal of Orthopsychiatry* 54: 530–543

Wolf, R. (1997) Germany: a nonpunitive model. In N. Gilbert (ed.) *Combating Child Abuse* Oxford: Oxford University Press

CHAPTER 2

THE MULTI-DISCIPLINARY CHILD PROTECTION SYSTEM

LEARNING OBJECTIVES

By the end of this chapter you will be able to:

- Refer to the legislation, guidance, and procedures which govern the operation of the current child protection system

- Identify child protection as a multi-disciplinary endeavour to safeguard children

- Identify the relevance/importance of the Framework for Assessment to meet the needs of and promote the welfare of children

- Describe the formal mechanisms for agencies working together in the child protection system

- Locate information about the roles and functions of a range of agencies and practitioners

- Value the input of colleagues from other professions/disciplines.

In the previous chapter we examined the rediscovery of child abuse and grappled with some of the complexity associated with changing perceptions and contested definitions of child maltreatment and child protection. It may be something of a relief, therefore, to examine the structure and organisation of contemporary child protection practice. By comparison this appears to offer clarity in proceeding with action to safeguard children. The focus in this section is upon the current operation of what is termed the child protection system. This term refers to the formal methods, backed by law and guidance, adopted by agencies and practitioners who respond to concerns about significant harm to children and young people.

The two overarching aims of the current system are to ensure that the welfare of children in need is *promoted* and *safeguarded*.

At the basis of the system is a core of legislation, guidance, policy and procedures, which aim to ensure that agencies and practitioners consistently fulfil their legal obligations and operate within the limits of their power.

CORE LEGISLATION

The core legislation relating to children and their families in England and Wales is the Children Act 1989 (CA89). The remit to promote and safeguard derives directly from this. Under Part III of this Act local authorities have a general duty, set out in section 17, to provide appropriate services to support children in need and their families.

GUIDANCE 2.1: SECTION 17 OF THE CHILDREN ACT 1989

States:

17. – (1) It shall be the general duty of every local authority (in addition to the other duties imposed on them by this Part) –

(a) to safeguard and promote the welfare of children within their area who are in need;

and

(b) so far as is consistent with that duty, to promote the upbringing of such children by their families, by providing a range and level of services appropriate to those children's needs.

© Crown copyright Reproduced with the permission of the Controller of HMSO and the Queen's Printer for Scotland.

Definitions of need were left intentionally broad under the Children Act but certainly encompass those children whose welfare is being undermined or put at risk by virtue of maltreatment. When concerns of this nature arise, the CA89 requires that action be taken to investigate and ascertain whether or not a child is suffering or at risk of suffering from significant harm. Section 47 of the Children Act lays a specific duty to make enquiries or cause enquires to be made, and to take action in response to reported concerns of significant harm.

These are not activities that social services can achieve on their own, nor were they ever intended to. The usual ways in which child welfare needs are met can involve many individuals and agencies, as you will see if you complete Development Activity 2.1.

We expect that you have included not only parents and family for each need, but also a range of agencies for many of them, including health services such as ante-natal and midwifery, health visiting, general practitioners and hospital specialists; education

– teachers and teaching assistants; and police. These represent statutory and public sector services, but you probably also included other sectors of the community such as neighbours and children's peers.

GUIDANCE 2.2: SECTION 47 OF THE CHILDREN ACT 1989

States:

The local authority is under a duty to make enquiries, or cause enquiries to be made, where it has reasonable cause to suspect that a child is suffering, or likely to suffer significant harm.

© Crown copyright Reproduced with the permission of the Controller of HMSO and the Queen's Printer for Scotland.

DEVELOPMENT ACTIVITY 2.1: MEETING THE NEEDS OF CHILDREN

Children's needs	*Usually met by:*
During pregnancy and birth	
Pre-school health and development	
General health through childhood	
Education	
In accidents and illness	
Social skills	
Leisure	
Warmth, love, affection	
Safety from harm	

GUIDANCE

In fulfilling these duties, agencies – local authorities and partners in health, education, police and probation – are assisted by guidance published by the Department of Health.

Working Together to Safeguard Children (Department of Health *et al.* 1999) directs inter-professional practice where children may be experiencing or at risk of significant harm. This guidance is far-reaching and includes:

- roles and responsibilities of different agencies and practitioners (paras 3.1–3.89)
- handling individual cases (paras 5.1–5.99)
- child protection in specific circumstances (paras 6.1–6.52)
- some key principles for practice (paras 7.1–7.52).

The guidance also identifies what you will need to know if you are a practitioner working with children (see Guidance 2.3).

GUIDANCE 2.3: WORKING TOGETHER – SUMMARY OF PRACTICE REQUIREMENTS

Professional staff who come into contact with children should know of the predisposing factors and signs and indicators of child maltreatment. They should be able to exercise professional skill in terms of effective information sharing and the ability to analyse this information. They should also have the knowledge and skills to collaborate with other agencies and disciplines in order to safeguard the welfare of children. Those involved in child protection work also need a sound understanding of the legislative framework and the wider policy context within which they work, as well as a familiarity with local policy and procedures. Individual agencies are responsible for ensuring that their staff are competent and confident to carry out their child protection responsibilities.

(Department of Health *et al.* 1999: 97)

© Crown copyright Reproduced with the permission of the Controller of HMSO and the Queen's Printer for Scotland.

The Framework for the Assessment of Children in Need and Their Families (Department of Health *et al.* 2000) lays down broad guidance on the conduct of various types of assessment wherever a child is brought to attention as a child in need or potentially in need. The purpose of such assessment is to establish:

- the level and nature of the need
- the appropriate services to meet the assessed need
- how, when and by whom such services will be delivered.

The *Framework for Assessment* (as we shall continue to refer to it) sets a standard for working with children, providing a practice tool and a Quality Assurance measure for both practitioners and agencies.

Together, both the *Framework for Assessment* and *Working Together* aim to ensure an integrated approach to support and safeguarding services by agencies working with children in need. A working knowledge of both documents is an essential requisite for health and social care practice and copies are freely available to download from the Department of Health website (see Further Reading).

WHAT IS THE DIFFERENCE BETWEEN LEGISLATION AND GUIDANCE?

You will come across a range of terms in official documents and literature and these can be confusing. Legislative duties are those that must be fulfilled by law (legislation). Guidance lacks the full force of laws that have been enacted. However, it is usually issued under section 7 of the Local Authority Social Services Act 1970 which directs local authorities to follow it. Legislation, in effect, defines the things that *must be done*, guidance the things that *should be done* unless, exceptionally, there are sound reasons for not doing so. For practice purposes, there is rarely any distinction. You will find a fuller discussion of these distinctions in *The Care of Children Principles and Practice in Guidelines and Regulations* (Department of Health 1989).

In the following sections, you can explore how this legislation and guidance come together in practice via snapshots of a safeguarding intervention in practice. You will find it helpful to refer to the *Framework for Assessment* flow chart (Figure 2.1) in conjunction with these.

SNAPSHOT 2.1: EXPRESSIONS OF CONCERN

David, 7 years old, was noticed by a teacher to have a series of inflamed welts across his back when he changed for sport at school. The school contacted their local authority social services department (SSD) by telephone to report concerns about possible physical maltreatment, saying that David had seemed evasive or uncertain as to what had caused the marks on his back and recalling that his attendance record was marred by a number of absences, which seemed to coincide with sports or PE sessions.

When the call was received, details of the referral were logged and the agencies' own records and the Child Protection Register were checked. Neither held prior information of David and his family.

Sahera, a qualified social worker, was allocated the referral to action.

David's school, in reporting its concerns, was acting in accordance with its legal duties under the Children Act and its role and responsibilities as directed in paras 3.11 and 3.12 of *Working Together*.

In allocating the case, the local authority was mindful of its duties under s.47, since allegations of injuries such as these raise the question of whether a child is suffering or at risk of suffering significant harm.

The situation needs to be explored and in doing this, Sahera will be undertaking an initial assessment as identified in the guidance (see Figure 2.1). Sahera will aim to bring an open mind to the referral and to determining David's situation and his needs.

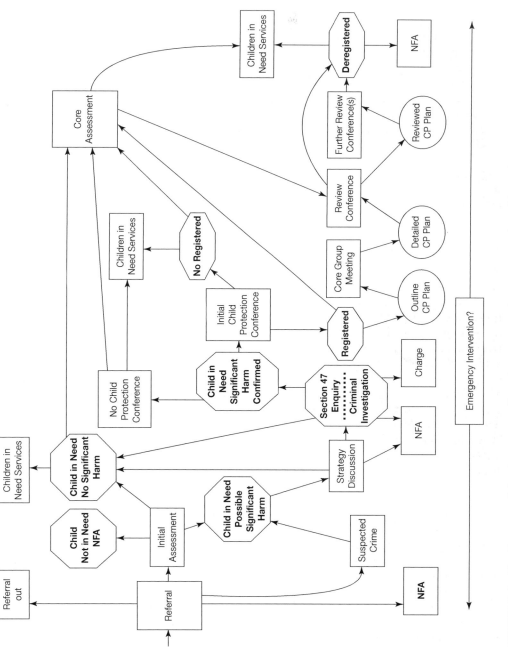

FIGURE 2.1   The Framework for Assessment flow chart Source: (Department of Health *et al.* 2000)

© Crown copyright Reproduced with the permission of the Controller of HMSO and the Queen's Printer for Scotland.

SNAPSHOT 2.2: BEGINNING THE INITIAL ASSESSMENT

Sahera's enquiries have included discussions with David's class teacher, meeting and introducing herself to David at school to explain her involvement, a visit to his home to meet and discuss the situation with Maxine and Steve, David's mother and father, and a visit to the local hospital where David and his mother were seen by a paediatrician. Maxine described David as 'hyperactive' and 'always throwing himself around' and 'getting himself covered in bruises'. Asked for her explanation of the regular marks, Steve suggested they were scratch marks from the family dog. The paediatrician's opinion was that the marks were not consistent with such an explanation and were not accidental in origin. Neither Maxine, Steve nor David offered an alternative explanation.

David's general health and physical development were reported by the paediatrician to be within normal limits and no treatment was required for the injuries. Following a strategy discussion over the telephone with the school teacher, the police child protection officer and her line manager, Sahera concluded that emergency action to safeguard David was not appropriate in this instance. She gave the family a lift home and described the continuing assessment process. Had their decision been otherwise, Sahera would have applied to local magistrates for an Emergency Protection Order, under the powers and duties vested in the local authority.

What if it had not been deemed safe for David to return home, and neither other family members nor local authority accommodation was forthcoming, a situation not unusual out of ordinary office hours? Sahera might have sought to negotiate an overnight stay for David in the hospital. Such a request is legitimated by both s.27 and s.47 of the Children Act which place duties on agencies to do the following:

- co-operate in the interests of vulnerable children (s.27) 'provided it is compatible with its other duties and functions' and
- assist any local authority with enquiries 'where there is reasonable cause to suspect that a child is suffering, or likely to suffer, significant harm' (s.47).

Resources are precious and frequently scarce, and requests with immediate financial implications on other agencies or departments might be more problematic. But knowledge of the legal duties at least allows such a request to be made and considered.

As it is, David goes home and Sahera informs the family that the initial assessment will continue.

Though families often fear that the arrival of social workers heralds the removal of children, the majority of children continue to live at home while assessments of need and risk are conducted.

In approaching and working with David and his family, Sahera has to use her skills in communication and engagement in order to do the following:

- explain the basis for her involvement
- ensure they have the necessary information about the processes of enquiries
- work in partnership
- progress an assessment of David's needs and welfare.

As has been noted, the basis for intervention with the family is the legal duty arising from sections 17 and 47 of the Children Act. Families can decline to co-operate with assessments, but to do so in circumstances of expressed concern about significant harm to a child could give rise to compulsion in the form of a legal order. Skill, sensitivity and professional authority are needed to convey information about the legal position and the assessment process while simultaneously establishing an effective working relationship that will promote the participation of parents and child in an assessment of need, and an examination of potential significant harm. Parents value open and straightforward communication (honesty), even-handedness (fairness, justice), answer-ability (you must be able to account for your decisions) and sensitivity (Shemmings and Shemmings 2001). These are pre-requisites for effective working relationships with mothers, fathers and carers. By informing David's parents at all times of what is happening and why, without allocating blame, Sahera is following these principles.

In doing this, Sahera keeps in mind that though such interventions are a routine and therefore a well understood process for her, they may well be unique occurrences having a considerable impact on the lives of children and families. In these circum-stances, information is not easily assimilated. Many local authorities provide booklets or pamphlets for parents and children where child-care concerns are being investigated. The best of such booklets come in a range of languages or formats (e.g. audiotape or Braille) and give clear information about rights, responsibilities, procedures and complaints which families can refer to at will.

Sahera must also keep in mind the broad duties that are owed to any child in need, so that judgements can be made as to how David's needs can be met most effectively. You will notice from the definitions of s.17 and s.47 that they both amount to a similar need: the impairment of health or development, and significant harm which is also the impairment of health or development. The difference, in practice, is that s.17 applies even where children have been significantly harmed if parents and carers are willing to work with the local authority and the risk of further significant harm is diminished. S.47 applies where the need is for more structured surveillance and a clearly defined child protection plan to which agencies and the family are accountable. In both cases, then, David requires some assessment of his needs using the *Framework for Assessment* as a guide which could result in convening a case conference.

Sahera consults with her line manager and the decision is taken to continue to work within s.17 at this time. In reaching that decision, they have considered the co-operation of David's parents so far and are drawing on both practice and research that informs an understanding of significant harm. This is usefully summarised in *Working Together* which gives some guidance on what to consider (see Guidance 2.4).

In other circumstances, perhaps a younger or more dependent child or in other teams, a different decision might have been taken. Such differences may reflect different perspectives on local thresholds. Some local authorities operate tighter criteria than others for deciding on whether to categorise a case as a section 47 enquiry. Provided a clear focus is retained on the needs and well-being of the child, the designation of the assessment (s.47 or s.17) may be largely incidental. Problems, however, could emerge where a s.17 assessment connotes a lower level of priority.

The observations and the inability of David's parents to accept or explain the injuries trigger a decision to formally move to a s.47 enquiry and to convene a child protection case conference to explore the possibility that David is suffering or likely to suffer significant harm.

GUIDANCE 2.4: SIGNIFICANT HARM

There are no absolute criteria on which to rely when judging what constitutes significant harm. Consideration of the severity of ill-treatment may include the degree and the extent of physical harm, the duration and frequency of maltreatment and neglect, and the extent of premeditation, degree of threat and coercion, sadism, and bizarre or unusual elements in child sexual abuse. Each of these elements have been associated with more severe effects on the child, and/or relatively greater difficulty in helping the child overcome the adverse impact of the ill-treatment . . . More often significant harm is a compilation of significant events, both acute and longstanding, which interrupt, change or damage the child's physical and psychological development. Some children live in family and social circumstances where their health and development are neglected. For them, it is the corrosiveness of long-term emotional, physical or sexual abuse that causes impairment to the extent constituting significant harm. In each case, it is necessary to consider any ill-treatment alongside the families' strength and support.

(Department of Health *et al.* 1999, para 2.17)

SNAPSHOT 2.3: HOME VISIT

Sahera accompanied David and his mother home following the hospital examination and explained the concerns that must always exist in the context of unexplained injuries. She outlined the continuing assessment process as a service to children in need and sought their agreement to the further enquiries that she would be making. Over the next few days Sahera spent some time with David at school, saw the family together at their home and collected and analysed information from other agencies.

Though the family home was clean and comfortably furnished, there was no evidence of a child's presence by way of toys, and no pictures from school or photographs of David were displayed, though there were several of the family dog. David's bedroom by comparison with the rest of the house was spartan, with bare boards, dirty and smelly bedding and the wallpaper by the bed was torn and discoloured.

Sahera's observations of family interactions raised some issues. Even allowing for the context (an imposed assessment) relations between the adults seemed distant and hostile and David was subject to a high level of criticism and disparagement, with Steve several times saying of his son 'He's a waste of space.' The injuries remained unexplained.

Keeping the family on board and promoting their participation in these circumstances demands that the practitioner be:

- respectful
- open
- direct.

The move to a s.47 enquiry does not preclude a core assessment but it alters the time frame. Whereas a core assessment under s.17 has a window of 35 days, it is expected that a case conference will be held within 15 working days of the strategy discussion. The process requires skilful time management and effective prioritisation. Sahera will need to draw on the support of her line manager and colleagues if any of her other cases present equally pressing demands.

SNAPSHOT 2.4: PREPARING FOR THE CASE CONFERENCE

Sahera informs the family of the decision to convene a child protection case conference, at which Sahera will present a written report based on her enquiries. She provides the family with written invitations to the conference, informs them who else will be invited (including a teacher from David's school and the paediatrician who examined him) and describes the way these multi-disciplinary meetings operate.

In the short period before the conference, Sahera continues to put together a rounded picture of David and his circumstances and to work with Steve, Maxine and David to understand how the injuries had occurred and how to safeguard him from future injuries and promote his development. She also needs to be sure that she is adequately reflecting any protective strengths in David's environment. Steve's mother lives two miles away and may be a source of support. This picture was the basis for her formal report, copies of which she shared with the family before the case conference.

SNAPSHOT 2.5: TALKING ABOUT THE CONFERENCE TO THE CHILD

Sahera talked with David about the conference and explained that the meeting would decide whether he had been hurt and if he had, what help would be needed to make his life better. She showed him a photograph of a case conference in action (this had come from a training pack in the office). She explained who each person was and helped David to identify the equivalent people in his own life. Together they anticipated what each person might say about David and his family. Sahera tried to encourage David to role play and talk to each person (this had worked well with a previous child she knew). He thought this was funny but kept saying 'I don't know'. The meeting didn't go too well and David was quiet. 'What should we do?' asked Sahera. 'Tell me what they decide,' replied David.

Sahera understands the potential impact on the family of attending a case conference. Briefing parents needs to be done in a way that will help to manage anxieties and help them prepare for and participate in the conference. She will include the views (as expressed) of David, Maxine and Steve, even where they are discrepant with her own.

Since David will not be attending the conference Sahera will ensure that his views are conveyed to the meeting. Though some young children may wish to write a letter for a conference, others might be better accommodated through an audiotape or a drawing or through telling their story to a protective parent, relative or a trusted teacher. Taking an imaginative approach to facilitating a child's voice being heard may do much to raise self-esteem and self-efficacy. Children will differ in their responses; some will want to participate more than others. The important point is to make sure opportunities have been given for participation. If they are old enough to understand, children generally want to know what is happening and want to be kept informed (Young and May-Chahal 2002).

Policy and good practice dictate that any case conference report should be available for the parents *before* the case conference, and in any case the content and the conclusion (the social worker's recommendation to the conference) should not be a surprise to the family. In practice, difficulties can arise, since many teams operate with low levels of administrative support. Making sure that draft reports are submitted in time for typing and distribution may result in a shorter period of time for information collection and analysis, or alternatively final copies coming hot off the photocopier an hour before the conference. Practitioners will need to have contingency plans, which may include supplying a handwritten draft or a taped reading.

SNAPSHOT 2.6: THE INITIAL CHILD PROTECTION CONFERENCE

The case conference received and discussed information. The designated teacher from David's school informed the conference that attendance at school was erratic and there was a record of bullying. Relationships with his peers were poor and he spent a lot of time on his own. His work was below average for the class group. The health visitor reported that when she had pre-school contact with David there were many concerns about both his development and his physical appearance. Though his growth chart was average, he was slow in reaching some milestones and continued to wet the bed regularly up to the age of 5. The teacher reported that David often smelt of urine at school, which she thought might be one reason other children wouldn't play with him. His grandmother and father were well known to the local authority and Steve had been fostered himself as a child as a result of his mother's mental illness. Little was known about Maxine and her family. Steve had met Maxine when he left care and moved to Manchester (120 miles away) where he became involved with drugs. The police reported that Steve had several previous offences for theft and that Maxine also had a previous offence for shoplifting. In their interactions with authorities (school, health visitor, police and probation) Steve had been either aggressive or defensive and Maxine was withdrawn or 'not interested'. The probation officer reported that Maxine was currently subject to a probation order following the shoplifting offence. She had worked hard to overcome her drug habit and had spent time in a rehabilitation unit. She did not know about Steve and whether he continued to use drugs. The health visitor referred to the GP's report which said that Maxine was receiving treatment for depression, that Steve was registered with the Community Drugs Team and was receiving prescribed methadone. He also noted that David had been treated twice at the local casualty department, once for a broken arm and once for poisoning having taken his mother's anti-depressants. On both occasions these were dealt with as accidents and in the latter case, a 'lucky escape'.

Steve and Maxine were invited into the conference after this information had been shared. The chair summarised the conference's concerns and asked Maxine and Steve to contribute. They agreed there had been problems in the past but these were under control. David was difficult, Steve said, but they did not hit him and still think the dog caused his injuries.

This context of substance use, an absence of adequate explanation for David's injuries, Steve's 'low warmth, high criticism' interaction with David, the health background and difficulties at school painted a worrying picture. This resulted in a decision to register David as a child 'At risk of Physical and Emotional Abuse', and in need of services, including a core assessment, and a plan of action to work to safeguard him, while he continued to live at home.

MECHANISMS FOR EFFECTIVE MULTI-DISCIPLINARY WORKING

The child protection system has developed a number of formal mechanisms for maximising multi-agency effectiveness in working together to safeguard specific children.

The strategy discussion or strategy meeting

In Snapshot 2.2 Sahera engaged in a strategy discussion over the telephone following David's medical examination. Strategy discussions were introduced to ensure that, where a number of professionals might be involved in a case, information was gathered in a way that met the needs of all concerned and retained the best interests of the child. Without strategy meetings it is possible that evidence for police investigations might be jeopardised. In a minority of cases the police may require evidence for a future prosecution. If someone speaks to the child about a possible offence (particularly alleged sexual abuse) and then later the child gives evidence in a videotaped interview, it could be said that the child had been coached, had ideas put into her head or the child may refuse to speak because she feels she has already told someone about what happened. Alternatively, relationships between professionals already involved with the family might be damaged unnecessarily. If a health visitor is working closely with a family and is aware of concerns but considers them to be minimal, she may agree to continue her involvement and monitor the situation, keeping the local authority informed. The strategy discussion is an early meeting of relevant professionals (in this case the teacher, the child protection police officer, the social worker and her manager) to plan the s.47 enquiries in terms of who needs to do what to ensure that all the right information is collected and shared. The police child protection officer agreed that it was not appropriate for her to get involved in David's case at this stage and all members of the group agreed that a case conference should be held.

If the concerns had arisen over sexual assault, serious physical assault or other circumstances in which a crime had been committed, the strategy discussion would have been guided by *Achieving Best Evidence in Criminal Proceedings* (HO *et al.* 2002), the guidance replacing the *Memorandum of Good Practice* (1992) to be followed for joint police and social work intervention. Though David's injuries could constitute a crime (assault), in practice prosecutions will be pursued only in sexual abuse or very serious maltreatment cases.

The multi-disciplinary child protection case conference

In Snapshot 2.3 a child protection case conference was convened. Child protection case conferences are formal meetings, chaired and minuted, open to and attended by a range of invited professionals and the parent or carers of the child concerned.

Exceptionally, there may be sound reasons why parents may not be invited, such as where a parent is charged with a criminal offence related to the referral. In this exceptional event, the matter should be referred to the case conference chair and the reasons for preclusion recorded. In our case study, David's mother and father were invited to and attended the conference. Ensuring parental attendance at a conference is more than a matter of issuing the invitation and will depend upon the extent to which social work efforts to engage parents are successful. Practical obstacles should not be underestimated. If there had been an issue of money or child care, Sahera could have facilitated their attendance by, for example, providing transport or bus fares or arranging for someone to look after other children in the family. Obstacles of a practical nature should never preclude parents from attending.

Sahera did briefly consider inviting David to the conference and discussed this with him, but judged that he was too young to understand or cope with it. She would have formed a different judgement if he had been older or if he or his parents had convinced her that it was in his interests to attend. In that case, she would have discussed this decision with the Chair in advance of the case conference to ensure the conference was as 'user friendly' as such an event can be for a 7-year-old child. The attendance of children or young people is not yet routine and professional judgement has to be exercised.

The purpose of an initial child protection case conference is to pool and examine a range of information (evidence) with a view to deciding:

- whether or not the child is at risk of further significant harm
- what the nature of such risk may be
- whether or not and what action is required to protect or promote the welfare of the child in the future.

Child protection case conferences are often referred to as 'quasi-judicial' bodies. This is a reminder that they are not democratic decision-making bodies. Parents and any child or young person attending do not 'have a vote'. Though the aim is to arrive at a consensus about the child's current welfare and safety and the best way forward on the evidence available, the decision to place a child on the register is open only to the professionals attending and there is no appeal against registration. Thus, conferences are 'rather like' (quasi) civil courts in the matter of decision making and the latitude on what constitutes evidence. Unlike courts there is no right of appeal, though a complaints procedure exists by which correct procedural operation may be reviewed. Where procedures have been correctly followed there will be no redress.

The multi-disciplinary case conference is only one part of the need to work together. There are many multi-disciplinary mechanisms routinely used in child protection. These are summarised in Table 2.1.

Open and effective communication between multi-disciplinary colleagues is central to effective child protection. The purpose of this communication is to do the following:

- share concerns about individual children
- pool information that is held separately
- provide as full a picture as possible about the current health, development and care of children
- ensure that services are appropriately targeted on children in need of them and not duplicated
- ensure that protective action is initiated and implemented when concerns arise.

CHILD PROTECTION PROCEDURES

How did Sahera know what to do? Knowing the legal framework is an important part of professional knowledge, but practitioners still have the task of putting the legislation and guidance into practice. For this they draw on procedures. Child protection procedures set out:

- key personnel and responsibilities
- actions to be taken
- the sequence of actions
- time-scales for action.

Child protection procedures are, simply, a set of guidelines for how to proceed when concerns arise about maltreatment or neglect of children in families. These guidelines are derived from and compatible with the range of legislative duties. Action to safeguard children requires a number of agencies and staff to work together in an orderly, efficient, timely manner. Without procedures, each and every action would have to be negotiated anew. They are also a means by which practitioners and agencies can be held accountable. A thorough grasp of local child protection procedure meant, for example, that:

- David's teacher knew how and where to transmit her concerns
- the local authority reception worker knew to check in-house records and the child protection register
- Sahera knew how to proceed when allocated a report of concerns about injuries to David and no explanation.

It is generally recognised that the current child protection system is heavily pro-ceduralised, and that reducing professional judgement gives rise to mechanistic practice. This is a potential danger in any activity bound by procedures.

TABLE 2.1 Multi-disciplinary working to safeguard children

Multi-disciplinary mechanism and purpose	Phase	Mode (any/all)
Liaison/Communication to refer or share concerns	Initial	Telephone, face to face, letter, fax, email
Strategy meeting to discuss best way to proceed	Early	Face to face, telephone
Liaison/Communication to share and/or pursue information about the child or children and to update colleagues about progress of enquiries and assessment	Early and middle	Telephone, face to face, letter, fax, email
Joint Interviewing – Police/Social Worker 'Achieving Best Evidence' interviews (formally Memorandum of Good Practice)	Early	Face to face and video
Initial Child Protection Case Conference – convened to share and discuss concerns emerging during a section 47 of the Children Act 1989 enquiry. The purpose: (a) to decide whether or not a child or children are to be registered. (b) to plan any necessary action for safeguarding or promoting welfare. Attended by multi-agency professionals, parents/carers and, on occasion, by child or children about whom the conference is convened	Within 15 working days of the initiation of a s.47 enquiry	Formal chaired meeting, with submission of reports written and verbal. Recorded/minuted. Conference minutes and decisions are distributed to all attending and to parents whether or not they attend

Core Group Meeting – small working parties comprising parent/s/carers, designated key worker (usually child's social worker), and those professionals or others most actively involved with the child and her family. Core groups carry forward the work necessary to safeguard children and promote their welfare	Post-Registration. (But also used when no registration has occurred, but needs for support/services identified)	Face to face meetings, often in family home, but also in family centres or other venues used by child/family and comfortable to them
Review Case Conference – convened to evaluate the current risk to registered children in light of work to date and to decide (a) whether or not continued registration is required to safeguard the child or children (b) What further work/services may be appropriate to meet changed circumstances	At scheduled intervals	Formal chaired meeting, with submission of reports written and verbal. Recorded/minuted. Conference minutes and decisions are distributed to all attending and to parents whether or not they attend
Core Assessment – the means of drawing together and analysing all necessary information to understand the difficulties and issues and establishing what is necessary to reduce or remove risk to a child. It also includes concurrently identifying and providing necessary services	May be instigated at any stage. 35 days allowed for completion under Framework of Assessment	Involves: direct work with child and family (e.g. interviews, family therapy sessions, compilation of genograms, eco-maps) Information gathering and sharing with other agencies Necessary service provision

GUIDANCE 2.5:   ARE PROCEDURES HELPFUL?

Ayre (2001) argues that legislative change, statutory guidance, recommendations from public enquiries and research findings: 'proliferated at such a rate that it was difficult for ordinary competent practitioners and managers to feel confident that they were aware of all the important guidance relevant to their work. It is not just the depth of the pile of guidance notes which causes concern, it is also their texture, in that they have become ever more closely woven. If an instance of error seems to have fallen through the net provided by existing guidance, we start to write on the spaces between the lines in the vain hope that we will eventually catch everything . . . The idea that we can control child protection and render it safe by writing increasingly detailed procedures describing right action is unfortunately fundamentally flawed. It rests heavily on the notion that if we could just get the system right, all would be well. However, we are here straying again into territory covered by the "myth of predictability". Unpredictability is of the essence of human behaviour, both that of abusers and that of the professionals who work with them.'

(pp. 893–894)

Procedures do not remove the need for professional judgement which is an inevitable feature of professional activity. Two illustrations will suffice.

The teacher's observation of David's injuries required her to make a judgement on:

- their nature and extent
- David's demeanour and response
- the lack of an explanation
- the context – his previous absences and behaviour in school
- the right thing to do.

In this instance she concluded, in consultation with the deputy Head Teacher (the designated teacher for child protection), that there was cause for concern. In other instances, other judgements could arise.

The action to return David home with his mother and father required a judgement about David's immediate safety. Here the social worker formed her judgement in consultation with the relevant professionals involved and her manager in a strategy discussion, but the decision depended significantly on her judgement of:

- David's feelings and wishes
- her observations of interactions between David and his mother
- the paediatrician's appraisal of his general health
- David's mother's and father's apparent willingness to co-operate.

Who is responsible for the development and implementation of procedures?

Broadly speaking, multi-disciplinary and inter-agency policies and practices for safe-guarding children are developed at the level of the local Area Child Protection Committee and implemented through agencies, which undertake responsibility for their own part in applying them. Child protection policies and practices nationally will share many similarities, but some local variations do exist. (You can get a feel for this by seeking opportunities to compare procedural handbooks across different local authorities.)

THE IMPORTANCE OF AGENCIES WORKING TOGETHER

At the heart of the system is the expectation that agencies must work together to safeguard children deemed at risk. No one agency or profession has the full range of services or information to meet the needs of children or to protect children from maltreatment. The most recent public enquiry concerning child protection (the Laming Inquiry appointed to examine matters leading to the death of Victoria Climbie) reinforces this central premise of child protection as a multi-disciplinary endeavour.

At local levels, the Area Child Protection Committee (ACPC) oversees the multi-disciplinary system. Its role is identified in para 4.1 of *Working Together*:

> The ACPC is an inter-agency forum for agreeing how the different services and professional groups should cooperate to safeguard children in that area, and for making sure that arrangements work effectively to bring about good outcomes for children.

An ACPC is formed by members of the agencies central to the system, and is responsible for providing local guidance and procedures, serious case reviews (previously Part 8 reviews) of all child maltreatment deaths or serious life-threatening injury and permanent impairment caused by maltreatment in their area, promotion of best practice and development of multi-disciplinary training. There is an expectation that members of the ACPC must have sufficient status to be able to commit their agency to decisions. Though there are local variations in level of agency commitment and support of an ACPC (Sanders *et al.* 1997), most acknowledge the central importance of this body. The agencies represented will include: local authority social services, health (both primary and hospital services), NSPCC, police, education and probation. Since its creation in 2001 the independent non-departmental body, the Children and Family Court Advisory Service (CAFCASS), is also represented.

The whole committee will often have standing sub-committees to drive forward different aspects of their business. Practitioners with an interest in shaping the practice of child protection and the operation of the system can do so by membership of such sub-committees. Following the Laming Inquiry ACPC work will be part of the Management Board for Services to Children and Families.

GUIDANCE 2.6:
THE RESPONSIBILITIES OF AN ACPC

ACPCs have three broad types of responsibility laid down by para 4.2 of *Working Together*. These are:

Overseeing local organisation of child protection

By:

Developing and agreeing local policies and procedures for inter-professional working to safeguard children in line with WT Guidance

Ensuring inter-agency agreement and understanding of operational decisions and thresholds for child protection interventions in the lives of children and their families

Setting out objectives and performance indicators for the system to work to and be evaluated against

Auditing and evaluating the performance of inter-professional working.

Promoting good practice to safeguard children

By:

Promoting good working relationships between agencies and professional groups

Advancing local working to safeguard children by implementing new knowledge gained from national and local experience and research

Conducting reviews in cases where children have died or been seriously harmed and maltreatment or neglect is a possibility or confirmed (serious case reviews)

Promoting the effective work of the system by specifying and ensuring delivery of inter-disciplinary training.

Promoting awareness of and involvement in promoting child welfare and safeguarding children within the local community

SNAPSHOT 2.7: ONGOING WORK AFTER REGISTRATION

A new social worker was allocated to be key worker, to co-ordinate the core group that would work to develop and implement the child protection plan. The core group members were identified as the key worker, Maxine, her Probation Officer, and the Education Welfare Officer whose work covers the school attended by David.

The assessment, the work to safeguard David and the initial case conference decision to register David as at risk are reviewed after three months by a meeting of the full multi-disciplinary case conference as directed by local procedures.

While Sahera's role as the worker for initial assessment means that she withdraws from the case after the conference, work with David and his family continues. This is co-ordinated by a core group of inter-professional colleagues, including another social worker. Family and professionals must now forge an effective working relationship to simultaneously progress the assessment, develop and deliver necessary services and safeguard David.

How effective is multi-agency working in safeguarding children?

Evidence from research (DoH 1995) indicates that multi-disciplinary working is better in the early stages of enquiries and work with children and their families where maltreatment is suspected or an issue, but less pronounced or apparent in implementing action plans.

The effectiveness of multi-agency working (and the child protection system as a whole) has never been evaluated in terms of outcomes for children either here or in the US (Chalk and King 1998). It is simply not known whether this is the best way of working because it is difficult to find comparisons. Countries that do not have multi-agency working, particularly in Europe, have sought to develop it and admire this aspect of the UK system. It seems to make good sense and is built on evidence from public and local authority inquiries which shows that when things go wrong it is usually because the professionals don't communicate well.

Obstacles and impediments to effective multi-disciplinary working

There is general agreement on the necessity for multi-disciplinary working. This agreement has existed since the Maria Colwell Inquiry, which instituted the formal structure of child protection case conferences. The fact that, thirty years later, deficiencies in multi-disciplinary working are still being highlighted in Child Death/Serious Injury Inquiries and Serious Case Reviews, alerts us to the fact that this is a problem more easily defined than solved. There is a better chance of making progress on this, when the problem is recognised as one of process as well as structures. As we have seen earlier, the system has well defined mechanisms to support professionals and agencies coming together to work to safeguard children. But protocols, procedures and mechanisms go only so far. The trust, commitment and skills of individuals and groups across the multi-agency arena to implement the mechanisms are a major factor in ensuring effectiveness.

The core information covering roles and functions is to be found in *Working Together to Safeguard Children* (Department of Health *et al.* 1999). Sahera certainly drew on her knowledge of the roles and functions of various multi-agency colleagues in her work towards safeguarding David. She knew, for example, that most adults and children would be registered with a local general medical practitioner (GP). If David or his mother or father had told her that David had been seen by his GP in respect of his injuries it is likely that she would have contacted the doctor before considering the need for a paediatric examination.

DEVELOPMENT ACTIVITY 2.2: IMPROVING MULTI-DISCIPLINARY WORKING

The following table highlights some issues identified in research and practice. You might like to use the third column to think about how multi-disciplinary working might be made more effective and what your own contribution will be.

Barriers/Impediments	Potential hazardous consequences	Ways forward
Status differentials (Stevenson 1989, DoH 1991, Hallett and Birchall 1992)	The contributions of low-status colleagues may be missed or played down, even though they may have 'expert' information about a specific child or children from regular direct contact and observation	
Confusion/uncertainty about own role/remit (DoH 1995)	Failure to act	
Confusion/uncertainty about others' roles/remit (DoH 1995)	Necessary actions or tasks not accomplished – because it is assumed that they fall to 'someone else' Inappropriate expectations of colleagues and the possible loss of trust and respect when tasks are not completed	
Different working practices, such that colleagues in different agencies may find it difficult to make contact with each other ('I've been trying to contact you all week . . .'), different agency priorities (Hallett and Birchall 1992)	May lead to failures to liaise with colleagues with essential/ helpful information May lead to important contributors being closed out of the information/ communication loop May lead to feelings of resentment/defensiveness	
Differences in communication practices and different understandings (Reder et al. 1993)	May assume other professionals understand when they do not or vice versa	
Lack of trust, fear of loss of autonomy (Hallett and Birchall 1992)	May hold back important information	

Overcoming or preventing such obstacles requires action at a number of levels: At the level of practitioners:

- there must be knowledge and understanding of individual roles
- there must be knowledge about the roles and functions of the range of colleagues with whom one works
- there must be recognition and respect for the contribution of all colleagues
- there must be a desire to reach a consensus about the problem and its solution. (Hallet and Birchall 1992)

Children under school age will generally be known to a health visitor, and health visitors will be a source of important information about the health, development and care of individual children. In the context of expressed concerns about the safety of young children, the absence of medical registration should be followed up. Though there may be sound reasons why a family with young children is not known to a local medical practice – new arrivals into a district may yet have to register, or having registered, their records may still have to be transferred – it is also possible that the reason is more problematic. David is beyond the usual age of routine contact with the health visiting service to children. Nevertheless, records remain, and in preparing her assessment report for the case conference Sahera found them a useful source of information. They can indicate David's health and development to date.

Some agencies and professionals will have much greater contact with children than others. Their involvement and information are particularly important because they can provide a more complete picture of a child, built up over time. This chronological information enables practitioners to note general trends and levels of well-being and alerts them to alterations or disruptions which may signify that all is not well. Concerns may be assessed and judged in this context. Many children of pre-school age, for example, will be attending day care, and day care workers tend to have a much fuller picture of a child than other professionals. Since children in day care are generally taken and collected by main carers, day care workers will also build up a picture of the wider family, and be aware on a daily basis of changes or difficulties within the family or family functioning. Children of school age will generally be attending school, or at any rate be enrolled with a school. Consequently teachers are often excellent contributors to a 'whole child' picture. In the case of David, the observation of the school teacher was critical in David coming to the attention of the social services. It must be acknowledged, however, that multi-agency working is a continuing challenge for all practitioners. In practice, effectiveness can depend on individual relationships and personalities.

PRACTITIONER CHECKLIST

☐ Am I familiar with the relevant legislation and guidance as detailed in this chapter?

☐ Am I familiar with the Child Protection Procedures Manual for my agency?

☐   Am I clear about the function of my agency and my particular role within it in relation to child-protection work?

☐   What additional knowledge and training do I need, and what action will I take to achieve this?

The introduction of the Post-Qualifying Award in Child Care seems set in statutory agencies to act as a benchmark for workers routinely working with more complex forms of child maltreatment. But safeguarding children is a feature of all child-care work and it is rarely possible to anticipate which cases may present complicity and thus shield beginning practitioners, whether in a statutory setting or in an independent sector organisation. The responsible worker will anticipate that familiarity with the local procedures is a necessary part of professional development.

SUMMARY

The structure and organisation of services to safeguard children are dictated by core legislation, guidance and policy. In particular, all practitioners need to be familiar with the Children Act 1989, *Working Together to Safeguard Children* (DoH *et al.* 1999) and the *Framework for the Assessment of Children in Need and their Families* (DoH *et al.* 2000). Following the Laming Inquiry these documents will be updated.

The *Framework for Assessment* sets a standard for working with children and provides a practice tool and a Quality Assurance measure for both practitioners and agencies. *Working Together* directs inter-professional practice where children may be experiencing or at risk of significant harm. A working knowledge of both the *Framework* and *Working Together* is an essential requisite for practice and copies are freely available to download from the Department of Health website as detailed in Further Reading.

Determining significant harm in respect of a child demands careful multidisciplinary assessment in line with the *Framework*.

In working to that legislative core and fulfilling their professional duties, practitioners are directed by local child protection procedures which cover: key personnel and responsibilities; actions to be taken, the sequence of actions, and timescales for action. Important mechanisms arising from the procedures include: strategy discussions or meetings, child protection case conferences, review conferences and core group meetings.

Child protection procedures are developed and monitored by local Area Child Protection Committees (ACPCs). ACPCs are inter-professional bodies with an important role in progressing the effectiveness of the child protection system.

Maximising effective interdisciplinary working is an ongoing challenge for all members of the child protection system, and practitioners have a part to play in valuing the contributions of multi-agency colleagues.

FURTHER READING

All practitioners, whatever their profession or discipline, need to be fully aware of the requirements of:

Department of Health/Home Office/Department for Education and Employment (1999) *Working Together to Safeguard Children. A guide to inter-agency working to safeguard and promote the welfare of children* London: The Stationery Office

This is available on the internet at: www.the-stationery-office.co.uk/doh/worktog/worktog.htm. This is a secure site and password protected. The following user name/password is needed to access:

USER NAME: worktog
PASSWORD: safeguard

Department of Health/Department for Education and Employment/Home Office (2000) *Framework for the Assessment of Children in Need and their Families* London: The Stationery Office

This is available on the internet at two sites: www.open.gov.uk/doh/quality.htm and www.the-stationery-office.co.uk/doh/facn/facn.htm. The second site contains the document in a fully searchable format with links to related publications. This is a secure site and password protected. The following user name/password is needed to access:

USER NAME: facneed
PASSWORD: r4ch7rd

Safeguarding Children: A Joint Chief Inspectors' Report on Arrangements to Safeguard Children (2002) Department of Health publications

Department of Health Child Protection: Clarification of arrangements between the NHS and other agencies: addendum to 'Working Together' under the Children Act 1989, Department of Health (1995).

REFERENCES

Ayre, P. (2001) Child protection and the media: Lessons from the last three decades *British Journal of Social Work* 31: 887–901

Chalk, R. and King, P. A. (eds) (1998) *Violence in Families: Assessing prevention and treatment programs* Committee on the Assessment of Family Violence Interventions Board on Children, Youth and Families, Commission on Behavioral and Social Sciences and Education National Research Council and Institute of Medicine, Washington, DC: National Academy Press

DoH (1989) *The Care of Children: Principles and practice in guidelines and regulations* London: HMSO

DoH (1991) *Child Abuse: A study of inquiry reports 1980–1989* London: HMSO

DoH (Department of Health/Social Services Inspectorate) (1995) *The Challenge of Partnership in Child Protection: Practice guide* London: HMSO

Hallett, C. and Birchall, E. (1992) *Co-ordination and Child Protection: A review of the literature* London: HMSO

HO/Lord Chancellor/CPS/DoH/The National Assembly for Wales (2002) *Achieving Best Evidence in Criminal Proceedings: Guidance for vulnerable or intimidated witnesses, including children* London: Home Office Communication Directorate

Reder, P., Duncan, S. and Gray, M. (1993) *Beyond Blame* London: Routledge

Sanders, R., Jackson, S. and Thomas, N. (1997) Degrees of involvement: The interaction of focus and commitment in area child protection committees *British Journal of Social Work* 27, 6: 871–892

Shemmings, Y. and Shemmings, D. (2001) Empowering children and family members to participate in the assessment process. In J. Horwath (ed.) *The Child's World: Assessing children in need* London: Jessica Kingsley Publishers

Stevenson, O. (1989) *Child Abuse: Professional practice and public policy* London: Harvester Wheatsheaf

Young, F. and May-Chahal, C. (2002) *Views of Children and their Carers of the Child Protection Quality Control Process* Blackburn with Darwen ACPC.

CHAPTER 3

RECOGNISING SIGNS OF HARM AND SAFETY

LEARNING OBJECTIVES

By the end of this chapter you will be able to:

▪ Recognise a range of indicators of possible maltreatment

▪ Understand the importance of home visits in providing clues to well-being

▪ Be alert to the needs of children

▪ Be familiar with some common systems failures.

As *Working Together* makes clear, everyone having contact with children and their families is tasked with safeguarding, and staff across a range of disciplines and settings must be able to recognise and respond to indicators that a child's welfare or safety may be at risk (s.5.2) and should know of the predisposing factors and signs and indicators of child abuse (s.9.1) (Department of Health *et al.* 1999).

It is equally important to be alert to signs of safety (Turnell *et al.* 1999). Looking for measures that demonstrate safety is part of working therapeutically with children and parents/carers (see Chapters 6 and 7). It is also a component of interpreting risk. The 'signs of safety' approach demands that the focus be not just the harm or likelihood of harm but the components present (or potentially present through therapeutic work) that can promote a safe environment for the child. These signs can be practical, for example locking prescription methodone in a secure cupboard. They can be interpersonal, for example recognising certain relationships as dangerous and personal, e.g. recognising when and how to get help. These signs will vary from case to case.

A significant measure of any child's welfare state is their overall development. The seven dimensions of child development as identified in the *Framework for*

Assessment are considered in greater detail in Chapter 4. Here we list them as areas to focus on when recognising signs of maltreatment and signs of safety.

GUIDANCE 3.1:
DIMENSIONS OF CHILD'S DEVELOPMENTAL NEEDS

Health

Includes growth and development as well as physical and mental wellbeing. The impact of genetic factors and of any impairment should be considered. Involves receiving appropriate health care when ill, an adequate and nutritious diet, exercise, immunisations where appropriate and developmental checks, dental and optical care and, for older children, appropriate advice and information on issues that have an impact on health, including sex education and substance misuse.

Education

Covers all areas of a child's cognitive development which begins from birth.
Includes opportunities: for play and interaction with other children; to have access to books; to acquire a range of skills and interests; to experience success and achievement. Involves an adult interested in educational activities, progress and achievements, who takes account of the child's starting point and any special educational needs.

Emotional and behavioural development

Concerns the appropriateness of response demonstrated in feelings and actions by a child, initially to parents and caregivers and, as the child grows older, to others beyond the family. *Includes* nature and quality of early attachments, characteristics of temperament, adaptation to change, response to stress and degree of appropriate self control.

Identity

Concerns the child's growing sense of self as a separate and valued person.
Includes the child's view of self and abilities, self image and self esteem, and having a positive sense of individuality. Race, religion, age, gender, sexuality and disability may all contribute to this. Feelings of belonging and acceptance by family, peer group and wider society, including other cultural groups.

Family and social relationships

Development of empathy and the capacity to place self in someone else's shoes.
Includes a stable and affectionate relationship with parents or caregivers, good relationships with siblings, increasing importance of age appropriate friendships with peers and other significant persons in the child's life and response of family to these relationships.

Social presentation

Concerns child's growing understanding of the way in which appearance, behaviour, and any impairment are perceived by the outside world and the impression being created.
Includes appropriateness of dress for age, gender, culture and religion; cleanliness and personal hygiene; and availability of advice from parents or caregivers about presentation in different settings.

Self-care skills

Concerns the acquisition by a child of practical, emotional and communication competencies required for increasing independence. Includes early practical skills of dressing and feeding, opportunities to gain confidence and practical skills to undertake activities away from the family and independent living skills as older children.
Includes encouragement to acquire social problem solving approaches. Special attention should be given to the impact of a child's impairment and other vulnerabilities, and on social circumstances affecting these in the development of self-care skills.

(Department of Health *et al.* 2000)

© Crown copyright Reproduced with the permission of the Controller of HMSO and the Queen's Printer for Scotland

These dimensions of development provide a starting point, a set of baseline indicators, for recognising signs of safety and harm. Clues to a child's welfare and well-being are also to be found in the other dimensions of the *Framework for Assessment*: parenting capacity and family and environmental factors.

HOME CIRCUMSTANCES

Secure, comfortable accommodation is a central feature in the well-being of everyone. A child's material living conditions are significant in terms of both their contributions to welfare and safety and the pointers they provide to how well needs are being met. Hence the importance of visiting children in their homes, whether, as in the majority of cases, children are living with parents or within families of origin, or living in out-of-home care or makeshift arrangements such as sleeping on friend's floors.

DEVELOPMENT ACTIVITY 3.1: MATERIAL HOME CIRCUMSTANCES (A) – WHAT CLUES ARE OFFERED ABOUT THE WELFARE AND SAFETY OF THIS CHILD?

Linda and Peter both have learning difficulties and attended the same special needs school, though they did not like each other very much at that time. They met again later, in their twenties and subsequently married. They now have an 18-month-old son, Ethan, and Linda is four months pregnant with their second child. They live in a two bed-room second floor maisonette reached by a steep stone staircase. There is a shared utility area on the ground floor and a shared back garden where the couple used to keep their ferrets and rabbits and which they also use as a run for their two dogs. Because the neighbours have complained about the smell of the animals, the ferrets and rabbits have been moved into the second bedroom and Ethan's bed is now in the parental bedroom. The two dogs spend time inside and their scratching has torn carpets and furniture. There is a strong smell on entering the home, accounted for by dog faeces and urine, the animal hutches and a bath full of stagnant water in which curtains and bedding have been soaking for about a fortnight. The kitchen floor is slippery with grease and old food and the kitchen sink is piled high with washing up. The house is very warm and an unguarded gas fire is kept on most days. Ethan is a boisterous child who spends as much time crawling as he does walking and he plays with both dogs and has been known to put his own food in their dishes before lapping it up. A favourite activity of Ethan's currently is hitting a large soft rubber ball for the dogs to chase, laughing uproariously when, as is often the case, this causes them to scramble widely over furniture. Ethan is encouraged in this game by both Linda and Peter who seem to enjoy it as much as him. He has burnt himself several times on the gas fire and has often been scratched and bitten by the ferrets and rabbits.

For many people, this would not epitomise comfortable home circumstances, but the question for practitioners is whether there are clues to be read about the well-being of Ethan and the forthcoming child. Certainly, there are clues here that Ethan's safety may be compromised by the unguarded fire and the family's animals, and the burns, scratches and bites give evidence of that. There are also clues that his health may be compromised – the unsanitary conditions could have implications for illness and disease. But so far, his sturdy constitution seems evidence that he is coping. One would be less sanguine about the physical resilience of a newborn child and there may be overcrowding if the second bedroom is not freed up by the time the expected baby is born.

Giving over Ethan's bedroom to the ferrets and rabbits might be a clue about family priorities, but on its own it is a hard clue to read. Perhaps Ethan is afforded a lower priority than the animals and perhaps the forthcoming baby is disregarded. Equally it could be an indication that the family is conscious of social obligations and, responsive to complaints, moving the animals indoors is a positive attempt to get on with neighbours and thereby secure family relations with the wider community. In which case, this could be an indication that parents can provide positive social and moral learning opportunities for Ethan and his future sibling.

The kitchen and bathroom suggest that one or both parents could be struggling with domestic routine and this may be a clue to parental health and well-being with consequences for their capacity to meet Ethan's needs. Or this may be a temporary feature – associated with Linda's pregnancy, the early stages of which can be associated for many women with tiredness and Peter's lack of recognition that he needs to do more to help. Alternatively, neither partner might set much store by domestic routine or more generally accepted standards of cleanliness and order. If so, this could have implications for establishing the necessary routine to meet the needs of two very young children once the baby is born and could have future consequences in terms of enabling children to fit easily into the routines of school attendance. These are signs of disorder, difficulties in coping and the need for support rather than signs of maltreatment. With the right help it would be relatively easy (though possibly time-consuming) to build safety and protective factors for Ethan and his expected sibling.

DEVELOPMENT ACTIVITY 3.2: MATERIAL HOME CIRCUMSTANCES (B) – WHAT CLUES ARE OFFERED ABOUT THE WELFARE AND SAFETY OF THIS CHILD?

Sadie is 14 years old, left home five months ago after a series of arguments and has been living with various friends or occasionally sleeping rough ever since. For the past three weeks she has been living with Lisa, Lisa's three children and Lisa's partner John in a three bedroom flat. Lisa is seven months pregnant and has now told Sadie she must leave, as she is causing trouble between herself and John.

Sadie's parents, Barbara and Mark, live in their own well kept two bedroom house with Sadie's brother Robin (16 years old). There are many photographs of Robin on display along with various certificates and medals he has achieved from his gymnastics and swimming. There is only one photo of Sadie, a joint portrait of her with Robin as a baby. When Sadie was at home she had the front living room for her bedroom. Shortly after her final departure, Barbara sold Sadie's bedroom furniture and the room was redecorated and refurnished as a family games room, with Mark's and Robin's pool table in pride of place.

Sadie's home circumstances are clearly insecure and have been for some time. She has proved herself resourceful and resilient, but her health and safety are currently seriously compromised. Living on the kindness of friends and acquaintances renders her vulnerable. It also seems likely that her educational needs are not being met. Questions arise as to how Sadie came to be living in this way and the clue of the new games room points to a complete breach of family relations, with Sadie metaphorically cut out of the family. The clue of the absent photos points in the same direction. This snapshot demonstrates signs of the likelihood of serious harm and exploitation through sleeping rough accompanied by a lack of parental and social support: Sadie is running out of people to turn to. There are few signs of safety in this picture and currently little indication of how safety could be developed without extensive work with Sadie and her family, who may not be willing to help.

PARENT/CHILD RELATIONS

While important clues can be read from the material home circumstances of any child, home visits are also crucial opportunities to see the child in the usual context of family interactions. In their various ways, the material home circumstances of both Ethan and

Sadie give cause for concern, but when we come to examine the dimension of family relationships the clues to their well-being point in distinctly different directions.

Ethan appears to be a well loved child, with both parents taking pleasure in his enjoyment and joining with him in play. Though there may be hygiene risks attendant upon him lapping his food from the dog's bowl, the action itself may be evidence of appropriate development in terms of pretend play. Similarly, although there are health and safety risks in the home, Ethan's mobility and boisterous play indicate a child interested in his environment and confident in exploring it, providing good evidence of appropriate physical and intellectual development.

Sadie's situation, however, is characterised by the breakdown of immediate family relations and the absence of secure alternative relationships. Evidence from research highlights the importance of secure attachment and warm, loving and supportive relationships to the well-being of children. Conversely, relationships characterised by insecurity, emotional distance and a high level of conflict and criticism can be damaging. Many factors can give rise to such relationships including:

- parental experiences of childhood
- early child/parent separation
- parental ill health
- domestic violence.

By definition, the problems are interactive, so that children growing up with hostility or rejection may adopt survival modes that increase the likelihood of them presenting as difficult to parent. Gilligan (2000) refers to virtuous circles (well-loved children will in turn be rewarding to a parent) and vicious circles (ill-loved children may in turn become unrewarding to a parent).

Where earlier clues are missed, problems can become entrenched. The actions of Sadie and her parents are suggestive of just such entrenched problems and practitioners should not expect to find an easy fix or quick solution. As a rule of thumb, the timescale for resolving relationship problems is likely to reflect their duration. Legislation, policy, limited alternative resources and recognition of the risks of harm that may occur in out-of-home placements, are powerful pressures to resist taking children into care. This is particularly pronounced in the case of teenagers, whose vulnerability is routinely downplayed compared to that of younger children. In Sadie's situation, a social worker in the first instance would be exploring the possibility of a return home. Though parents *might* bow to pressure – the iteration of their legal obligations or the financial contributions they would be required to make if Sadie was accommodated – and Sadie may be temporarily at the end of her resourcefulness, the clues from the home suggest that caution is needed. Without resolution of entrenched problems it is hard to see how secure such an arrangement would be, and the risk is that Sadie would be missing from home in a very short time.

Once immediate physical safety and care are secured, it will be necessary to explore the nature of the problems giving rise to relationship breakdown between Sadie and family members. Ongoing adjustments of the parent/child relationship are an ordinary feature of life and necessary to ensure that different life stage needs are met as children develop. Adolescence is associated for many with the potential for greater friction between parents and young people as they negotiate, for example, increasing independence and wider social activity. But where adolescent/parent conflict gives rise to complete breaches as in this example, it may be a clue to deep-seated problems which could include the possibility of emotional maltreatment. Emotional harm is notoriously difficult for practitioners to define and to work with (Iwaniec *et al.* 2002), though it can thread through many other forms of maltreatment. When children survive to adolescence in the presence of unrecognised long-standing emotional maltreatment, taking their chances away from home may be their chosen survival strategy, especially when the maltreatment is associated with physical or sexual abuse.

CHILD AND FAMILY/HOUSEHOLD RELATIONSHIPS

Important clues for the welfare and safety of children are contained in the quality of the wider family relations and household composition. Once again, visiting the home can render these visible. Siblings and other family members can be sources of positive value, acting as buffers or support in the face of adversity consequent upon parental maltreatment. Alternatively, for some children they may be potent sources of harm. Increasingly, the evidence base is building concerning the risk of sexually intrusive or inappropriate behaviour by siblings. In Sadie's case, for example, the pattern and apparent finality of home breakdown could alert practitioners to the possibility of sibling maltreatment.

The child

Clues and evidence of maltreatment may be read directly from a child in terms of:

* health
* physical appearance
* behaviour and demeanour
* what they tell.

In some instances the clues will be highly visible and the evidence compelling.

SNAPSHOT 3.1:
AN ACUTE PRESENTATION OF CHILD HARM

A distressed mother brought Rosie her 18-month-old daughter into the casualty department of her local hospital in the early hours of the morning. The child has received traumatic life-threatening injuries to the head and although she lives, she is brain damaged and paralysed in all four limbs. The mother, age 24, who is six months pregnant with her second child, is unable to account for the injuries, as are the 17-year-old babysitter and the father. Both parents went out for the night. The mother describes Rosie as absolutely fine when she was put in her cot upstairs after the babysitter arrived. At some point on their return, her partner walked the babysitter back home and much later the mother woke in the night, and looking in on Rosie described finding her cold, with open unfocused eyes and something evidently amiss. During the police investigation some of the accounts change, but no one acknowledges responsibility for violently shaking Rosie, which the paediatrician and consultant radiographer agree would be the most probable explanation for her current condition. Nor is there any explanation for an old spiral fracture to her right arm shown up by skeletal survey and indicative of non-accidental injury.

The fact that Rosie's life is in peril and there is high-order medical evidence are fairly incontrovertible indicators of severe physical assault and this presentation is in many ways typical of serious injuries with discrepant explanation (SIDE) presentations (Dale *et al.* 2002). The difficulty here lies not in reading the clues, but in framing a suitable child protection plan when/if she recovers sufficiently to leave the hospital, where she is currently receiving emergency intensive treatment. In reviewing their research into SIDE cases, Dale *et al.* (2002) make the point:

> These findings indicate that when previously seriously injured children (where the circumstances and responsibility for the injuries remain unclear) are returned to parents/carers, the outcomes are mixed. Some children do very well in terms of safety and standards of care, while others are re-injured, sometimes fatally. (p. 309)

Signs of safety would begin with one or more people (mother, father, babysitter) giving a clear account of how the injury occurred. In such an extreme case this is provoked by the nature of the injury. There are many other cases where signs of injury are more ambiguous though no less dangerous. For example, when infants are brought into hospitals having stopped breathing, there can be many causes including attempted suffocation. In just the same way as the cases of Ethan and Sadie demonstrate, where children die or almost die it is important not to interpret aspects of parental appearance, employment or financial status or home circumstances as indicative of safety (May-Chahal *et al.* 2002).

Explanations of the child's condition can be varied, but they need to be compatible with medical opinion if work is to begin to prevent harm from happening again. A difficulty at the present time is that there is no incentive for mothers, fathers or carers to admit to harming or killing children. In fact, there is every incentive not to, since if no person can be held responsible the legal system cannot respond.

These are, however, extreme cases. The majority of maltreatment, physical or otherwise, is by no means of this order of severity in terms of acute life threat to the child.

Though Mickey (in Snapshot 3.2) is certainly physically assaulted, it is in the context of a wider maltreating environment that many aspects of his health and development are at risk. Though Mickey has survived this harsh regime to date, it is likely that his behaviour is a consequence of that regime. Hill makes the point:

> Children who come to the attention of social workers do of course share many of the characteristics and views of children in general, but they usually have additional experiences of problems or responses by specialist services.

They tend to be doubly disadvantaged in that they have more serious problems and the support provided by their informal networks is often deficient. Nevertheless it is important to remember that they are children *with* problems and not problem children. Also, even when family or friends have contributed to their difficulties, these often remain the main sources of loyalty and trust.

(1999: 140)

SNAPSHOT 3.2: A MASKED PRESENTATION OF HARM

Mickey, 12 years old, though one of the smallest children in his class, has acquired a reputation as a bully at school. He has been referred to educational psychology as part of a statement of educational needs. His fingernails are bitten to the quick and his habitual scratching of hands and face leaves his skin in these parts inflamed, though this is usually obscured by grazing and bruises, some of which are the result of aggressive play and fighting. He has frequent discharges from his ears and bruising and torn lobes indicative of 'boxed' ears. He is rarely without bruising from different time periods including, on occasion, linear welts on his back and fingertip marks on the side of his face.

In fact, Mickey's body is eloquent with clues of the harsh regime he experiences at home where he is frequently slapped, beaten with a metal stair rod and pulled around the house by his ear lobes. He is never certain when such treatment will occur and he has been unable to detect any pattern to it. Sometimes he has been beaten for making a noise while his father is listening to music, but on other occasions he has been manhandled for 'creeping round the house like a ghost'. He is routinely addressed derogatively, but again there are inconsistencies. When school phoned home to report Mickey fighting, he heard his father telling the teacher that 'boys will be boys' and that his son was right to fight when goaded. Then later, he was told by his father that he would be 'put away' if he brought trouble home again.

Mickey's behaviour feeds a dominant view of him as a bully that obscures the clues to the maltreatment he endures. Unless or until these clues are read and acted upon, Mickey will have to rely on his own resilience to manage the situation he finds himself in. Many schools have well-developed polices to combat bullying, but unless they address maltreatment as one of the possible causes of bullying, the needs of children like Mickey will remain unserved.

RECOGNISING CHILDREN'S EXPERIENCES OF MALTREATMENT

An early task for practitioners in recognising harm, injury and assault is accepting that it happens. This may seem an unnecessary injunction, given the widespread publicity that has existed about child maltreatment over many years. However, researchers suggest that this publicity may have a negative effect because it generally portrays what are known as 'rear end' cases: the most extreme versions of maltreatment (Thorpe 1994). In focusing on severe and unusual cases, the public image of child abuse becomes one that 'doesn't happen here in my family' or 'not what's happening to me'. In addition, the focus on extremes suggests that maltreatment will be visible: if it's happening it will be noticed. In both cases the reverse is more likely to be the case. Repetitive, publicly hidden, maltreatment is more likely to be the norm (Cawson *et al.* 2000).

This knowledge needs to be reviewed in conjunction with the notion that parents and carers, in the majority of cases, attempt to do their best for their children. The assumption is enshrined in legislation, such as the Children Act 1989, which states as a guiding principle that most children are best served by being brought up by their parents or in their families of origin. This principle is well supported by the fact that most children are, in fact, reared in families which provide the necessary care and protection, and even in those families where care may falter or maltreatment may occur, it is desirable for children to remain at home with the support of intervention and services to bring about necessary change.

Other visible clues on the child are listed in Table 3.1.

The problem here is that though some of the clues may be highly visible (e.g. suicide or giving birth under-age), others are susceptible to being overlooked (e.g. faltering growth) and most of them are indicative of a range of possible causes. However, all of them are clues to something being amiss in the life of the child and, on that basis, deserving of attention and professional response. This is simple to say, but a continuing challenge for all those working with or having contact with children.

It is salutary to note, from the evidence of inquires, inspections and research, the recurring features associated with systems failure in relation to safeguarding children. Table 3.2 draws on some failures identified during the Laming Inquiry (2002) into the death of Victoria Climbie, but they could be identified in almost every inquiry to date.

How can failures be minimised and children better safeguarded?

Though it is always possible to adjust policy to take account of a developing evidence base, to refine administrative systems, to tighten or reformulate procedures – and such things *are* important – they cannot be the whole picture. Equally important is the commitment of individual staff members across all disciplines who must take responsibility for being alert to the welfare of children, recognising the clues that may indicate maltreatment, and where they are detected, working to ensure safety.

In subsequent chapters, you will examine all of these strands in greater detail.

SUMMARY

As *Working Together* makes clear, everyone having contact with children and their families is tasked with safeguarding, and all staff must be able to recognise and respond to indicators that a child's welfare or safety may be at risk.

TABLE 3.1 Clues that a child might be maltreated

Presentation	Clues	What they might connote
Health	Pregnancy in under-age girls or sexually transmitted disease in any under-age child in the absence of fully consensual sexual activity	In the case of younger children these do connote sexual abuse and may also connote neglect. Can also be the result of consensual sexual activity although this is illegal.
	Faltering growth/failure to thrive (FTT)	Such clues are highly visible in young children where centile charts are kept up to date and measurements are accurate. FTT may be indicative of physical and/or emotional neglect; or cruel and unusual treatment including (more rarely) fabricated illness (Iwaniec *et al.* 2002, Gray and Bentovim 1996). There are organic reasons (e.g. illness) that can explain the condition
	Persistent ill health and soiling/wetting (encopresis/enuresis) not associated with any underlying/organic condition	In younger children, may indicate neglectful care, poor nutrition or physical or emotional maltreatment. In older children this may indicate that any of the above are now chronic and/or in addition homelessness or substance misuse. There are organic reasons (e.g. illness, impairment and genetic conditions) that can explain these signs.
Physical appearance (excluding physical injury)	Consistently poor condition of skin, hair, eyes, teeth, nails not associated with any underlying/organic condition, and/or frequent presence of infestations (e.g. head lice, fleas, scabies) that go untreated	In younger children this connotes neglectful care – physical and/or emotional. In older children, these may connote chronic neglect, emotional or sexual maltreatment and/or in addition mental ill health, homelessness or substance misuse
	Other signs include persistent/septic nappy rash, rank body odour/bad breath, hair loss (alopecia)	
Physical injury	Any action by a parent/carer necessitating medical treatment or which leaves visible marks beyond 24 hours, e.g. broken bones, knife/blade wounds, burns, scalds, bites, scratches, bruises and weals, forcible or negligent ingestion of harmful substances, needle stick injuries, strangling, suffocation	Any such injuries to babies and pre- or non-ambulant (walking) children necessitate medical examination to assess harm. In the absence of clear accidental explanations, these strongly connote maltreatment or neglect

TABLE 3.1 Clues that a child might be maltreated

Presentation	Clues	What they might connote
	Frequent or systematic injuries to soft body parts not associated with illness or organic conditions	Ordinary active play and exploration give rise to a range of accidental injuries throughout childhood. Where these injuries are atypical and consistent explanations are missing they may connote harm through cruel and unusual treatment
	Frequent/systematic injuries other than to palms of hands, knees, elbows, shins, forehead (bony protuberances)	
Behaviour/demeanour	Behaviours that are markedly different from those of peers, i.e. falling outside the normal distribution for the child's age and ability (e.g. frequent scavenging for food or eating paper or stones, sexual precocity)	For example consistently 'ultra good' or 'ultra naughty' or highly disruptive are atypical of ordinary patterns of child development and may represent survival responses to maltreatment
	Behavioural or personality changes not linked to ordinary developmental phases (e.g. 'troublesome twos and threes') or explicable in terms of known adversity (e.g. the normally vivacious child afflicted by illness or bereavement) or life stage change (e.g. birth of a sibling)	May indicate the onset of physical, sexual or emotional maltreatment or neglect
	Markedly different patterns of behaviour in different contexts where the difference is not accounted for by the setting or the situation (e.g. wariness or absolute compliance in presence of particular individual)	May connote survival strategy in response to domestic violence, physical or emotional maltreatment
	Incongruence between demeanour and expressed views not accounted for by the context	
	Ritualistic/obsessive behaviour in absence of specific syndromes (e.g. rocking or head-banging)	
	Self-harm including 'cutting up', para-suicide and suicide	
What they tell/try to tell	Reports of physical ill treatment.	If children do report, they should always be taken seriously. There is no evidence to confirm that cared for children lie about such matters, and considerable evidence to suggest that they do not tell (Cawson et al. 2000) or their attempts to tell are not heard.
	Reports of sexual maltreatment	

TABLE 3.2 Safeguarding failures identified by the Laming Inquiry

Type of failure	Example
Failure to act	*November 1999*: H. police and social workers failed to investigate claims from Kouau of sexual abuse by her boyfriend Carl Manning
	August 1999: A letter from Dr R expressing 'enormous concern' for Victoria was ignored by H. social services
	April to July 1999: E. social services department failed to act when Victoria's great-aunt Marie Therese Kouau visited social services on at least fourteen different occasions – seven of them with Victoria
	June 1999: B. social services department failed to act thoroughly upon warnings from a distant relative E. A. that Victoria's life was in danger
Failure to follow through/ follow on	*June 1999*: Doctors at N. M. Hospital discharged Victoria after thirteen days in hospital following a scalding incident without arrangements to see her again
	June 1999 onwards: Health visitors failed to see Victoria after she was discharged from N. M. Hospital
Failure to transmit information	*July 1999*: Staff at E. Council area office did not pass on concerns about Victoria's appearance
	September 1999: Another letter from Dr R. to social services mentioning injuries from possibly looped wire did not get through to the relevant social worker
Failure of professional knowledge base (to ask pertinent questions, to accurately diagnose)	*August to October 1999*: H. social worker did not ask why Victoria was not in school despite two home visits
	July 1999: Doctors at C. M. Hospital diagnosed bruising on Victoria's body as scabies after she was taken to hospital by her childminder
Precipitate case closure	*August 1999*: Staff at NSPCC T. child and family centre closed Victoria's case after being told the family had moved away without ever having seen her in the four months since the case was referred to them
	February 25, 2000: H. SSD manager closed Victoria's file not knowing she was pronounced dead that day

Any child's overall development will be an important measure of her/his welfare and safety.

Practitioners should recognise the important clues to well-being or otherwise that can be read in home and family circumstances and relationships. Observation during home visiting plays an important part in ensuring that such clues are identified.

Clues to maltreatment may be read from the child's health and behaviour/demeanour, through injury and physical appearance and, more rarely, through what they tell or try to tell.

In other cases such clues may be absent, obscured or contradictory.

No matter how compelling or visible the clue, a core assessment will need to be conducted if the full picture is to be obtained.

Though knowledge and understanding are important in recognising possible or actual maltreatment, responding appropriately is of equal importance. Organisational arrangements and resources are critical factors here.

But equally important is that all staff, whatever their role or position, take responsibility for initiating action and following up concerns.

FURTHER READING

Bee, H. (1989) *The Developing Child*, 5th edn, New York: HarperCollins

Browne, K. D., Hanks, H., Stratton, P. and Hamilton, C. (eds) (2002) *Early Prediction and Prevention of Child Abuse: A handbook* Chichester: John Wiley & Sons

Corby, B. (2000) *Child Abuse: Towards a knowledge base* 2nd edition, Buckingham: Open University Press

Fawcett, M. (1996) *Learning Through Child Observation* London: Jessica Kingsley

Wilson, K. and James, A. (eds) (2002) *The Child Protection Handbook*, 2nd edn, Edinburgh: Bailliere Tindall

REFERENCES

Brandon, M. Thoburn, J., Lewis, A. and Way, A. (1999) *Safeguarding Children with the Children Act 1989* London: The Stationery Office

Cawson, P., Wattam, C., Brooker, S. and Kelly, G. (2000) *Child Maltreatment in the United Kingdom: A study of the prevalence of child abuse and neglect* London: NSPCC

Cleaver, H., Unell, I. and Aldgate, J. (1999) *Children's Needs – Parenting Capacity: The impact of parental mental illness, problem alcohol and drug use, and domestic violence on children's development* London: The Stationery Office

Dale, P., Green, R. and Fellows, R. (2002) *What Really Happened? Child protection case management of young children with serious injuries and discrepant parental explanations* London: NSPCC

Department of Health/Department for Education and Employment/Home Office (2000) *Framework for the Assessment of Children in Need and their Families* London: The Stationery Office

Department of Health/Home Office/Department for Education and Employment (1999) *Working Together to Safeguard Children. A guide to inter-agency working to safeguard and promote the welfare of children* London: The Stationery Office

Gilligan, R. (2000) Adversity, resilience and young people: the protective value of positive school and spare time experiences *Childhood and Society* 14: 37–47

Gray, J. and Bentovim, A. (1996) Illness Induction Syndrome: paper 1 – A series of 41 children from 37 families identified at the Great Ormond Street Hospital for Children NHS Trust *Child Abuse and Neglect*, 20, 8: 655–673

Hill, M. (1999) What's the problem? Who can help? The perspectives of children and young people on their well-being and on helping professionals *Journal of Social Work Practice* 13, 2: 135–145

Iwaniec, D., Herbert, M. and Sluckin, A. (2002) Helping emotionally abused and neglected children and abusive carers. In K. Browne *et al.* (eds) *Early Prediction and Prevention of Child Abuse: A handbook* Chichester: John Wiley & Sons

Jones, D. and Ramchandani, P. (1999) *Child Sexual Abuse Informing Practice from Research* Oxford: Radcliffe Medical Press

May-Chahal, C., Hicks, S. and Thomlinson, J. (2002) *The Relationship Between Child Maltreatment and Child Death* London: NSPCC

Thorpe, D. (1994) *Evaluating Child Protection* Buckingham: Open University Press

Turnell, A., Edwards, S. and Berg, I. K. (1999) *Signs of Safety: A solution and safety oriented approach to child protection casework* New York: Norton

CHAPTER 4

RISK ASSESSMENT AND VULNERABLE CHILDREN

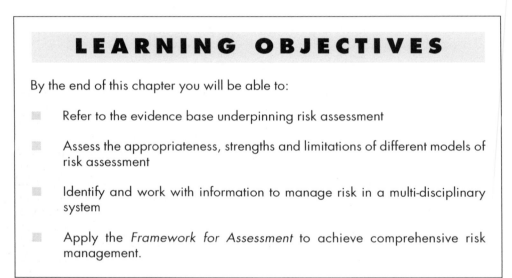

LEARNING OBJECTIVES

By the end of this chapter you will be able to:

- Refer to the evidence base underpinning risk assessment

- Assess the appropriateness, strengths and limitations of different models of risk assessment

- Identify and work with information to manage risk in a multi-disciplinary system

- Apply the *Framework for Assessment* to achieve comprehensive risk management.

> A risk factor does not mean that a consequence will automatically follow. It means that protective actions are needed to try to reduce the child's vulnerability to such consequences occurring.
>
> (Adcock 2001: 90)

There are several approaches to risk assessment, and all will agree it is not an exact science. It never could be, of course, because it refers to assessing whether something is likely to happen. Likelihood can never be known with certainty, by definition. Imagine what our insurance system would look like if it were possible to know exactly when someone was going to have a car accident and to calculate the extent of the damage. Professionals who work with children, like insurers, must always and inevitably work with uncertainty. The question that is central to risk assessment then becomes how to manage this uncertainty.

Some practitioners claim that uncertainty should be managed, as insurers do, by using actuarial models. This involves identifying factors associated with the expected harm and rating them according to their importance. A judgement about the likelihood of harm happening is then made on the basis of how many of these factors, or which of the most important, are present in a child's situation. For example, a parental history of maltreatment combined with domestic violence may indicate risk. Some models adopt a 'strengths and hazards' approach that include buffer or mediating factors that can minimise the effects of the negatives. To use an insurance example again, if you live in a high crime area but you have a house alarm, your premiums will reduce because it is known that alarms deter burglars. Likewise for child maltreatment, if a child is living with someone who has been convicted of an offence against children (known as a Schedule 1 offender), they may be considered 'at risk'. If they also have a safe carer who knows about the offence and takes measures to monitor and protect the child, the risk of further maltreatment will be assessed as lower than if the safe carer was not present. These models appear to offer certainty, but the appearance is misleading (see Table 4.1).

Although the evidence base is limited, it can offer a background to decision making, so long as it is understood within these limitations. The following factors have been reviewed as relevant in assessment:

- *social class*: Children who are reported to services have a different profile from children who are known to experience maltreatment. The former tend towards social and economic disadvantage with an estimated 95 per cent of children on child protection registers described as 'poor' (Department of Health 1995). The latter are drawn from all socio-economic groups although there is a tendency for serious physical maltreatment and absence of care to be over-represented in social classes DE (Gelles and Cornell 1990, Cawson *et al.* 2000). There is no evidence of social class trends for sexual abuse, psychological maltreatment or absence of supervision.
- *financial difficulty*: Cross-sectional studies show that money problems are twice as likely to be reported by those who experience serious physical or emotional maltreatment or absence of physical care, and approximately one-third of this group report that money worries contributed to their maltreatment. It must be remembered that 'money worries' are not equivalent to poverty and that they are probably experienced by all families at some point.
- *family relationships*: The NSPCC prevalence study found that children who were maltreated within their own families were more likely to have certain relationships with their parents. They tended not to regard their parents as good examples or role models to look up to, and they were less likely to receive affection and more likely to live in households where violence between carers was constant or frequent (Cawson 2002). Other studies have also reinforced links between domestic violence and maltreatment (McGee 2000).
- *age*: Children under 1 year old are more likely to suffer fatal or serious physical maltreatment (Creighton 1992).
- *mental or physical impairment or disability*: Where parents or carers experience mental or physical illness, including the misuse of alcohol or drugs, this can affect parenting capacity (Cleaver 2001). Disabled children are more vulnerable to maltreatment than children in the general population (Westcott and Cross 1996, Cawson 2002).

TABLE 4.1 Shortcomings of the actuarial approach and related models

Assumptions of actuarial models	Problems	Commentary
Based on evidence rather than opinion	Insecure evidence base for child maltreatment	Many of the factors have been found from establishing correlations in clinical populations. Children who are referred to services differ markedly from the wider population of maltreated children, particularly in terms of social class, ethnicity and disability. Even where factors are assessed from prevalence studies that examine this wider population, however, they are limited because little is usually known about how they related to the maltreatment
Based on statistical tests	Correlations are not causes and there may be other reasons for the maltreatment that are not asked about	For example, it is usual to ask about family structure and to find a correlation between children who live in single parent or reconstituted families with maltreatment. However, it is not known whether the maltreatment was part of the child's life before or after the family separated
Identify key risk factors	Factors that have been identified through the evidence base are generally too broad to be helpful	Single parenting, gender, poverty, stress are all correlated with populations of maltreated children, but they also apply to a much larger section of the population. To continue with our insurance analogy, it is helpful for insurance companies to apply broad risk factors to assess risk. For one thing they can charge more money, for another they have to deal with general populations. Social workers working with maltreated children are working with a small minority of children. They have to assess those who are most at risk of future significant harm out of that small population so the factors need to be more specific

Maltreatment can be identified	There is a problem with the nature of maltreatment itself
	What is commonly known as child 'abuse' amounts to a vast array of behaviours and conditions that can have a number of causes, explanations and contexts. The actions depend on their context for definition. Children may fall down the stairs because they are too young to manage steps and there is no stair gate (possibly neglect) or because they are pushed (possibly physical maltreatment) or because they throw themselves down (self-harm possibly as a result of emotional maltreatment). In addition, the range of possible injury will stretch from none to death
Can help with prediction/prevention	Factors identified in actuarial models to risk assessment lack the ability to deal with the complex relationships and variations between context and harm.
	The actuarial approach may improve as the evidence base increases, but the complexity of maltreatment makes this unlikely. The benefits are better focused on general populations (as in insurance). For example, taking the whole population, what is the chance that any one child will be assaulted by their parents, sexually abused by an uncle or left unsupervised overnight under 10 years of age? That information helps to develop broad prevention programmes but is of little use in assessing the chance of significant harm *to a specific child* reported to social services

timisation: A history of previous maltreatment is an indicator of future rm (Further Reading, Hagell 1998; Department of Health 1991). This inding in the crime prevention literature, where it is established that crime are more likely than non-victims to be victims again (Pease 2001).

practitioners is to develop effective and appropriate ways of using such evidence in routine risk management. One application has been the development of a range of checklists and rating scales as tools for practice. Though such instruments have long been a feature of the tool boxes in some applied areas of psychology and health, they have been less favoured in social care. Where checklists and rating risk factors have been applied to child protection intervention, as in the US, evaluations have found them to have limited use (see, for example, Doueck *et al*. 1993). The guidance accompanying the *Framework for Assessment* directs practitioners to a number of checklists and rating scales and while uncritical use is to be avoided, these are likely to find a place in practice with families. Current advice is to use them as structured protocols for gathering consistent information and ensuring that the safety of the child is the primary focus of decision making rather than being applied to predicting future behaviour (Weber 1997).

RISK MANAGEMENT IN PRACTICE

All strategies for risk management must balance costs against the perceived reduction in risk. Never travelling by air will certainly render the risk of death through air crash minimal (though it will not eliminate the possibility altogether if you are struck by a crashing airplane), but it will also reduce the possibilities of maintaining contact with family or friends living in distant countries. In some instances, the costs are minimal relative to the reduction in risk – wearing a seat belt when travelling by car, for example, is widely accepted – while in others the costs are more finely balanced and in still others, the costs may outweigh the benefits.

Processing information in a systematic way to manage risk

Risk and need are both fundamentally based on the quality of information. Where information is lacking, risk can be assessed as being very high, when the situation may not present a negative risk to a child at all. For example, an anonymous caller phones in and leaves a message saying they saw a child through a window in a neighbouring house with blood running down their face, screaming, and heard a man shouting and banging about. The caller is giving minimal information that could indicate high risk or low risk of danger to the child. Without better information it is impossible to find out.

Assessing risk and decision making depend significantly on the quality of information available. Making judgements about whether harm will occur in the future to an individual child involves decision making about specific information. In the absence of certainties, or clearly defined risk factors, it is important to guard against faulty professional judgement and unsound decision making. Public inquiries and research have shown that decision making can be influenced by certain factors, such as:

- *the 'rule of optimism'* – hoping that the treatment of a child will improve but the evidence may be saying different (Dingwall *et al.* 1983)
- *cultural relativism* – assessing behaviour in the context of cultural stereotypes (Dingwall *et al.* 1983)
- *moral judgements* – approval or disapproval of service user lifestyle or behaviours rather than evidence in a case becomes the basis for decisions (Parton *et al.* 1996)
- *refusal of dissonant information* – forming an assessment and then failing to understand the importance of new information when it contradicts it (Department of Health 1991)
- *'intuitive reasoning'* – decisions on basis of gut feelings unlinked to wider current evidence base or poorly explicated (Munro 2002).

Children can remain at risk of significant harm once they have come to the attention of child protection services (i.e. once they have been referred) because of the decision-making processes and practices of professionals. Cleaver *et al.* (1998) identify ten 'pitfalls' from research into child protection (see also Department of Health *et al.* 1999). The research indicates the following:

1 Pressures from high status referrers or the press, with fears that a child may die, lead to over-precipitate action.
2 Professionals think that when they have explained something as clearly as they can, the other person will have understood it.
3 Assumptions and pre-judgements about families lead to observations being ignored or misinterpreted.
4 Parents' behaviour, whether co-operative or uncooperative, is often misinterpreted.
5 Not enough weight is given to information from family, friends and neighbours.
6 Not enough attention is paid to what children say, how they look and how they behave.
7 Attention is focused on the most visible or pressing problems and other warning signs are not appreciated.
8 When the initial enquiry shows that the child is not at risk of significant harm, families are seldom referred to other services which they need to prevent longer-term problems.
9 When faced with an aggressive or frightening family, professionals are reluctant to discuss fears for their own safety and ask for help.
10 Information taken at the first enquiry is not adequately recorded, facts are not checked and reasons for decisions are not noted.

(Source: Cleaver *et al.* 1998: 4)

Although these factors do not increase risk to the child – that falls within the alleged perpetrator/child relationship – if all of these factors are addressed, the likelihood of future significant harm to a child, once the child becomes known to services, will be reduced. Adopting a systematic framework for gathering information (Department of Health *et al.* 2000) and keeping an open mind and non-judgemental stance (Butler Sloss 1988) may increase the likelihood of avoiding such pitfalls.

SNAPSHOT 4.1: TAKING A REFERRAL

Jenny is a newly qualified social worker in an intake team. Her team takes referrals from the general public and other professionals or agencies when they have concerns about a child and carry out initial assessments. It is 10.00 on a Tuesday morning and she receives a telephone call from Amar.

Amar has been aware of something wrong with her 3-year-old daughter Jasbir for a week or so. Jasbir has been holding herself and saying she's sore 'down below'. Amar says that Jasbir is waking up at 'all hours' petrified. Last night she woke up at 2.30 a.m. Her sister Kamlesh (aged 6 years) was in bed with her and reported that Jasbir was bringing her knees up, spreading them and crying. She has told Amar that 'Granddad touches me when I'm asleep'. Amar has been working Thursday, Friday and Saturday nights. The children stay at their grandparents while she works.

Jenny's task is to get information that will facilitate assessment and she decides to use the guide to 'Referrals Involving a Child' (Cleaver *et al*. 1998) when talking to Amar. This is a chart designed to help gather comprehensive information at the point of referral in a manner conducive to sound decision making.

An important feature of this process is to establish what exactly the referrer is looking for from the agency. Consequently, Jenny is careful to question what help Amar is seeking in response to her call. "What would be helpful for you at this time?' and 'How can we best assist you?' are typical of questioning that must occur within any initial referral. Such questions are important in establishing relevance to the agency remit – is the caller looking for something that falls within the agency's role – but are also fundamental to an enabling and empowering social work approach to service users. Sometimes referrers may be seeking information or advice or the opportunity to 'ventilate' or talk over a concern with someone independent of the caller or their family. It is possible to lose sight of this, particularly when callers are expressing or practitioners are experiencing high levels of anxiety or distress. The pitfall in such situations is for practitioners to 'take over' responsibility for the problem and its resolution – interpreting the fact of contact and the level of anxiety as the tacit mandate for doing so. This can be counter-productive and serve to do the following:

- undermine service user's own problem-solving capacity
- heighten anxiety (worker's and service user's)
- leave potentially pertinent information undisclosed
- shape or distort inconclusive information
- precipitate hypotheses in advance of the facts
- impair decision making
- precipitate action.

Pressures to 'get it right' and a climate of heightened anxiety about harm and injury can trigger a 'knee-jerk' response that may catapult the child and family into the child protection system in advance of any hard or clear evidence to warrant it. Practitioners will need to keep firmly in mind that though social work interventions must always be timely and appropriate, social work is not one of the emergency services.

DEVELOPMENT ACTIVITY 4.1: WHAT HELP DO YOU THINK AMAR IS REQUESTING FROM THE FOLLOWING OPTIONS?

On the basis of Snapshot 4.1, identify the range and type of help Amar might be seeking.

- material resources (e.g. housing, beds, clothing, money, other)
- practical help for a parent/carer (e.g. respite care, other)
- support for parent/carer (e.g. someone to talk to, advice/information, other)
- support for referrer (e.g. advice/information, discussion of current concern, other)
- practical help for child (e.g. accommodation, school place, specialist equipment, other)
- support for child (e.g. befriending, counselling, youth scheme, other)
- protection for child (e.g. home visit, immediate shelter, other).

(Source: Cleaver *et al.* 1998)

At this early stage Amar is asking for advice: Is this a normal problem or does Jasbir's behaviour indicate there is something seriously wrong? She is also seeking protection for her daughter. Jenny reinforces the feeling that Amar is right to be concerned about Jasbir. Her behaviour indicates that she is distressed and there is a possibility of sexual abuse, although there may be other explanations. At the beginning of the assessment sexual abuse remains a possibility and all options must be considered. Jenny moves to the next section of the chart: Is there a child in danger? Jenny has information that there are two children in the family and a child-centred focus demands that the well-being of both children be considered, even though Amar's concerns are expressed only in relation to Jasbir.

Table 4.2 lists the questions that Jenny needs to ask Amar and the answers she is given. The information helps to both assess risk of harm to Jasbir and Kamlesh and at the same time enables Jenny to assess what help is required and what she needs to do next.

On the basis of her detailed referral taking, Jenny has already identified further information (shaded in the table) necessary for the risk management process. The question now arises, how best to proceed with such action given the dual duty to promote (s.17 CA89) and protect (s.47 CA89) the welfare of children in need? Again, professional judgement must be brought to bear.

TABLE 4.2 Is there a child in danger?

Question	Amar's response	Jenny's assessment
1. Source of information Was the problem observed by referrer?	Yes, Amar has seen soreness, Jasbir holding herself and waking up at 'all hours'	The information source (the child's mother) appears to be reliable and evidence of the problem is first-hand
Has the child talked to referrer?	Jasbir has said she is sore and that her grandad touches her when she is asleep	
Has someone else told the referrer of their concern?	Kamlesh has reported Jasbir waking up, bringing her knees up, spreading them and crying	
If the referrer has general concerns – why refer now?	Amar has explained she has been worried for a few days but has only just got round to phoning because she has been at work. Also she has been thinking about what to do for the best	
2. Why is the referrer worried? Is there a need for immediate medical treatment?	Jenny asks Amar if she has taken Jasbir to the doctor. Amar replies she has not but she has been putting cream on Jasbir's vagina	Jasbir will need a medical examination to satisfy Amar that she is not in need of further treatment and also to see if there are signs of an infection or possibly sexual abuse
Is there a physical injury?	Amar reports that Jasbir's vagina is red and swollen	
Is the child neglected?	Not knowable at this stage	
Is there lack of supervision?	Not knowable at this stage	Supervision at grandparents needs checking out
Is the child a victim of sexual assault?	Jenny puts this question to Amar who says she just does not know what to think. She has talked to her husband about it (he is working away) but he became angry when she suggested his father might be responsible and refused to speak further	
Is the child emotionally maltreated?	Not knowable at this stage	

Is there a person present who has been convicted of an offence against a child?	Amar states that her father-in-law was reported to the police a couple of years ago because a friend of another grandchild made an allegation about inappropriate touching but nothing came of it	Jenny notes that she needs to check out any previous reports to the police
Is there an alternative explanation?	Amar says that Jasbir has had urine infections in the past so she might have one again	
Details of:		
Child's current whereabouts	Jasbir is currently at home with Amar. Kamlesh is at school	Jenny notes Jasbir is not at immediate risk; she is in a safe place with her mother
Date child was last seen	Today	
Any previous concerns	None reported	
Background to current concern	As above	
Any specific injury or event causing concern?	As above	
When did it happen?	As above	
Child's parent's/carers account	As above	
Identity of alleged perpetrator – personal details to assist police checks	Jenny asks Amar for her father-in-law's name, address and age. She also asks how long he has been living at his current address	
Alleged perpetrator's current whereabouts	Amar thinks her father-in-law will be at his home address	
Any supporting medical or forensic evidence	None other than Amar's account of Jasbir's soreness	
Is there any other possible explanation the referrer can offer for their concern?	Jasbir may have an infection but Amar does not know of any other problems that she is having that might explain why she is waking up at night. However, she has not asked Jasbir about this	Jenny notes that she needs to check out whether Jasbir is having problems in other areas (Nursery? Relationship with sister?)
Additional information: Willingness of referrer to be interviewed	Amar is happy for Jenny to visit and talk to herself and the children	
Discrepancies or inconsistencies in report		Jenny cannot see any discrepancies or inconsistencies at this stage

Source: Cleaver *et al.* 1998

S.47 OR S.17 ENQUIRY?

At the same time as knowing that children who are maltreated do not generally get referred to child protection services, we also know that the majority of children reported into children's services are in need but may not be suffering from significant harm (Thorpe 1994, Department of Health 1995). An immediate question, because of this context, is whether a referral should be treated as an enquiry under s.47 of the Children Act, 1989 or section 17. Does the local authority have a duty to make enquiries about likely future significant harm or is this a child in need under the broader provisions of the Act? Thorpe and Bilson (1998) offer criteria for making this decision as follows:

S.47 – Child protection

1   Information has been offered that clearly indicates a child has been harmed or injured, or an adult has behaved in a way that would normally cause harm or injury, and an investigation is needed to clarify this information.
2   It is necessary to clarify whether the alleged actions were deliberately intended to cause harm or injury or were the consequence of an accident or excessive discipline.
3   It is necessary to investigate if allegations have been received from a number of different sources.
4   It is necessary to determine if reports are required from other professionals in health, education and criminal justice who have first-hand evidence of the alleged harm or injury.

S.17 – Child concern

1   Parents are having difficulties and support is required to help look after children.
2   An assessment is needed to clarify the type of support required and which agency is most appropriate to deliver this support.
3   The moral character of parents is given as reason for concern over care of the children.
4   General concerns are expressed about care of the children but no direct allegation of harm is made.

There are many reasons why a child may be classified as being 'in need' that are not linked to maltreatment, including disability. However, Thorpe and Bilson (1998) are attempting to distinguish between reasons that might previously have led to a child protection enquiry by providing a third category 'child concern'. Such cases can sound like quite serious child protection reports when they are referred, but when the information is questioned, for example by using the referral guide as Jenny did, allegations often turn out to be concern rather than maltreatment. In Jasbir's case, however, the information given by Amar *does* indicate that she may have been harmed or injured. Amar is not having difficulties, or asking for support in caring for her children, and her moral character has not been used as a rationale for referral. The concerns are quite specific and need to be checked out. At this stage there is no question that the children are in need for any other reasons.

SNAPSHOT 4.2: GETTING COMPREHENSIVE
POST-REFERRAL INFORMATION

Jenny decides to hold a strategy discussion (see Chapter 2) with the local child protection police officer, Chris, and the family's health visitor, Amneka. She also discusses the case with her line manager. In addition to getting as much of the right information as possible, managing risk is also about sharing decision making, involving the expertise of others and ensuring there is support for the decisions that are taken. The *Framework for Assessment* sets a timescale of seven days for an initial assessment, so there is some time to allow for this meeting. Jenny is aware that the weekend is looming and Amar would normally leave the children with her parents-in-law on a Thursday night. If the concerns turn out to be linked to sexual abuse, this increases the risk that something might happen to Jasbir.

Jenny decides to hold the strategy meeting over the phone that afternoon. All parties to the strategy discussion agree that s.47 enquiries should be initiated and that the children should be interviewed jointly by a child protection police officer and a social worker using the guidance of *Achieving Best Evidence* (Home Office *et al.* 2002). They also agree that the children should be medically examined. In the meantime checks would be made about previous criminal records of family members, progress at nursery and school and health records.

Jenny telephones Amar to tell her of this decision and to get further details. She discovers that her husband, Anil, works in a town 250 miles away each Monday to Friday. Jenny then makes arrangements for both the interview and the examination to happen on the following day. She explains that their purpose is to find out what, if anything, had happened and to reassure Jasbir and Amar that the right medical treatment was being received. She also explains that this is part of a wider assessment that would address whether there were any other reasons for Jasbir's signs of distress.

As the snapshot illustrates, the decision to pursue action under s.47 will have specific immediate consequences for Jasbir, Kamlesh, their parents and family. The likely impact of what amounts to an unusual and significant disruption in all their lives is being balanced against the potential risk of harm to children and the possibility that a perpetrator has been identified. Jenny will need to make time available to support Amar, especially if she is to avoid the pitfall of overestimating Amar's understanding of the process she now finds herself in. Even as a relatively new practitioner, Jenny is still inevitably far more familiar and comfortable with child protection procedures and operations than Amar whose situation, in the space of a very few days, is set to radically alter from private concern about the safety of her daughter to public involvement with a range of professional strangers.

As the social worker with responsibility for this case, Jenny must now progress her assessment alongside the s.47 enquiry, while working to support Amar and engage with Jasbir, Kamlesh and Anil. Depending on the outcome of the s.47 enquiry, Jenny may need to organise a child protection case conference. In some areas, local policy and practice have routinely resulted in child protection case conferencing following from a s.47 enquiry. However, as we observed in Chapter 2, the crucial factor is the maintenance of effective multi-disciplinary involvement and decision making. Consequently, if the outcome of the s.47 enquiry is inconclusive and no further risks surface, a further strategy meeting could fulfil requirements.

The initial assessment, as well as giving rise to the s.47 enquiry, also highlighted the possibility of wider child-care and family needs existing whatever the outcome of that enquiry. Exploring these will form the basis of a core assessment which Jenny will have responsibility for co-ordinating. She will also need to brief the social work colleague who will be jointly interviewing Jasbir and Kamlesh. As a recently qualified social worker, Jenny has not yet completed the training programme deemed necessary by her agency and the local ACPC for conducting joint interviews in cases of suspected sexual abuse. Interviewing children in such cases is skilled and sensitive work. Guidance (Home Office *et al.* 2002) and best practice dictate that children should not be subject to repeat or over-lengthy interviews. Such interviews must achieve the difficult synthesis of

- achieving sufficient rapport between the interviewers (adult strangers) and the child
- eliciting information that will confirm or disconfirm that a crime has been committed
- ensuring the evidential value of any information obtained for criminal prosecution purposes
- establishing the child's capacity as a witness
- remaining sensitive to the child's therapeutic needs.

SNAPSHOT 4.3: INCONCLUSIVE OUTCOMES – WORKING WITH UNCERTAINTY

The interview and the medical have inconclusive outcomes and no new information emerged. Jasbir voluntarily repeated her account that grandfather 'touches me when I'm asleep' but would not say more than this. Jasbir's physical symptoms were confirmed by the medical and it was also found that Kamlesh had irregularities in her hymen.

An interview with Jasbir's grandfather by the police also provides inconclusive evidence. He admitted that he may have rubbed the children's vaginas a little too hard while bathing them but strongly denied any sexual contact with either child. Police records give no evidence of any previous suspicion of sexual abuse, though there is a brief note of a referral to a local police station by a family friend, which was recorded as 'family disputes – cultural'. This referral was not passed on to the police protection team. The police decide that no further action will be taken by them at this time, but they will review their decision if other issues arise.

While the joint interviews were in progress, Amar disclosed to Jenny that she was sexually abused as a child and she thought that this was why she was being 'hyper vigilant'. She has never told anyone about this, including her husband. Following the interviews and medicals, Amar continues to be concerned about Jasbir and is now worried that something may also have happened to Kamlesh.

The private views of the two workers who conducted the interviews differ somewhat – though both agree that something is amiss, one is 'quite certain' that there has been sexual abuse while the other is undecided.

A strategy meeting to conclude the s.47 enquiry decides that no useful purpose can be served at this time by convening a child protection conference, especially in light of an ongoing core assessment. Doing so was considered to be unhelpfully burdensome and punitive of Amar who has sought and is accepting help in protecting her daughters. She has in any case arranged to take leave from work until alternative arrangements can be made for child care and has agreed to participate in the core assessment.

Jenny intends to proceed with the core assessment (action made possible by Amar's co-operation) to establish whether there are ways of ensuring Jasbir and Kamlesh's safety given that the risk they may have been sexually abused remains. She also wants to attend to Amar's disclosure, which introduces a new dynamic to the situation. Amneka agrees to undertake the assessment with Jenny as she speaks Punjabi and can contribute expertise in terms of health and development.

This situation described in Snapshot 4.3 is typical of many, mostly but not exclusively, child sexual abuse cases, where workers and family members are left to contend with serious concerns in a context of uncertainty. Only Jasbir, Kamlesh and their grandfather have absolute certainty about what has happened.

Amar's decision to take leave from work and the fact that the grandparents live under a different roof take some of the pressure off the agencies, but may do little to reduce pressures on Amar. Her work is important for the finances it brings into the family and cutting herself off from ordinary family interactions is not a desired option. In similar situations where a family member suspected of being the alleged perpetrator resides in the home, the aim of agencies is often to achieve separation, with the person moving out or, failing that, the protective parent and children. This can present tensions and difficulties for children and protective parents, who are almost invariably mothers. It is not surprising therefore that sometimes mothers decide the costs incurred in moving are difficult to balance against the benefits of reducing an apparently unprovable risk. Meanwhile, neither Jasbir nor Kamlesh can be immune to the crisis in the family and the question arises what messages either child will take from the experience. It is easy to forget that children also 'manage risk' as part of daily life and 6-year-old Kamlesh may conclude that disclosing maltreatment is too costly.

Jenny will need to be sensitive to all of these difficulties and tensions as the core assessment progresses and must avoid the pitfall of wrongly interpreting positions and responses adopted by family members.

To date, Anil, the girl's father, has not been directly involved in events. The invisibility of fathers in child-care interventions is a common phenomenon, even when, as in this case, the father resides in the family home. However, any risk management process will be seriously undermined without the involvement of male parents or partners, whether or not they are resident in the family. If Anil cannot be persuaded to take time off work and return home for weekday sessions (and Jenny may need to look to the agency to provide transport costs or reimbursement for lost pay to facilitate this), she will need to consider sessions held over a weekend and negotiate clear arrangements for her to take time off in lieu.

The inconclusive outcomes of the medicals and interviews mean that a core assessment has become the major plank in Jenny's strategy for working to safeguard and promote the welfare of Jasbir and Kamlesh. Amar's co-operation to date renders this a possibility. Jenny and Amneka will need to exercise skill, sensitivity and patience to maintain Amar's participation and to bring Anil on board. In cases of proven harm or clearer risk, parental participation may be enforced through legal action in care proceedings or seeking an Assessment Order. In this instance, where harm is unproven and evidence of risk is clouded – it is doubtful, for example, what weight would be given to 3-year-old Jasbir's statement – there would be little to support such an application. Jenny is aware that, as matters stand, she has little to legitimate her involvement other than the power of persuasion.

In the wider, core assessment, Jenny and her multi-disciplinary colleagues will be guided by the principles outlined in the *Framework for Assessment* (Department of Health *et al.* 2000). These principles are listed in Table 4.3 along with how the principles might apply to Jasbir's case.

DIMENSIONS OF THE CHILD'S DEVELOPMENTAL NEEDS

Health

Amneka reports that Jasbir's growth and development are within the normal range for her age. Clearly, her physical and mental well-being are currently causing concern. It is normal for young children to have nightmares and many factors can cause them. At this age it is possible that Jasbir is not distinguishing between her dreams and day-to-day reality. This does not, however, explain her distress or the cause of the nightmares. The medical reveals that Jasbir probably has an infection but the doctor cannot say how this has been caused. Kamlesh also has growth and development within the normal range for a 6-year-old. The irregularities of her hymen can have many causes. Both children's development and growth checks and immunisations are up to date.

Education

Education covers all areas of a child's cognitive development that begins from birth. Jasbir has the opportunity for play and interaction with other children at her day nursery, which she attends two mornings a week. Kamlesh was below average in her SATS and there has been concern about her reading ability at school. She also does not mix well with the other children, who are predominantly white.

Emotional and behavioural development

Emotional and behavioural development is demonstrated in feelings and actions by a child, initially to parents and caregivers and, as the child grows older, to others beyond

TABLE 4.3 Assessment principles

Assessments should:	Considerations applied to Jasbir's case
Be child-centred	What do the children know? What choices do they have? What are their needs?
Be rooted in child development	The children are aged 3 and 6 and are both girls. Activities and communication must be age appropriate
Be ecological in their approach	The assessment will collect information on the individual children, the parent's capacity to care and the wider social and physical environment, including the extended family
Ensure equality of opportunity	The family's first language is Punjabi, although Kamlesh speaks perfect English. Translation issues therefore arise. If either child were disabled it may be appropriate to use an advocate
Involve working with children and families	Anil is working away and an extended family member is implicated in the allegation. Both the father and other extended family members will need to be involved
Build on strengths as well as identify difficulties	There are no concerns about the children, other than the allegations of sexual abuse
Be inter-agency in their approach to assessment and the provision of services	Jenny is already working closely with the police and the health visitor from the Primary Care Trust (PCT). She will also need to involve the school, nursery and any other professional who has contact with the family
Be a continuing process, not a single event	An interview has been arranged as *part* of the first stages of assessment. A broader, core assessment, which must be completed within 35 days, will also be undertaken
Be carried out in parallel with other action and providing services	The Best Evidence Interview and police investigation are ongoing. A need for other services may emerge during the assessment
Be grounded in evidence-based knowledge	The evidence base will include information that is known about the family and the family's environment, the children and their development, understanding of decision-making processes and research on risk relevant to child sexual abuse

the family. This is the most problematic area for Jasbir and her family. Observations of the children and their parents reveal little demonstrated affection between them. This must be interpreted within the context of the Sikh culture, but also with the knowledge that low levels of expression of affection are associated with families where sexual abuse is prevalent (Macdonald 2001, Cawson 2002). Amneka reports that she would expect Amar to show more physical affection towards the children, even though Anil may not be expected to – although this is by no means unilateral, as many Sikh fathers do demonstrate obvious affection. Nonetheless, Jasbir demonstrates secure attachment behaviour with both parents. Kamlesh seems to be quite independent and is described by Amar as almost a 'little parent' to Jasbir. This is explained within the context of normal child-rearing for this family since it is expected that older siblings take on responsibility for younger children. Amar is not abdicating her responsibility to Kamlesh, but instead encouraging her to behave in culturally appropriate ways.

Identity

Identity concerns the child's growing sense of self as a separate and valued person. The assessment identifies this as an area for further work, particularly for Kamlesh. While Jasbir is beginning to be aware of differences between her own skin colour and other children in the nursery, Kamlesh has reached a point where she is having to deal with racism in school. At this stage she needs extra help to develop a positive view of herself. The grandfather has admitted to excessively scrubbing the children in the bath and it is possible that her skin colour has been linked with lack of cleanliness either directly or indirectly. Racism and identity difficulties can make children more vulnerable, which, in turn, can increase feelings of isolation and having no-one to trust if maltreatment is present.

Family and social relationships

Family and social relationships include a stable and affectionate relationship with parents or caregivers, good relationships with siblings, increasing importance of age-appropriate friendships with peers and other significant persons in the child's life and response of the family to these relationships. Here there are some positives and negatives. The children appear to have a stable relationship with both parents though it is relatively low in affection. Kamlesh has a very protective relationship with Jasbir. She also has a peer friendship with a child who lives nearby, though as the racism at school has increased she has seen this friend less often.

Social presentation

Social presentation concerns the child's growing understanding of the way in which appearance, behaviour, and any impairment are perceived by the outside world and the impression being created. Both children are dressed appropriately on the several occasions that they are seen. At home they tend to wear traditional Indian dress, while at school and nursery they are dressed in English clothes. Amar takes great pride in her daughters' appearance.

Self-care skills

Self-care skills are all found to be appropriate for their age while at home. The discovery that (by his own admission) the grandfather is still bathing Kamlesh signals concern since Kamlesh is able to bathe herself, though under supervision. Jasbir is beginning to dress herself with help and gets upset if Amar interferes before she asks for help. It is agreed that Jenny will work with Kamlesh and Jasbir on personal safety skills.

DIMENSIONS OF PARENTING CAPACITY

- *basic care*: Providing for the child's physical needs, and appropriate medical and dental care
- *ensuring safety*: Ensuring that the child is adequately protected from harm or danger
- *emotional warmth*: Ensuring that the child's emotional needs are met and giving the child a sense of being specially valued and a positive sense of their own racial and cultural identity
- *stimulation*: Promoting the child's learning and intellectual development through encouragement and cognitive stimulation and promoting social opportunities
- *guidance and boundaries*: Enabling the child to regulate their own emotions and behaviour. The key parental tasks are *demonstrating* and *modelling* appropriate behaviour and control of emotions and interactions with others, and *guidance* which involves setting boundaries
- *stability*: Providing a sufficiently stable family environment to enable a child to develop and maintain a secure attachment to the primary caregiver(s) in order to ensure optimal development.

(Source: Department of Health *et al*. 2000)

Erooga and Print (2001) following Smith (1994) suggest that certain areas must be attended to in any assessment of parental capacity in cases of alleged sexual abuse. We consider each of these in relation to Jasbir's case and include the implications for risk management (see Table 4.4).

FAMILY AND ENVIRONMENTAL FACTORS

The third domain identified in the *Framework for Assessment* concerns the child's immediate environment: who they live with, where they live and who has contact with them or influence on their lives. The dimensions of this domain are considered in Table 4.5 in relation to risk management and Jasbir's case.

TABLE 4.4 Parental capacity and child sexual abuse

Factors to consider (Source: Erooga and Print 2001)	Assessment framework: Dimensions of parenting capacity	Application to Jasbir's case	Implications for risk management
Response to disclosure: Is it accepted that sexual abuse has occurred? If not, what further information is needed to improve acceptance?	Emotional warmth and stability	Amar accepts that sexual abuse has occurred. Anil does not	Anil's denial constitutes a source of risk. If he cannot accept that maltreatment may have occurred he is less likely to co-operate with measures to regulate contact with his father
Feelings towards the child who disclosed. Initially feelings may be confused. The child may be blamed or scapegoated	Emotional warmth and stability	Amar has developed an empathetic understanding of Jasbir's experiences. Anil is blaming Amar for using the incident to create division in his family	Neither parent is blaming Jasbir at this stage but this might change over time, given the inconclusive outcome of the current investigation. The conflict between her parents, however, may increase the risk of breakdown in their relationship and make both children more vulnerable
Role in the disclosing process: Willingness to report concerns will depend on understanding the maltreatment and also family relationships	Ensuring safety	Amar has demonstrated her willingness to report. Anil has not	Although the initial report was made, conflict between the parents may make further reports less likely
Position regarding responsibility and blame: Initially the child themselves may be blamed but it is important to recognise full responsibility lies with the perpetrator	Ensuring safety, emotional warmth and stability	Amar considers that her father-in-law is fully responsible. Anil blames Amar and considers that she is responsible for bringing shame on the family	Anil must accept that Amar was acting to protect her children. Future risk of harm would decrease if Anil could accept that the children may have been abused and his father may have been responsible

Perceived options: What options do the safe carers consider they have, how appropriate are they and how likely are they to use them?	Ensuring safety	Amar does not see how she can take protective action without Anil's support. Her power within the family can only be exercised through him	Anil must support Amar in taking protective action, e.g. supervising any contact between the children and their grandfather
Co-operation with statutory agencies	Ensuring safety	Amar has demonstrated that she wants to co-operate with agencies. Anil has been less co-operative	This is not essential to risk management, though informal monitoring by the Health Visitor must be co-operated with
Relationship history: Can the safe carer prioritise the needs of the child over their own relationship?	Ensuring safety and stability	Amar is financially and socially dependent on Anil and his family. She does not want to separate from Anil and he does not want to separate from her	The desire to keep the marital relationship intact along with Amar's desire to protect her children may optimise co-operation in protective action and contain the risk
History of sexual abuse: Unresolved memories and feelings may be reactivated in the safe carer. Help may be needed to deal with these before the child's needs can be fully met	Ensuring safety, warmth and stability	Amar disclosed her own abuse when the children were being interviewed	Amar is vulnerable and needs extra help to deal with her own feelings and experiences
Other vulnerabilities: For example, physical disabilities, mental health problems, substance misuse. May require extra help	Basic care, ensuring safety	Jasbir's family are Sikh. The grandparent's and parent's first language is Punjabi. They live in a predominantly white area where they know few people. Their extended family and friends do not know about the abuse	The family is relatively isolated in terms of physical location and language. The two households have been a significant mutual support network – now undermined. Amar has already expressed her mental turmoil over events and there is a risk of serious depression or emotional breakdown

TABLE 4.5 Risk management in relation to family and environmental factors

Dimension	Risk management
Family history and functioning	Amar and Anil have so far managed to provide a stable family environment for their children. Amar's disclosure of her own abuse and the uncertainty surrounding the possibility of sexual assault to the children may threaten this stability. A key issue for the team will be how to maintain stability while protecting against possible future harm and supporting Amar and Anil to deal with the past
Wider family	Relations with the parents-in-law will inevitably change. This will have repercussions for other extended family members
Housing	This has not been identified as a problem area in any aspect of the assessment
Employment	Anil has agreed to consider finding a job closer to home in order to offer more support to Amar. If this is not possible, Amar has agreed to either give up her job or find alternative child care
Income	Not currently a major concern, though if employment changes it could become one. Jenny needs to ensure that the family is in receipt of all its benefit entitlements
Family's social integration	The family are integrated into a community network but not in the immediate locality. The problems of racism at school need addressing. Kamlesh's teacher agrees to take this up but he will need support from the LEA
Community resources	Amneka encourages Amar to join a mother and toddler group and to take up a training course in IT at the local FE college. She will continue to visit regularly as the family's Health Visitor

RISK MANAGEMENT FOLLOWING THE INITIAL ASSESSMENT

The *Framework for Assessment* states that the conclusion of an assessment should result in:

* an analysis of the needs of the child and the parenting capacity to respond appropriately to those needs within their family context

- identification of whether and, if so, where intervention will be required to secure the well-being of the child or young person
- a realistic plan of action (including services to be provided), detailing who has responsibility for action, a timetable and a process for review.

The difficulty in this case and in many others is that cause of the harm cannot be proved: the outcome is inconclusive. The assessment of safety highlighted several areas for further work:

- personal safety around appropriate and inappropriate touching
- body image, identity and self-esteem
- supporting the parents to deal with the potential of sexual abuse
- supporting the parents to work through their own history
- creating a safe extended family environment: one in which more than one relative shares and knows of the concerns
- racism at school.

Each of these will reduce the likelihood of significant harm. The parents and children (where they can understand) should be informed of the outcome of the assessment and given an opportunity to record their views. The outcome may be:

- no further action – there is no likelihood of future significant harm. Applies where the alleged harm is false or services provided and actions taken during the initial or core assessment have minimised risk (e.g. a Schedule 1 offender leaves the household)
- informal monitoring by universal services – the likelihood of future significant harm cannot be proved by the minimum legal test of the balance of probabilities and the parents do not want to co-operate with further action
- a plan of work with the family – to reduce the likelihood of future significant harm and to meet the needs of the children (as defined under s.17), which would not be met without services
- the children become looked after – imminent significant harm is clearly likely unless the children are removed and this is the only remaining option. The 'no order' principle must apply (see Chapter 8) and this will usually also involve a plan of work with the family.

It must also be made clear which professional will have responsibility for taking forward the plan. This does not have to be a social worker. In Jasbir's case both Jenny and Amneka have responsibility for taking the plan forward in partnership with the parents. The authority for working with this family began under s.47 but without conclusive proof further involvement depends on the voluntary commitment of the parents. If co-operation is not forthcoming, then services will not be provided. If that had happened in this case it is likely that the outcome would have been to request that the PCT (via Amneka) and the school continue to monitor the children. Then, if further concerns arose they would be reported. This informal monitoring is difficult to sustain, particularly where there are frequent changes of staff and children can again be put at risk. Partnership with parents is therefore crucial to managing risk.

With the exception of the first outcome (no further action), good risk management means reviewing intervention after an agreed period. Where there is a legal mandate or the child's name is placed on the child protection register, the review period is specified by procedures (see Chapters 2 and 8). In other cases the review period needs to be agreed. In this way ensuring safety becomes a process, subject to evidence which is compiled as different interventions are tried and evaluated. Figure 4.1 illustrates the process.

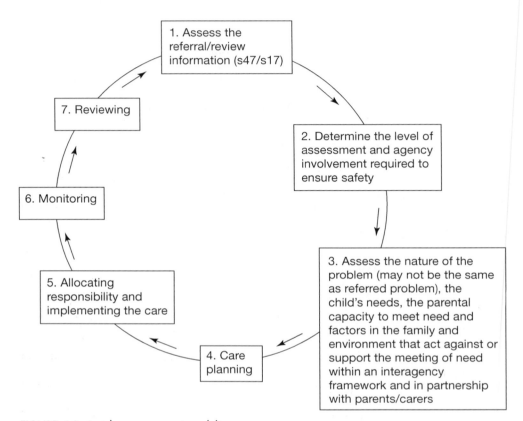

FIGURE 4.1 A risk management model

SUMMARY

A risk factor does not mean that a consequence will follow. Assessing risk inevitably means, by definition, that you will be dealing with uncertainty.

There are no criteria that definitively identify whether a child will be harmed or injured. Models that use such criteria are at best providing a 'cognitive map' or an 'aide mémoire'. Factors that have been linked to maltreatment can alert practitioners to explore these further in a comprehensive assessment, where the complex relationship between harms and contexts can be better understood.

The safety of children can be pursued through the systematic gathering of information at all stages:

- at referral (we recommend using the NSPCC Guide to Taking a Referral (see Table 4.2 and Cleaver *et al.* 1998)
- immediately post referral (we recommend using Thorpe and Bilson's criteria (1998) to decide whether the information constitutes a child protection referral or a 'child concern' case)
- initial assessment and core assessment using the *Framework for the Assessment of Children in Need and their Families* (Department of Health *et al.* 2000)
- joint investigation with the police using the guide *Achieving Best Evidence* (Home Office *et al.* 2002)

The safety of children is best ensured through

- being child focused, keeping the child's needs and voiced concerns at the centre of any assessment or intervention and ensuring that they are visible throughout the process
- partnership with parents/safe carers
- working closely, accountably and meaningfully with other professionals and agencies involved with the family
- subjecting interventions to evaluation and review on a regular basis (Are they working? Is the risk of harm reduced? How do I know? How do interventions need to change?)
- keeping an open mind and a non-judgemental stance, especially when new information arises.

FURTHER READING

Adcock, M. and White, R. (eds) (1998) *Significant Harm: Its management and outcome*, 2nd edn Croydon: Significant Publications

Horwath, J. (ed.) (2001) *The Child's World: Assessing children in need* London: Jessica Kingsley Publishers

REFERENCES

Adcock, M. (2001) The core assessment: How to synthesise information and make judgements. In J. Horwath (ed.) *The Child's World: Assessing children in need* London: Jessica Kingsley Publishers

Butler-Sloss, E. (1988) *Report of the Inquiry into Child Abuse in Cleveland in 1987* London: HMSO

Cawson, P. (2002) *Child Maltreatment in the Family: The experience of a national sample of young people* London: NSPCC

Cawson, P., Wattam, C., Brooker, S. and Kelly, G. (2000) *Child Maltreatment in the United Kingdom: A study of the prevalence of child abuse and neglect* London: NSPCC

Cleaver, H. (2001) When parents' issues influence their ability to respond to children's needs. In J. Horwath (ed.) *The Child's World: Assessing children in need* London: Jessica Kingsley Publishers

Cleaver, H., Wattam, C. and Cawson, P. (1998) *Assessing Risk in Child Protection* London: NSPCC

Creighton, S. (1992) *Child Abuse Deaths*, NSPCC Information Briefing, No. 5, London: NSPCC

Department of Health (1991) *Child Abuse: A study of inquiry reports 1980–89* London: HMSO

Department of Health (1995) *Child Protection: Messages from research* London: HMSO

Department of Health, Department for Education and Employment and the Home Office (2000) *Framework for the Assessment of Children in Need and their Families* London: The Stationery Office

Department of Health, Home Office, Department for Education and Employment (1999) *Working Together to Safeguard Children* London: The Stationery Office

Dingwall, R., Eekelaar, J. and Murray, T. (1983) *The Protection of Children: State intervention and family life* Oxford: Basil Blackwell

Doueck, H.J., Levine, M. and Bronson, D.E. (1993) Risk assessment in child protective services: An evaluation of the child at risk field system *Journal of Interpersonal Violence* 8, 4: 446–467

Erooga, M. and Print, B. (2001) Assessing parental capacity when intra-familial sexual abuse by an adult is a concern. In J. Horwath (ed.) *The Child's World: Assessing children in need* London: Jessica Kingsley Publishers

Gelles, R. J. and Cornell, C. P. (1990) *Intimate Violence in Families* Newbury Park, CA: Sage

Hagell, A. (1998) *Dangerous Care: Reviewing the risks to children from their carers* London: Policy Studies Institute and the Bridge Child Care Development Service

Home Office, Lord Chancellor, CPS, DH, National Assembly for Wales (2002) *Achieving Best Evidence in Criminal Proceedings: Guidance for vulnerable or intimidated witnesses, including children* London: Home Office Communications Directorate

Macdonald, G. (2001) *Effective Interventions for Child Abuse and Neglect: An evidence-based approach to planning and evaluating interventions* Chichester: Wiley

McGee, C. (2000) *Childhood Experiences of Domestic Violence* London: Jessica Kingsley

Munro, E. (2002) *Effective Child Protection* London: Sage

Parton, N., Thorpe, D. and Wattam, C. (1996) *Child Protection: Risk and the moral order* Basingstoke: Macmillan

Pease, K. (2001) Distributive justice and crime *European Journal on Criminal Policy and Research* 9, 4: 360–365

Smith, G. (1994) Parent, partner, protector: conflicting role demands for mothers of sexually abused children. In T. Morrison, M. Erooga and R. Beckett (eds) *Sexual Offending Against Children: Assessment and treatment of male abusers* London: Routledge

Thorpe, D. (1994) *Evaluating Child Protection* Buckingham: Open University Press

Thorpe, D. and Bilson, A. (1998) From protection to concern: Child protection careers without apologies *Children and Society* 12: 373–386

Wattam, C. (1996) Can filtering processes be rationalised? In N. Parton (ed.) *Child Protection and Family Support: Tensions, contradictions and possibilities* London: Routledge

Weber, M. (1997) The assessment of child abuse: a primary function of child protective services. In M. E. Helfer, R. S. Kempe and R. D. Krugman (eds) *The Battered Child*, 5th edn, Chicago: University of Chicago Press

Westcott, H. and Cross, M. (1996) *This Far and No Further: Towards ending the abuse of disabled children* Birmingham, Venture Press

CHAPTER 5

DIVERSITY AND ANTI-OPPRESSIVE PRACTICE IN CHILD PROTECTION

LEARNING OBJECTIVES

By the end of this chapter you will be able to:

- Examine your own value/knowledge base

- Be alert to the impact of the range of structural and institutional oppressions on children and families

- Identify the challenges for agencies and practitioners in achieving anti-oppressive practice in relation to ethnicity and disability in child protection

- Develop/apply practice tools for achieving anti-oppressive practice in child protection.

In Chapter 1 we introduced the UN Convention on the Rights of the Child. The CRC asserts the right of *all* children to be protected from maltreatment and contains articles that relate to this right, including Article 2 which states that children should be treated without discrimination. These are legally enforceable principles that are relatively easy to sign up to but extremely difficult to put into practice. Social work has a long tradition of including anti-oppressive practice in its training and competencies. Other professionals working with children, such as nurses and teachers, will all now be aware of the importance of working positively with diversity in an anti-oppressive way. Despite this, there are constant reminders that discrimination against and oppression of certain children and young people continue.

In the NSPCC child-rearing study (Cawson *et al.* 2000) 7 per cent of respondents felt they were discriminated against when they were children and 13 per cent considered they were 'made to feel different'. Over 40 per cent of the sample experienced bullying or discrimination by other children. When asked why they thought this had occurred, reasons given included size, class, intelligence, hobbies and 'race' (see Table 5.1). Most of this bullying and discrimination involved verbal abuse, though for a minority it included physical violence. Almost all of the perpetrators were other children and young people.

TABLE 5.1   Why children were bullied or discriminated against

Reason	Total %
Size	25
'Class'	21
Intelligence	19
Interests/hobbies	10
The place you lived	8
'Race'	7
Don't know/not stated	22
Weighted base:	1,199

This table demonstrates how prevalent discrimination is for children and the variety of reasons that can be given for this. Twenty-two per cent of this sample either did not know or did not state a reason to explain their oppression. There can be many other reasons that are not included in this list, including sexuality, appearance, disability, gender and age. Some of these oppressions are so embedded within the cultural fabric of society that even those who experience them cannot identify them directly. Inequalities can be entrenched. However, although we can see the evidence of inequality on the broad canvas of society and demonstrate the complicit role of institutions, people also experience their power or powerlessness individually. If society is the canvas, no one can be merely a spectator, we are all the paint that makes the picture. The child protection system and those who work with it and within it are no exception.

ACHIEVING ANTI-DISCRIMINATORY PRACTICE

For services to be anti-discriminatory, they must be accessible to and address the needs of children from all groups and communities. Though all local authorities and health authorities are required to have equality policies and some may have developed a good standard of service to potential users, the overall picture is inconsistent. Certain groups of children remain poorly served. In particular, services continue to struggle to meet the needs of children who are:

•   from black and minority ethnic communities
•   disabled
•   refugees and asylum seeking

- from traveller communities
- developing an other than heterosexual identity.

Nevertheless there is an expectation that agencies and practitioners will continue to strive to achieve inclusive services and anti-discriminatory practices. This expectation is now enshrined in the national objectives for social services and identified with the benchmarks of modernising welfare. Linking anti-discriminatory practice to required standards is an important strategy for developing services that can challenge exclusion and promote social inclusion. The reason for doing this is helpfully summarised in the *Framework for Assessment*:

> Since discrimination of all kinds is an everyday reality in many children's lives, every effort must be made to ensure that agencies' responses do not reflect or reinforce that experience and indeed should counteract it.
>
> (Department of Health *et al.* 2000: 12)

An important first step is to improve our understanding of how disadvantage and social exclusion work. Seeing snapshots in the form of work with individual service users provides glimpses but doesn't give the whole picture. One explanation is that social exclusion is rooted in the structure of society, in which power – whether economic, political, social or ideological – is concentrated in some groups and classes (white, male, middle-class, wealthy, able-bodied, heterosexual, early to middle-aged) at the expense of other groups and classes (black and minority ethnic, female, working-class, poor, disabled, gay, lesbian, children and older people). This unequal distribution of power shapes the organisation and institutions of society and gives rise to broad patterns of disadvantage or oppression (wage and job opportunity differences by gender, ethnicity and disability, for example) and recurrent themes of inequality (for example, in health, criminal justice and education). These themes of inequality demonstrate social injustice and power differentials. Indeed, the public institutions and practices of society become a significant mechanism for perpetuating these inequalities – maintaining what is known as the 'status quo'. Though institutional racism has most recently been highlighted by the Macpherson Report (Home Office 1999), other inequalities are similarly entrenched.

Power and social exclusion are both dynamic. By this we mean that they can change from situation to situation and across time. Social theory has moved away from a static notion of power held by institutions or individuals, such as 'government' or the 'prime minister'. Instead power is best thought of as being exercised in relationships and interactions, through communication. People do not fit easily into 'powerful' or 'powerless' groupings (Fook 2002); rather, people can exercise power in some situations but not in others. Similarly, people may be socially excluded in one way but not in another and they may move in and out of exclusion (Room 1998). If you reflect on your own life you will remember times when you had little power and times when you had a great deal, times when you felt left out or unable to access something and others when you could get something other people could not. One implication of a dynamic model for child protection is that for many children, even though they experience disadvantage and exclusion, there will be sites of positive reinforcement, positive power and inclusion that practitioners can work with to build resilience. Dominelli (1997) also makes the point that:

Individual people can be both oppressed and oppressing. Making connections between these roles facilitates people learning how to use their experience of oppression along one dimension to develop their skills of countering it along others. Their deepened understanding of different forms of oppression can be the outcome of transferring skills from one area to another. Transferability of skills is useful in extending good practice.

(p. 223)

DEVELOPMENT ACTIVITY 5.1: EXPLORING SOCIAL INJUSTICE AND POWER DIFFERENTIALS

Consider your own or a relevant organisational setting (college/education, health, social services, criminal justice) and look for evidence of power differentials. Places to start might be the numbers of men and women, BME or white, disabled or non-disabled in senior positions or full- and part-time work. Alternatively, start with the buildings: Are they built to meet the needs of all groups who can legitimately work in the organisation, e.g. is there a prayer room/area, disabled access to all facilities? What information is on the walls? Does it prioritise a certain group or reflect certain stereotypes (e.g. white, heterosexual, young adult)? You could also consider working arrangements: Are they flexible, family friendly, respectful of different religious requirements, adequately supported for people with complex needs? What do your answers tell you about power differences and social injustice?

EXAMINING YOUR OWN VALUE/KNOWLEDGE BASE

In Chapter 1 we suggested it was important to understand how your own experiences affect what you consider to be acceptable and unacceptable treatment of children. For similar reasons it is essential that you allow yourself time to examine your own attitudes towards diversity and oppression. One way to do this is to consider the development of your own identity and what that means in terms of how you understand the world and behave towards others, including children whom you may come into contact with. Development Activity 5.2 is derived from the work of NCBI (National Coalition Building Institute) International who work towards welcoming diversity, reducing prejudice and developing conflict resolution. One theory underpinning the NCBI's approach is that:

- guilt is the glue that holds prejudice in place
- every group counts, we all get hurt
- we welcome diversity
- we take pride in who we are
- the best way to help people become better advocates for others is to help them heal their own hurts.

(Brown/NCBI 2001)

DEVELOPMENT ACTIVITY 5.2: THE NCBI APPROACH TO RECOGNISING AND UNDERSTANDING IDENTITIES AND INTERNALISED OPPRESSION

1. Everyone can be described as belonging to a number of different categories. For example: gender, age, marital status, geographical location, class/economic background, religious group, physical attributes, parent status, language community, education/school, food preference (e.g. vegetarian), sexuality, criminality, housing status, victim/survivor, 'race'/ethnicity (think of others that could apply to you).

Make a list of the categories you are part of. How many of these are you happy to tell anyone about, how many would you tell to a confined set of people and how many would you not tell anyone about?

NCBI state that 'We cannot escape being identified as belonging to some groups. For example female/male, Black/Asian/White etc. But there are others that are less visible, nonetheless a great deal of discrimination is directed at them . . . It is possible to be completely proud of being a member of a group and yet decide not to share that information . . . Every group counts and every group is important when we think about welcoming diversity' (p. 8).

Drawing on your own experience, think about why people feel the need to keep some identities hidden.

2. *Internalising the negatives*

Choose one group you selected as being relevant to you. Make a list of the stereotypes, positive and negative, associated with that group.

NCBI state that 'Most people, when they think of prejudice reduction work, think of the stereotypes we have about other groups. But one of the most painful results of discrimination is that we also end up internalising many of these stereotypes and taking them out against members of our own group . . . Many of the things we can't stand about our own groups are simply an internalisation of what people from outside our groups have said about us . . . the things we hate about our own groups are the scars our groups carry from being mistreated. As we build greater unity with our own groups, we can also build greater unity across group lines' (pp. 11–12).

How true do you think this statement is for you?

3. *Being proud of your identities*

'When some people hear the word "pride" they think it means that someone thinks they are better than someone else. That is chauvinism. Chauvinism is claiming that my group is better than yours to conceal my feelings of inferiority. Real pride welcomes diversity. I feel good about my group: so I can welcome you to feel good about your group' (NCBI 2001: p. 13)

Try saying 'It's great to be . . .' go through each of the categories you identified in 1 above.

Share this exercise with a friend.

(Source: Brown/NCBI 2000)

It would be impossible to cover all forms of discrimination here and readers are directed towards useful texts in the recommended reading. This chapter will focus on two sources of discrimination: ethnicity and disability. Many of the considerations relating to these two groups are common to all forms of discrimination and oppression. One such area has to do with correct terms. It is important in any area of anti-discriminatory practice not to be inhibited in talking about the difficulties facing socially excluded groups because of terminology. It is better to talk about terminology with children, families, other professionals and colleagues than to be silenced by political correctness. Each of our sections begins with a definition but these are contested domains.

CULTURE AND ETHNICITY

> Ethnicity refers to a person's distinct sense of cultural and historical identity based on them belonging by birth (or in some cases marriage) to a particular ethnic group.
>
> (Dadzie 2000: 90)

Everyone has a culture, though the traditions and rituals associated with some cultural patterns are more explicit or dominant than others in the context of UK society. Despite this, ethnicity is usually taken to refer to a minority group. 'Ethnic minority' or 'minority ethnic' are terms used to refer to people who can be identified as different from the majority ethnic group. In some areas groups that are referred to as ethnic minorities can be close in numbers to the majority. For example, in Greater London ethnic minorities constitute 44.6 per cent of the resident population. This reinforces the fact that a defining feature of being a 'minority ethnic' person is the perception of difference as seen by the dominant group (Banks 2001). The power of the majority group to define is a prevailing feature for all minorities.

Ethnicity has tended to replace the term 'race', which is considered to be inaccurate and misleading. There are some concerns about this, because a fundamental problem facing society and all its institutions is racism. Talking only in terms of ethnicity can have the effect of diluting challenges to racism while it still remains endemic (Dutt and Phillips 1996).

Culture, ethnicity and 'race' encompass diverse child-rearing practices and the relationship between culture and child maltreatment is complex (Korbin 1997: 29). Difficulties in practice relate to:

- defining what is maltreatment
- discriminatory practices in responding to maltreatment, and
- culturally sensitive practices in relation to supporting children and families when maltreatment has occurred.

Over the past twenty years efforts have been made to develop culturally competent child protection practice, but there is still a long way to go.

Early debates concerned the influence of cultural relativism and the importance of not imposing one set of cultural standards on another group. The emergence of the sociology of childhood, which viewed childhood as a social/cultural construction, reinforced concerns that white Eurocentric versions of childhood were becoming the benchmark by which other childhoods were measured (James and Prout 1997). This leads to caution about stating that any one culture is better than any other (cultural relativism). However, arguments arising out of child death inquiries signalled problems with cultural relativism. Dingwall *et al.* (1983) identified cultural relativism as one criterion used by health and social care professionals when they assessed parents. They found that judgements about parenting were made in the context of what could be expected of a particular family, living in a particular place or coming from a particular background. Sometimes these judgements were based on stereotypes, for example the idea that an Asian father would not show his child affection. After their research was published, the tragic case of Jasmine Beckford hit the headlines. She was an 8-year-old black child who was murdered by her mother's boyfriend. The inquiry agreed that making judgements on the basis of 'cultural relativism' may have happened in Jasmine's case and thus contributed to her death (London Borough of Brent 1985).

SNAPSHOT 5.1: AN EXAMPLE OF CULTURAL RELATIVISM

Joan is a primary school teacher. She has four boys in her class who are Muslim. On Tuesday morning it was PE and the children were asked to report to the Hall in the bare feet. When they arrived, Joan noticed very clear bruises and welts on the feet of the four boys. She asked them how they got the marks and they told her they were beaten on the feet by the Iman at the Mosque because they did not learn the Koran. She discussed this with the Head Teacher who referred it to the local Social Services Department. After a few days, and having heard nothing further, Joan decided to phone Social Services to find out what happened. She was told that the matter had been dealt with by the Police Community Liaison Officer who had 'had a word' with the Iman. If she noticed bruising again she was to let them know. Joan was shocked at this and said that if she had been accused of bruising children she would have automatically been suspended while a full investigation took place.

Snapshot 5.1 is based on a real case, although names and identifying details have been altered. It raises a number of questions to which there are no absolute right or wrong answers. These are issues of professional judgement: something that is frequently required in child protection practice. In Chapter 4 we referred to criteria that help distinguish between what might be a child protection referral ('likelihood of significant harm') and child concern (Thorpe and Bilson 1998). One of the criteria for s.47 was when it is necessary to clarify whether the alleged actions were deliberately intended to cause harm or injury or were the consequence of an accident or excessive discipline. In this case it would appear that the injuries were a result of excessive discipline by someone outside the home. At the very least, then, under the current guidelines of the *Framework for Assessment*, a home visit should have been made to the parents of these children and an initial assessment carried out. The assessment would need to be conducted by someone who was familiar with Muslim culture and could speak the parent's first language, if this was not English. There are also critical gender issues. The allegation involves a male Iman and his treatment of male children. It would be important to speak with both the mother and father on this matter to explore their views on this treatment of their children. It is possible that they agreed with the Iman's actions and that they administer excessive corporal punishment at home. Banks (2001) helpfully suggests that the terms used to describe discipline techniques, such as 'beating', 'whipping', 'thrashing', should be demonstrated wherever possible since meanings can vary. The issue of discipline would need to be dealt with in a culturally sensitive way but the parents must also be informed of the limits. Although it is legal in the UK to hit children, it is not legal to assault them and cause actual bodily harm. In this case the children's ethnicity is a consideration in terms of language, religion and culture, but not the behaviour of hitting that causes injury. In addition there are generic concerns that would apply to all such cases: gender and the limits of parental discipline.

There are differences between cultural groups in terms of child-rearing practices but there are some practices that, even when understood in the context of these groups, are inherently harmful. The example of excessive corporal punishment is one. Another is the 'sexual use' of children, a term which refers to culturally accepted practices that involve children and young people in sexual activity. Sexual use is set apart from the sexual abuse of children that clearly contravenes cultural norms. One form of the sexual use of children is that of child marriage, an acceptable custom in many cultures. Social pressure reproduces such customs, even where laws are passed against them. Parents and friends will not publicly oppose child marriage arrangements for fear of the social ostracism that might follow. In addition the practice continues because economic factors play an important role in encouraging early marriages. However, this does not mean that effects are not potentially harmful. According to one study, in a country where child marriage is experienced by one-quarter of 14-year-olds, females under 15 years of age are four times more likely to die during childbirth than those aged between 15 to 19 (Levesque 1998).

DEVELOPMENT ACTIVITY 5.3: DEVELOPING CULTURALLY COMPETENT PRACTICE

Areas to consider	*What do you need to do?*
The need for cultural familiarity – children cannot be assessed or worked with outside of their cultural context	How many different cultures are you familiar with? Do you take opportunities to attend events or meetings held by minority ethnic groups? Be able to say you do not know.
Use of language – wherever possible, children and their parents/carers should be communicated with in their language of choice. It is never acceptable to use other children as interpreters where there are child protection concerns	What languages can you speak? Do you know how you would find an interpreter? Remember there may be problems if the interpreter is from the same living community as the referred child.
Cultural misattribution – stereotyping and fear as a consequence of	Challenge any stereotypes you may have. Mix more with people of cultures and

misunderstanding self-presentation and behaviour. Banks gives the example of feeling intimidated by a father who has dreadlocks (p. 145)	ethnicities different from your own. Reflect on what makes you fearful and why. Ensure that any interaction is not influenced by your personal bias, including 'absolving guilt' for being 'racist' (Ridley 1995)
Over-reliance on cultural explanations	Try to assess personal contributions to the problem. Avoid seeing all behaviour as arising from the culture, as this pathologises culture. Keep the focus on the child
	(Source: Banks 2001)

White (1999) identifies three kinds of cultural relativism:

1   A theoretical position which, in effect, says cultures are not to be compared but only understood in their own terms
2   A moral and political doctrine that asserts that rights and rules are established and legitimated within cultures and consequently should only be judged from within. In effect, they are exempt from criticism or interference from those outside the culture
3   A practical analytic position 'which insists we remain sensitive to differences simply as a practical analytic tool. Relativity then becomes, in addition to a general principle of respect for the ways of life of others, a tool of learning and understanding . . . a way of shaking-up and questioning supposed universalist ideas and opening up the possibility of others'. (White 1999: 137)

Ultimately the child protection test for whether a behaviour is acceptable or not must be the test for significant harm (see Chapter 3). Although 'significant' is not defined by the Children Act 1989, White (1998) suggests that the dictionary definition of 'considerable, noteworthy or important' is helpful. Sometimes, in reaching judgements, it is helpful to know what is not included. Significant does not refer to 'minor shortcomings in health care or minor deficits in physical, psychological or social development' (Department of Health 1990). Harm is defined as impairment of health or development. Though culture may provide us with some grey areas, these are fairly specific criteria which, if attitudes such as cultural relativism and cultural misattribution don't get in the way, can be measured and justified socially, morally and legally. Ultimately all cases will depend on a degree of professional judgement and it is important to improve the skills required to make such judgements. In relation to ethnicity, the SSI report *Excellence Not Excuses* (2000) provides a series of key questions that have been incorporated into Development Activity 5.4 at the end of this chapter. These questions can be applied at an individual, personal level or to agencies and organisations more generally.

Finally, it is important to remember the potential effects of racism and discrimination on children who may be referred for child protection concerns. The Home Office *et al.* (2002) have set out some considerations to take into account when interviewing black and minority ethnic children (Guidance 5.1). These can also be applied to interventions and treatment services.

GUIDANCE 5.1: SOME POSSIBLE EFFECTS OF RACISM

- Fear
- Lowered self-esteem
- Fear of betrayal of community
- Mistrust of people from outside own community
- Difficulty in establishing positive (racial) identity
- Increased vulnerability to racist abuse.

(Source: Home Office *et al.* 2002, *Achieving Best Evidence in Criminal Proceedings: Guidance for vulnerable or intimidated witnesses, including children,* Box 2.6. HMSO: London)

© Crown copyright Reproduced with the permission of the Controller of HMSO and the Queen's Printer for Scotland

CHILDREN WITH COMPLEX NEEDS

Marchant (2001) points out that there is considerable debate regarding definitions of disability and that the social environment, history and medical advances can alter conditions and circumstances that define what is a complex need or a disability. She gives a helpful definition of the distinction between complex needs and disability:

Complex needs is used to refer to:

- Children who have major health care needs in addition to their impairments, including children with life-limiting conditions;
- Children who have more than one impairment affecting their communication or more than one impairment having other major impact on their lives;
- Children whose impairments have been caused by maltreatment, including those children whose disability is a consequence of the parent inducing or fabricating the child's illness.

Most children with complex needs will, then, be disabled, but not all disabled children have complex needs.

(Marchant 2001: 209)

On the grounds of equality of access and opportunity, child protection services should be as open to disabled children as they are to non-disabled children. However, there are additional reasons to consider disabled children as a special case. Research has shown that disabled children are more vulnerable to maltreatment than the non-disabled (Westcott and Cross 1996). Just over 4 per cent of the total in the NSPCC's random probability prevalence study (Cawson *et al.* 2000) declared they were disabled or experienced a long-term illness before they were 16. Their experience of maltreatment was proportionally higher for serious physical abuse, emotional abuse, serious absence of care and sexual abuse by a known person or stranger (see Table 5.2). The researchers did not talk to young adults who lived in institutions because sampling was conducted through postcode address files, nor did they have the facilities for assisted communication. Thus, a large proportion of people with complex needs may have been missed and the findings are likely to be an underestimate. This is a further example of exclusion because of a reluctance to put in the extra resources to facilitate inclusion. It illustrates the social model of disability, which proposes that disabled people are not disabled by their impairment(s) but by social factors that create barriers, including the additional investment needed for participation.

TABLE 5.2 Disability and maltreatment

Child-rearing study: Respondents research assessed or self-assessed as maltreated

Type of maltreatment	Whole sample	Respondents with a disability or long-term illness before 16 years
Sample weighted base	2,869 100%	129 100%
Serious physical abuse	7%	10%
Emotional abuse	6%	10%
Serious absence of care	6%	8%
Serious absence of supervision	5%	5%
Sexual abuse parents	1%	1%
Sexual abuse other known person	15%	22%
Sexual abuse stranger/person just met	4%	8%

(Source: Cawson *et al*. 2000)

For all excluded groups there are issues about service accessibility. Availability of service and accessibility do not mean the same thing. We already know that the majority of children who experience maltreatment do not access services, even though technically they are available (see Chapter 1). Failure to access may be due to how appropriate services seem, fear of losing control, loss of confidentiality or a lack of confidence that the service will be able to help. In addition to these factors, impediments to uptake of services can include:

- lack of information (about service provision and legal entitlement)
- communication barriers
- historically negative relationships
- current discriminatory practices and procedures.

Safeguarding disabled children requires additional resources, concentrated effort and, once again, fine professional judgement. Some disabled children will find it even harder to talk about maltreatment than non-disabled children because they need assistance in communication and may not have access to anyone they can talk to about it. Children with complex needs are more dependent on their carers, and the boundaries between abusive behaviour and care can become blurred in some cases. Marchant (2001) gives the example of a child known to her who had dual sensory impairment and learning disabilities. This child spent prolonged periods tied to furniture as her carers thought this was the only way to prevent her harming herself or others (p. 210). A child in such a situation may accept the treatment as normal and for this reason may not consider telling anyone else about it. Access to opportunities to tell, a choice of people to talk to about maltreatment and understanding that what is happening to you is wrong, are features of maltreatment for all children. However, they may be of heightened importance for children with complex needs.

A further difficulty can be described as the 'dominant mode of understanding' a child's situation. This was highlighted in a review of inquiry reports into child mal-treatment cases during the 1980s (Department of Health 1991). It refers to the way in which new information cannot be heard because the case has already been framed in a certain way. For disabled children the dominant mode of understanding may centre upon their disability. When signs of maltreatment arise they may be interpreted within the existing framework or missed altogether. Several authors have recommended that health and social care professionals who specialise in working with disabled children should also be trained in child protection to combat this problem (see for example, Marchant and Page 1993).

SNAPSHOT 5.2: A CHILD WITH COMPLEX NEEDS

Kwan Ye, 6 years old, lives with his mother and 13-year-old sister, his father having died three years ago. The family live in a rather cramped flat above the 'Take Away' family business which Kwan Ye's mother now runs with a cousin. Kwan Ye is hearing impaired, partially sighted, has severe learning disability, and has Hepatitis C (a viral disorder of the blood transmitted at birth via his mother who is a carrier). He is developmentally delayed across all dimensions but has yet to receive any schooling – his statement of educational needs was delayed by the family being out of the country for eighteen months and there are difficulties locating an appropriate place with the Hepatitis a complicating factor for some schools. His mother's first language is Hakka (one of the distinct but minor languages of Hong Kong, her country of origin) and she has some understanding of spoken English, but she relies on her daughter to supplement this and to translate written communications. Kwan Ye has no language but communicates through noise, gesture and behaviour. He is described by various professionals who have had contact with him as 'loud and unruly', 'unmanageable' and 'feral' (wild).

Neighbours and people using the 'Take Away' have reported concerns about emotional and physical maltreatment of Kwan Ye to several agencies, but inconsistent or cursory follow-ups have failed to identify the fact that Kwan Ye is regularly left alone during business hours constrained by a harness which is linked to a modified animal cable that allows him to move back and forth across a largely empty attic room with a television turned on but just beyond his reach. A similar harness arrangement exists downstairs where Kwan Ye has a run in sight of the food preparation room and spends time out of opening hours.

Kwan Ye is clearly a child with complex needs, certainly fulfilling two and possibly all three of Marchant's criteria listed earlier. Furthermore, a dominant mode of understanding appears to be at work here, impeding recognition of what is clearly cruel and unusual treatment. It is ironic that staff reports describe Kwan Ye in terms that accurately flag up this treatment, if only questions were asked about his quality of life. Whereas it seems likely that the focus of attention is not Kwan Ye – his life – but rather, Kwan Ye – the problem. A core assessment could have the merit of achieving a child-centred focus, but as matters stand Kwan Ye is in an administrative limbo, awaiting a school place (another dominant mode) and the previous medical and educational needs assessment hold sway.

Perhaps of equal significance is a dominant view whereby communication is linked primarily to spoken language, usually English. Limited diversity in the welfare workforce generally means that meeting the needs of other than English-language speakers, including sign language (BSL) users, requires exceptional arrangements to be made. Though most agencies now have policies about meeting such needs, many struggle to implement them, and where agencies lack developed protocols and well-established links to interpreting services, inertia can set in, leaving staff and service users to manage somehow, with attendant risks to vulnerable children and adults. However, the issues are compounded when language (spoken or signed) as in Kwan Ye's case is not the vehicle of communication. Here, the scale of the challenge to professional skills and resources can give rise to panic (Wonnacott and Kennedy 2001) abated only by resigned acceptance ('s/he can't talk' becomes 'we can't do anything') or avoidance ('s/he can't talk' becomes 'there's nothing to be discovered').

The Home Office *et al.* (2002) give some examples of the possible effects of discrimination based on impairments when children do tell others about maltreatment. These effects can act to silence disabled victims of maltreatment or make their search for help more difficult.

DEVELOPMENT ACTIVITY 5.4: THE SILENCING OF DISABLED CHILDREN OR CHILDREN WITH COMPLEX NEEDS

Achieving Best Evidence identifies a number of potential effects of discrimination based on impairment(s) which may serve to silence children in the matter of maltreatment or neglect. Drawing on Snapshot 5.2, consider the relevance of each possible effect in relation to the silencing of Kwan Ye.

Possible effects on child	*Relevance for specific child*
• lack of autonomy, patronisation	
• difficulty in establishing positive self-identity as a disabled child	
• isolation (geographical, physical, social)	
• dependency	
• increased vulnerability to maltreatment.	

Possible effects on professionals

- child perceived as 'voiceless object'
- child perceived as 'asexual'.

(Home Office *et al.* (2002) Box 2.7)
(from Shakespeare and Watson (1998) and Westcott 1993)

It seems likely that a number of these factors are working to silence Kwan Ye – and we expect you readily identified lack of autonomy, isolation, dependency and a perception of him as 'voiceless object'. But there is cause for considering that he may be struggling to identify a positive self-image – it is difficult to see where he might be obtaining positive models of disability and the descriptions of him as 'feral' might be indicative of negative self-identity. Conversely, his wildness may reflect a determined resistance to the adversity of his situation which may be the basis for a more positive self-image and there is a slight possibility that the unfettered access to television has provided some useful material for identity building. Similarly, there is a case to be made for increased vulnerability to abuse – the failure of a range of professionals to recognise his experiences gives permission for the cruel and unusual treatment to continue. The failure to address his needs renders him vulnerable to further significant harm in the form of illness or injury or third-party maltreatment.

Safeguarding children with complex needs in such situations requires confident, skilled staff and resources, in addition to a resolutely child-centred approach. For example, *Positive Practice Standards* (Department of Health 2002) highlights the point that, 'Though all children can communicate, most workers have a limited language or communication repertoire and it will be necessary for workers to address their deficiency' and states that 'the conduct of child protection assessments with deaf children might require at least 3 different types of worker:

- A specialist in child protection
- A qualified social worker for deaf people / deaf advocate
- A communication support worker (e.g. a BSL interpreter).'

Clearly there are training and workforce implications to be addressed by agencies, but practitioners have professional responsibilities for identifying the 'limits of their repertoires' and considering, through staff appraisal, how these could be extended.

SUMMARY

The UN Convention on the Rights of the Child asserts the right of *all* children to be protected from maltreatment and contains articles that relate to this right, including Article 2 which states that children should be treated without discrimination.

Ensuring fair access to services is identified with National Objectives for children's services and linked to national occupational standards. Thus, organisations and individual practitioners have responsibilities for countering discrimination.

Countering discrimination requires practitioners to consider their own values and attitudes across all dimensions of diversity.

For services to be anti-discriminatory they must be accessible to and address the needs of children from all groups and communities. Though all local authorities and health authorities are required to have equality policies and some may have developed a good standard of service to potential users, the overall picture is inconsistent. Certain groups of children remain poorly served. In particular, children who are: from black and minority ethnic communities, disabled, refugee and asylum-seeking, from traveller communities, or developing an other than heterosexual identity.

DEVELOPMENT ACTIVITY 5.5: EXCELLENCE NOT EXCUSES

Practice question	Yes/No	How do/will I/we (the organisation) achieve this?
Do you ensure that your practice is anti-racist/anti-discriminatory?		
Do you recognise racial harassment as a child protection/children in need issue?		
Can you recognise when discrimination becomes a children in need issue?		
Do you ensure that a child's religion, racial, cultural and linguistic background are taken account of in any decision-making process?		
Do you record ethnicity, language and religion of *all* children and families?		
Do you record ethnicity, language and religion of some children and families?		
Do you ensure that refugees and asylum seekers are treated fairly?		
Do you ensure that all looked-after children have positive role models and that these are appropriate to their ethnicity, disability and gender?		
Do you ensure that all children in the child protection, children in need or looked-after systems have access to advocates?		
Are these advocates gender, disability or ethnicity appropriate?		
Do you address racism and ways of developing anti-oppressive practice?		

Working with children and families from diverse backgrounds demands that practitioners develop culturally competent practice – which allows for a child-centred focus and sensitivity to children and their families' cultural context. But practitioners will need to avoid the pitfall of cultural relativism, which leaves some groups of children at risk because maltreatment is stereotypically associated with their cultural background.

Children with complex needs and some children with disability are at increased risk of maltreatment – in particular: for serious physical abuse, emotional maltreatment, serious absence of care and sexual abuse by a known person or stranger.

Dominant modes of understanding – whereby all aspects of a child's life are explained or understood in relation to their disability or complex needs – can increase the risk that maltreatment or neglect is discounted.

Children with complex needs are more dependent on their carers and the boundaries between abusive behaviour and care can become blurred in some cases.

Some disabled children will find it even harder to talk about maltreatment than non-disabled children because they need assistance in communication and may not have access to anyone they can talk to about it.

FURTHER READING

Barter, C. (1999) *Protecting Children from Racism and Racial Abuse – A research review* London: NSPCC

Cawson, P. (2002) *Child Maltreatment in the Family* London: NSPCC

Cross, T., Bazron, B., Dennis, K. and Isaacs, M. (1989) Towards a culturally competent system of care: A monograph on effective services for minority children who are severely emotionally disturbed. In Valtonen, K. (2002) Social work with immigrants and refugees: Developing a participation-based framework for anti-oppressive practice part 2 *British Journal of Social Work* 32: 113–120

Dominelli, L. (1997) *Anti-Racist Practice*, 2nd ed., Basingstoke: BASW/Macmillan

Dutt, R. and Phillips, M. (2000) The assessment of black children in need and their families. In Department of Health (2000) *Assessing Children in Need and their Families: Practice Guidance* London: The Stationery Office

Fortnum, H. and Davis, A. (1997) Epidemiology of permanent child hearing impairment in the Trent region 1985–1993 *British Journal of Audiology* 31: 409–446

Lau, A. (1991) Cultural and ethnic perspectives on significant harm: its assessment and treatment. In M. Adcock, R. White and A. Hollows *Significant Harm* Croydon: Significant Publications

Measures, P. (1992) Abuse – The disability dimension *Social Work Today* 17 (30/1/92)

NSPCC/Department of Health (1997) *Turning Points: A resource pack for communicating with children* Leicester: NSPCC

Parry, G. (1996) BACDA Newsletter cited in Department of Health (2002) *Deaf Children: Positive practice standards in social services – Executive summary*, online DOH/Quality Protects website

Race Equality Unit (1998) *Black and Ethnic Minority Children and their Families – A review of research studies for the SSI* London: REU

Stalker, K. (2000) *Supporting Disabled Children and Their Families: A review of policy and research* York: Joseph Rowntree Foundation

Thompson, N. (1997) *Anti-Discriminatory Practice*, 2nd edn, London: Macmillan

Thompson, N. (1998) *Promoting Equality: Challenging discrimination and oppression in the human services* London: Macmillan

Thompson, N. (2000) *Theory and Practice in Human Services* Buckingham: Open University Press

REFERENCES

Banks, N. (2001) Assessing children and families who belong to minority ethnic groups. In J. Horwath (ed.) *The Child's World: Assessing children in need* London: Jessica Kingsley Publishers

Brown, C. R. (2001) *Welcoming Diversity and Prejudice Reduction Workshop and Conflict Resolution Models: Trainers' notes* Washington, DC: National Coalition Building Institute International.

Cawson, P., Wattam, C., Brooker, S. and Kelly, G. (2000) *Child Maltreatment in the United Kingdom: A study of the prevalence of child abuse and neglect* London: NSPCC

Dadzie, S. (2000) *Toolkit for Tackling Racism in Schools* Stoke on Trent: Trentham

Department of Health (1990) *Volume 1 Department of Health Guidance (Court Orders)* London: HMSO

Department of Health (1991) *Child Abuse: A study of inquiry reports 1980–89* London: HMSO

Department of Health (2002) *Deaf Children: Positive practice standards in social services – Executive summary*, online DOH/Quality Protects website

Department of Health, Department for Education and Employment and the Home Office (2000) *Framework for the Assessment of Children in Need and their Families* London: The Stationery Office

Dingwall, R., Eekelaar, J.M. and Murray, T. (1983) *The Protection of Children: State intervention and family life* Oxford: Basil Blackwell

Dutt, R. and Phillips, M. (1996) In *Childhood Matters*, Report of the National Commission of Inquiry into the Prevention of Child Abuse, Volume 2, Background Papers London: HMSO

Fook, J. (2002) *Social Work: Critical theory and practice* London: Sage

Home Office (1999) *The Stephen Lawrence Inquiry, Report of an Inquiry by Sir William Macpherson of Cluny Advised by Tom Cook, The Right Reverend Dr John Sentamu, Dr Richard Stone* London: The Stationery Office

Home Office, Lord Chancellor's Department, Crown Prosecution Service, Department of Health and National Assembly for Wales (2002) *Achieving Best Evidence in Criminal Proceedings: Guidance for vulnerable or intimidated witnesses, including children* London: The Stationery Office

James, A. and Prout, A. (1997) *Constructing and Reconstructing Childhood*, 2nd edn, London: Falmer Press

Korbin, J. E. (1997) Culture and child maltreatment. In M. E. Helfer, R. S. Kempe and R. D. Krugman, *The Battered Child*, 5th edn, Chicago: University of Chicago Press

Levesque, R. J. R. (1998) *Sexual Abuse of Children: A human rights perspective* Bloomington: Indiana University Press

London Borough of Brent (1985) *A Child in Trust, The Report of the Panel of Inquiry into the Circumstances Surrounding the Death of Jasmine Beckford* Middlesex: Borough of Brent

Marchant, R. (2001) The assessment of children with complex needs. In J. Horwath (ed.) *The Child's World: Assessing children in need* London: Jessica Kingsley Publishers

Marchant, R. and Page, M. (1993) *Bridging the Gap: Child protection work with childen with multiple disabilities* London: NSPCC

Ridley, C. (1995) *Overcoming Unintentional Racism in Counseling and Therapy: A practitioner's guide to intentional intervention* Thousand Oaks, CA: Sage Publications

Room, G. (1998) *Social Exclusion, Solidarity and the Challenge of Globalisation*, CASP Working Papers No. 27, Centre for the Analysis of Social Policy University of Bath: Mimeo

Shakespeare, T. and Watson, N. (1998) Theoretical perspectives on research with disabled children. In C. Robinson and K. Stalker (eds) *Growing Up with Disability* London: Jessica Kingsley Publishers

SSI/O'Neale, V. (2000) *Excellence Not Excuses: Inspection of services for ethnic minority children and families* London: DOH (available online via www.doh.gov.uk/scg/socialc.htm)

Thorpe, D. and Bilson, A. (1998) From protection to concern: Child protection careers without apologies *Children and Society* 12: 373–386

Westcott, H. (1993) *Abuse of Children and Adults with Disabilities* London: NSPCC

Westcott, H. and Cross, M. (1996) *This Far and No Further: Towards ending the abuse of disabled children* Birmingham: Venture Press

White, B. (1999) Defining the intolerable: Child work, global standards and cultural relativism *Childhood* 6, 1: 133–144

White, R. (1998) Significant harm: Legal applications. In M. Adcock and R. White (eds) *Significant Harm: Its management and outcome*, 2nd edn, Croydon: Significant Publications

Wonnacott, M. and Kennedy, M. (2001) A model approach *Community Care* 8 March: 27

CHAPTER 6

WORKING THERAPEUTICALLY WITH CHILDREN

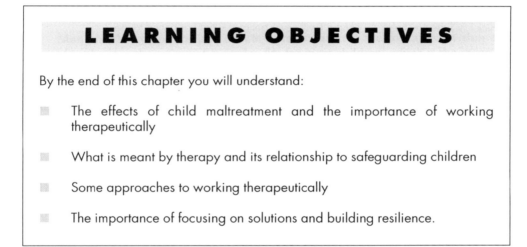

LEARNING OBJECTIVES

By the end of this chapter you will understand:

- The effects of child maltreatment and the importance of working therapeutically

- What is meant by therapy and its relationship to safeguarding children

- Some approaches to working therapeutically

- The importance of focusing on solutions and building resilience.

Children who experience maltreatment may suffer a wide range of effects. Though some children are resilient and some forms of maltreatment appear to be less harmful than others, it is likely that the majority will feel some effects from their experiences. There will be physical and emotional health consequences, but whereas in most cases the physical injuries will heal, the mental effects can last a lifetime. When the National Commission of Inquiry into the Prevention of Child Abuse asked survivors to write about their experiences, over 1000 people replied and 54% talked about a wide range of effects including their ability to form and keep relationships, to trust, to have children, to care for their children as well as reports of chronic illness both physical and mental (Wattam and Woodward 1996). By definition, all those who wrote to the Commission had, in some way, survived and lived with these effects from day to day. Three examples are given in Snapshot 6.1. They demonstrate the length of time that effects stay with survivors and how, without the right therapeutic help, many find it difficult to move on.

DEVELOPMENT ACTIVITY 6.4: BREAKING THE 'TRAUMA BOND'

Goals	How might you help Karen achieve this?
Identifying the relationship as 'victim' and 'offender' – helping the child to see she is not responsible for the offender's actions	
Releasing the victim from the power of the offender – understanding methods used by the offender to keep the child in the abusive relationship	
Relieving guilt about consequences – particularly where the family breaks up or the child becomes looked after	
Building self-esteem – through body image and identity work, small successes and learning to hear positive things about themselves	
Breaking down patterns of behaviour that can lead to future abusive relationships – e.g working on internalised scripts 'I'm bad I deserve to be hurt/get nowhere/be miserable' Needing to hear or feel pain to feel alive/loved	
Moving from victim to survivor – no longer seeing themselves as unable to avoid maltreatment and negative experience	
Moving to seeing and taking choices, making mistakes is the way to learn, acceptance	

FOCUS ON SOLUTIONS RATHER THAN PROBLEMS

A more recent turn in therapeutic approaches has been that of 'solution-focused therapy' (De Shazer 1988). This has interesting potential for working with maltreated children, though it has mostly been applied to adults (see, for example, Parton and Byrne 2001). The underlying principle is quite simple: rather than focusing on the problem, the target is solutions. So, for example, in Karen's case the therapist or helper could ask what she would like to change, what she has done so far to make that change come about and what more she could do. The principles are outlined in Table 6.1.

WORKING ETHICALLY

Hurley sums up good ethical practice in the following way:

> There are elements of ethical practice such as openness, sensitivity, accuracy, honesty, objectivity, privacy and confidentiality with which most consultants, researchers and practitioners would concur. An important function of adhering to these elements of ethical practice is to ensure that when closure of the discussion occurs no members of the group are left feeling anxious, upset, or apprehensive either about what happened in the group or about what will happen after the group.
>
> (1998: 26)

There is a clear responsibility for ethical practice on the part of the practitioner. In addition to practice that maintains confidentiality and privacy, essential elements of a therapeutic framework are considered to be

- predictability and consistency
- therapist neutrality
- therapist anonymity

(Daniels and Jenkins 2000)

Considering Karen's case, what do you think would be important ethical issues to attend to when applying a solution-focused approach?

BUILDING RESILIENCE

Research shows that some children will experience more profound effects than others (Wattam and Woodward 1996). Effects will be influenced by the type of maltreatment, particularly if a child experiences more than one type over an extended period of time, its intensity and the relationship of the perpetrator to the child (Cawson 2002). However, we also know that resilience can mediate these effects (Gilligan 2000). Certain factors can help buffer the child and reduce the impact of maltreatment. These factors have been described on three levels: intra-personal, inter-personal and contextual

TABLE 6.1 Principles of solution-focused therapy

Principles	*Possible applications to Karen's case*
1. Focusing on change and possibilities, e.g. between now and the first group meeting please observe any positive changes that you would want to carry on, however small	She finds she is feeling more positive because she is looking forward to getting help. She is feeling less afraid, knowing her mother will have to let her go to the group as part of the assessment agreement
2. Creating goals and preferred futures. If applied to a group, finding group goals, e.g. everyone agrees they want to be less angry	'I want to stop getting into trouble at school.' 'Why do you want to do that?' 'So I can make my Mum happy.' 'How about you? What would make you happy?' 'Getting on better with other people at school, having a good friend.'
3. Building on strengths, skills and resources, e.g. adopting a collaborative stance and positively reframing negative behaviour. This must be genuine and appropriate and can apply to an individual or a group	'You must have been very afraid about coming to the group and meeting new people for the first time, being here shows how brave you are.'
4. Looking for 'what's right' not 'what's wrong', e.g. identifying successes, talents, abilities. Focus on hearing 'what's working' when listening, rather than what isn't. Don't ignore the negative, but try to find the positive within it	Karen complains that her mother hates her so much she won't let her enjoy doing anything on her own. 'Hate is a strong feeling. Your mum has a lot of feeling for you. If she let you do anything you wanted would that mean she doesn't care?'
5. Being respectfully curious. Questions are used to generate ideas	'What would your life be like if your mother didn't hate you? What would be different? How would you be different? How do you cope with the way your mother treats you? Who/what helps you?'
6. Creating co-operation and collaboration	'My mother isn't going to change no matter what you say.' 'Yes, it is you who agreed to come to the group. Things can change for the better for you because you want them to change. Your mother might change with help, but are there changes that would make life happier for you even if she doesn't?'
7. Using humour and creativity	In one session Karen describes what her mother looks like when she gets really angry. Sensing her fear, the leader asks the group to think of their own example of someone getting really angry and draw the person as a cartoon animal mask. One group member then takes Karen's mask (a snake) and Karen chooses another (a crocodile). The group put on the other masks and role play getting angry in their animal role. The group help the crocodile to outwit the snake, all feeling a little stupid but having a lot of fun in the process.

Source: Sharry (2001: 17)

(Killian 2002). It makes sense when working therapeutically with children to promote resilience by focusing intervention on some of these characteristics. If you are working directly with the child the intra-personal resilience factors should be promoted. For some excellent ideas about doing this see Daniel and Wassel (2002) (Further Reading).

Intra-personal therapeutic work to build resilience would focus on:

- fostering a temperament that elicits positive responses from family and strangers
- developing self-esteem and a positive sense of self
- good problem-solving skills
- a sense of meaning and purpose to life
- areas of personal competence; having interests, sports, hobbies, etc.
- being in control of the past by being able to talk or play through difficult past experiences, but not dwell on painful memories.

Working therapeutically at an inter-personal level would mean focusing on:

- secure attachment relationships
- establishing clear parent–child boundaries (e.g. child not expected to parent)
- identifying at least one person who can give support and care that match the child's needs
- building social support and helping to access it
- finding a positive role model who can contribute to the child's life.

The presence of beneficial factors, such as advantaged socio-economic backgrounds and doing well at school, may not in themselves be sufficient to buffer negative effects. Resilience also depends on 'human agency', the will of an individual to use beneficial factors as sources of help. This human agency is itself related to 'cumulative protective processes', meaning that the development of coping builds from one protective element to the next (Gilgun 1999). Resilence builds resilience and some, though by no means all, children will be starting from quite a fragile base.

SHARING INFORMATION

A key ethical principle of working therapeutically is the importance of keeping confidentiality. It is not always easy to do so, and knowing when and how to retain or disclose confidential information is an essential skill of working therapeutically with children. The position on sharing information can be viewed as a continuum: on one end there is the legal position of mandatory reporting and at the other complete confidentiality, characterised by confession to a priest. The therapeutic position for work with children fits somewhere in between, making professional judgement a central issue. In the US and many other countries there are mandatory reporting laws that make it illegal not to report suspicions of maltreatment. However, even where these laws exist, professionals use their judgement about when to act and how much to report. This is particularly so for medical and therapeutic professionals, who admit that they do not report maltreatment in some cases because they fear the consequences of reporting will make the situation worse. In some European countries, for example France, practitioners are authorised to keep the 'professional secret'. This means that so long as the practitioner is working with the child to deal with the maltreatment and the child's safety can be ensured, there is no legal impetus to tell anyone else. If, however, the child dies or is seriously harmed, the practitioner is liable and once again the professional must use their judgement to decide how to proceed.

In sharing information about maltreatment the wishes and rights of children are often ignored or overridden (Daniels and Jenkins 2000). Young children understand the concept of secrecy from quite an early age. Adults depend on this to enable them to keep maltreatment hidden. Though secrecy is sometimes associated with fear (if you tell anyone I'll kill you/your pet/your sister/your mother), it is also linked to trust and complicity (this will be our special secret, just between you and me). Knowledge about how children understand secrecy underpins personal safety work on good and bad secrets. Good secrets are those that bring nice surprises and make people happy; they are secrets that everyone can know about at the right time. Bad secrets make you feel bad and make others feel bad if they know; they are secrets that cannot be told for fear of hurting someone. Teaching children what is a good secret (e.g. knowing what Mum is getting for her birthday but not telling her) and what is a bad secret (e.g. knowing your friend stole a bike and covering up for them) can be a helpful prevention tactic. Though it is mostly applied to sexual abuse, where secrecy is often part of the abuse, secrecy work can apply to all forms of maltreatment because the continuation of maltreatment often depends on the child not telling anyone.

In asking an adult to keep a secret, or requesting confidence, children demonstrate that they understand the rules and principles of confidentiality. Adults have the power to break these rules and children know this. To combat this power they disclose information in ways that help them keep control of it, by saying a little at a time, by being oblique and ambiguous and by stating they will deny the information if it is passed to anyone else (Wattam 1998). Sometimes the only solution that appears available to them when this happens is silence and/or denial. Working therapeutically with children demands that confidentiality be understood from their perspective (active empathy) and be negotiated therapeutically in a way that at worst does not disempower them and, at best, empowers them to 'break the silence'.

Working in this way takes time, skill and trust. In a *minority* of cases time is not available, as emergency action will need to be taken. In all other cases there is the possibility of working within the law to carefully negotiate the complex area of confidentiality. Guidance in this country can appear contradictory with regard to sharing information that children do not want to share. For example, the criminal legal position demands that if a practitioner has knowledge that a crime has been committed they should report it. Technically all maltreatment can be framed in criminal law terms; although maltreatment *per se* is not a crime, its components of assault, indecency, neglect, cruelty and so forth can all be covered by statute. The civil law position requires that the wishes and feelings of children should be taken into account and that children where they have sufficient 'understanding and intelligence' are competent to make their own decisions about seeking help. Within each position there is discretion, leeway and decision making to be done.

Disclosure of personal information is subject to common and statute law. *Working Together* (Department of Health *et al.* 1999) makes it clear that:

- personal information should only be disclosed with the consent of the child
- if this is not possible, the safety and welfare of a child should dictate whether the information should be shared
- disclosure should be justifiable in each case and legal advice should be sought in cases of doubt
- children are entitled to the same duty of confidence as adults provided that they have the ability to understand the consequences
- where it is believed that a child is being exploited or maltreated, confidentiality *may* be breached, following discussion with the child
- personal information *may* be disclosed for the purposes of the prevention or detection of crime, or the apprehension or prosecution of offenders, in cases where failure to disclose would be likely to prejudice those objectives.

This guidance reflects the contradictory positions of the wishes of the child and the demands of the law and gives practitioners their discretion. You will note that nowhere is it stated that practitioners *must* breach confidentiality or must disclose information to the police for prosecution purposes. Given this licence, however, the onus is on the practitioner (and his or her agency) to justify why they do not do so if the decision turns out to be against the best interests of the child or the public interest. While advising practitioners to balance their duties to protect children from harm with their general duty towards the child and his or her carers, *Working Together* clearly states that,

> where there are concerns that a child is, or may be at risk of significant harm, the needs of that child must come first. In these circumstances, the overriding objective must be to safeguard the child.
>
> (Department of Health *et al.* 1999: 88 para 7.28)

GUIDANCE 6.1:   THE DATA PROTECTION ACT

The Data Protection Act 1998 requires that personal information is obtained and processed fairly and lawfully; only disclosed in appropriate circumstances; is accurate, relevant and not held longer than necessary; and is kept securely. The Act allows for disclosure without the consent of the subject in certain conditions, including for the purposes of the prevention or detection of crime, or the apprehension or prosecution of offenders, and where failure to disclose would be likely to prejudice those objectives in a particular case.

(Department of Health *et al.* 1999: 89 para 7.34)

Later it is stated that

A party seeking to rely on this exemption needs to make a judgement as to whether, in the particular circumstances of an individual case, there would be a substantial chance that one or both of those objectives would be noticeably damaged if the personal information was withheld.

(Department of Health *et al.* 1999: 123)

The European Convention on Human Rights is also relevant to decision making. Breaking confidence without consent might be in breach of Article 8, which states that everyone has the right to respect for his private and family life, his home and his correspondence. This right can only be interfered with

> in the interests of national security, public safety or the economic well-being of the country, for the prevention of disorder or crime, for the protection of health or morals, or for the protection of the rights and freedoms of others.
> (Department of Health *et al.* 1999: 89 para 7.35)

The Data Protection Act limits the amount of personal information that can be held about a child or family (or you!) by stating that it be adequate and not excessive in relation to the purpose for which it is held. The information should also be deleted once its purpose is served, and it can only be used for the purposes for which it was given.

SUMMARY

Research demonstrates that children can experience a wide range of short- and long-term effects including the ability to form and keep relationships, to trust, to become parents themselves, self-harming behaviour, depression, PTSD and chronic illness, both physical and mental.

The bulk of health and social care professionals working with children are not therapists but practitioners who can work therapeutically in all their interventions. Not all children will require specialist help. In the main, practitioners will be working with 'fairly ordinary' children who are in need because of the harm they have experienced.

Throughout child protection practice there is a degree of inevitable conflict between competing legal and therapeutic demands. Child protection must be practised in an inter-agency framework in the context of law and procedures that can sometimes cut across therapeutic ideals.

Listening to and understanding the maltreated child's framework form the starting point for working therapeutically. Children's understandings of themselves need to be explored. Often they are not seeing the world in the wrong way but are seeing it *their* way through 'internalising' negative and damaging experiences.

Keep the 'whole' child in view: children are more than the maltreatment they experience and they will want to talk about many aspects of their lives, some of which will be relevant to the maltreatment and some of which won't be.

Practitioners must work not only therapeutically but ethically as well. Elements of ethical practice include openness, sensitivity, accuracy, honesty, objectivity, confidentiality, ensuring that no child is left feeling anxious, upset, or apprehensive as a consequence of intervention, predictability, consistency and neutrality.

Building resilience is crucial to mediate longer-term effects and to promote the health and well-being of children.

The position on sharing information can be viewed as a continuum: at one end there is the legal position of mandatory reporting and at the other complete confidentiality, characterised by confession to a priest. The therapeutic position for work with children fits somewhere in between, making professional judgement a central issue.

FURTHER READING

Daniel, B. and Wassell, S. (2002) *Assessing and Promoting Resilience in Vulnerable Children*, 3 vols: *The Early Years, The School Years, Adolescence* London: Jessica Kingsley Publishers

Daniels, D. and Jenkins, P. (2000) *Therapy with Children: Children's rights, confidentiality and the law* London: Sage

Redgrave, K. (2000) *Care-Therapy for Children: Direct work in counselling and psychotherapy* London: Continuum

REFERENCES

Brown, D. and Peddar, J. (1991) *Introduction to Psychotherapy: An outline of psychodynamic principles and practice*, 2nd edn, London: Routledge

Butler, I. and Williamson, H. (1994) *Children Speak: Children, trauma and social work* London: Wiley

Callias, M., Miller, A., Lane, D. A. and Lanyado, M. (1992) Child and adolescent therapy: A changing agenda. In D. Lane and A. Miller (eds) *Child and Adolescent Therapy: A handbook* Buckingham: Open University Press

Cawson, P. (2002) *Child Maltreatment in the Family: The experience of a national sample of young people* London: NSPCC

Choquet, M., DarvesBornoz, J. M., Ledoux, S. *et al.* (1997) Self-reported health and behavioral problems among adolescent victims of rape in France: Results of a cross-sectional survey *Child Abuse and Neglect* 21, 9: 823–832

Claussen, A. H. and Crittenden, P. M. (1991) Physical and psychological maltreatment: Relations among the types of maltreatment *Child Abuse and Neglect* 15, 12: 5–18

Craig, E. (1995) Starting the journey: Enhancing the therapeutic elements of groupwork for adolescent female child sexual abuse victims. In A. Keslake (ed.) *Readings on Groupwork Intervention in Child Sexual Abuse* London: Whiting and Birch

Crittenden, P. M. (1992) Children's strategies for coping with adverse home environments: An interoperation using attachment theory *Child Abuse and Neglect* 16, 3: 329–343

Crouch, J. L. and Milner, J. S. (1993) Effects of child neglect on children *Criminal Justice and Behavior* 20, 1: 49–65

de Shazer, S. (1985) *Keys to Solution in Brief Therapy* New York: Norton

de Shazer, S. (1988) *Clues: Investigating Solutions in Brief Therapy* New York: Norton

Department of Health/Department for Education and Employment/Home Office (2000) *Framework for the Assessment of Children in Need and their Families* London: The Stationery Office

Department of Health/Home Office/Department for Education and Employment (1999) *Working Together to Safeguard Children: A guide to inter-agency working to safeguard and promote the welfare of children* London: The Stationery Office

Edgardh, K. and Ormstad, K. (2000) Prevalence and characteristics of sexual abuse in a national sample of Swedish seventeen-year-old boys and girls *Acta Paediatrica* 89, 3: 310–319

Egeland, B. and Erickson, M. F. (1987) Psychologically unavailable caregiving. In M. R. Brassard, R. Germain and S. N. Hart (eds) *Psychological Maltreatment of Children and Youth* Elmsford: Pergamon

Egeland, B., Sroufe, L. A. and Erickson, M. (1983) The developmental consequences of different patterns of maltreatment *Child Abuse and Neglect* 7: 459–469

Erickson, M. F., Egeland, B. and Pianta, R. (1989) The effects of maltreatment on the development of young children. In D. Chicchetti and V. Carlson (eds) *Child Maltreatment: Theory and research on the causes and consequences of child abuse and neglect* New York: Cambridge University Press

Gilgun, J. F. (1999) Mapping resilience as process among adults with childhood adversities. In H. I. McCubbin *et al.* (eds) *The Dynamics of Resilient Families* Thousand Oaks, CA: Sage

Gilligan, R. (2000) Adversity, resilience and young people: The protective value of positive school and spare time experiences *Children & Society* 14, 1: 37–47

Glaser, D. (1992) Abuse of children. In D. Lane and A. Miller (eds) *Child and Adolescent Therapy: A handbook* Buckingham: Open University Press

Hill, M. (1999) What's the problem? Who can help? The perspectives of children and young people on their well-being and on helping professionals *Journal of Social Work Practice* 13, 2: 135–145

Hindman, J. (1989) It's all relative: Family incest treatment. Unpublished paper presented at the Fourth Annual Treatment Conference in South Carolina, 21 February

Hurley, N. (1998) *Straight Talk: Working with children and young people in groups* York: Joseph Rowntree Foundation

Kerslake, A. (ed.) (1995) *Readings on Groupwork Intervention in Child Sexual Abuse* London: Whiting and Birch

Killian, B. (2002) Is child protection possible in areas of war and violence? In P. Lachman *et al.* Challenges facing child protection *Child Abuse and Neglect* 26, 6/7: 587–618

Macdonald, G. (2001) *Effective Interventions for Child Abuse and Neglect: An evidence-based approach to planning and evaluating interventions* Chichester: Wiley

Page, J. and Ross, T. (illustrator) (2001) *It's Not Funny!* London: Corgi Children's Books

Parton, N. and Byrne, P. (2001) *Constructive Social Work* Basingstoke: Macmillan

Rogers, C. R. (1951) *Client-Centered Therapy* Boston: Houghton Mifflin

Sharry, J. (2001) *Solution-Focused Groupwork* London: Sage

Wattam, C. (1998) Confidentiality. In N. Parton and C. Wattam (eds) *Child Sexual Abuse: Responding to the experiences of children* Chichester: Wiley

Wattam, C. and Woodward, C. (1996) 'And do I abuse my children – No!' In *Childhood Matters*, Report of the National Commission of Inquiry into the Prevention of Child Abuse, Volume 2, Background Papers, London: HMSO

Wieland, S. (1998) *Techniques and Issues in Abuse-Focused Therapy with Children and Adolescents* Thousand Oaks, CA: Sage

Woodward, J. (2000) The uses of therapy: Understanding and treating the effects of childhood abuse and neglect. In C. Itzin (ed.) *Home Truths About Child Sexual Abuse* London: Routledge

CHAPTER 7

WORKING EFFECTIVELY WITH PARENTS

LEARNING OBJECTIVES

By the end of this chapter you will be able to:

- Recognise the importance of establishing effective working relations with parents and families in safeguarding children

- Contribute to accurate and dynamic assessments of parental capacity

- Work to sustain and promote parental capacity

- Critically appraise notions of partnership and empowerment

- Identify strategies for working with conflict and resistance to change

- Work within time limits dictated by the time-scale of children.

In the previous chapter we considered working therapeutically with children. Many of the principles of working therapeutically also apply to parents, including the following:

- listening and active empathy
- taking a non-judgemental stance
- attending to confidentiality and restrictions about sharing information
- being open and honest
- focusing on solutions without minimising the problem.

When considering working with parents, it is important to understand the main reasons why parents and their children are referred to child protection services. A large proportion (between a third and a half) of all referrals will concern single female parents attempting to cope on their own in difficult conditions (Thorpe 1994, CAPCAE 1998). In these cases, then, we are talking about working with mothers rather than parents. Often these mothers will be young and unsupported by social networks. The majority will be white British and are likely to be referred for reasons of general concern about neglect and/or physical maltreatment. Another significant group of parents will be biological parents (mothers and fathers) who are characterised by their use of violence as a conflict resolution strategy, including violence between the parents and regular use of corporal punishment (CAPCAE 1998). Children of these parents are likely to be referred for physical maltreatment caused by excessive corporal punishment. A smaller group of parents/carers will be referred for reasons of sexual and/or emotional maltreatment. Each of these parents/carers will have different needs and will require different forms of support.

Just as with children, practitioners who work with parents are generally not specialist mental health professionals; resources for these types of intervention are limited and only occasionally relevant. In this chapter we focus on generic knowledge and skills for working therapeutically and legally with parents/carers, particularly single parents and mothers and fathers living in violent contexts.

PARENTAL RESPONSIBILITY

The Children Act 1989 makes it clear that primary responsibility for the care and protection of dependent children rests with parents. 'Parental responsibility' refers to the duties and obligations of biological mothers and married fathers at the birth of a child. This may be extended to others by agreement (for example unmarried fathers) or by court order (for example a s.8 residence order to a relative or foster carer or care order to a local authority) but can only be extinguished with the making of an adoption order.

The discharge of parental responsibility (how people parent) is usually open to scrutiny only within the privacy of the family. When questions of significant harm arise, this becomes the explicit focus of concern and parents are accountable to external judgement. In this context it should be remembered that if all parents in the country were exposed to the same assessment as those referred for child protection concerns, many may fall short of expectations.

In Chapter 4 we considered the dimensions of parenting capacity as criteria to attend to in managing risk:

- basic care
- ensuring safety
- emotional warmth
- stimulation
- guidance and boundaries
- stability

(Source: Department of Health 2000)

These responsibilities are not static – each child is unique and as children grow, their needs and capabilities change. The needs of infants are not the same as the needs of adolescents. Consequently, parenting must be responsive, adaptive and 'good enough' to meet each child's needs.

Few of us set out to be bad or inept at the things we undertake, and parenthood is no different. Most parents about whom there are child protection concerns set out with the common expectation of being good or good enough parents to their children. However, the presence of enduring difficulties or critical events can challenge the capacity of parents and undermine their efforts. Many factors can make parenting more than ordinarily difficult (see Table 7.1).

TABLE 7.1 Factors that may undermine or challenge parental capacity

Impact level	Examples
Intrinsic to parent	Severe and enduring mental illness
	Severe and enduring physical and learning incapacity
	Chronic/Chaotic substance misuse
	Chronic criminality
	All of which can render the parent absent or unavailable to the child for significant periods
	Harmful or negligent care in own childhood
Interpersonal	Social isolation
	Domestic violence – between partners and inter-generational
	Conflicted relationships including childcare, residence and contact disputes
	Single parenting
External/structural	Chronic/enduring poverty; deleterious neighbourhoods; sub-standard housing or homelessness; racism; war
Associated with the child	Unwanted at birth or subsequently in re-formed families
	Children with multiple additional or special needs
	Children associated by family or community with shame or stigma
	Children presenting 'out of control' behaviours

Difficulties can be interactive and cumulative. For example, domestic violence can result in single parenting, social isolation, residence and contact disputes, while severe and enduring illness can lead to chronic poverty and homelessness. Set against this, many people demonstrate skills and resilience in contending with adversity and any assessment of parental capacity aims to identify and build on such strengths and resourcefulness. Parenting capacity refers to the skills and resources of the individual parent *and* the resources available *to* and utilised *by* any parent in caring for a child (see Table 7.2). Parenting capacity is most accurately described as interactive.

TABLE 7.2 Resources for parental capacity

Skills and resources of individual parent	Includes time, emotional warmth, interest, energy, patience, knowledge of child care, sense of humour, flexibility
	Ability to use resources to overcome difficulties
	Insight into problems, being child focused, motivation, determination
Skills and resources available within the family	Other pairs of hands, and partners in care – available and accessible to provide or amplify all of the above
Skills and resources available external to the family	Local community groups and associations, childcare services, support and treatment services

Though research evidence highlights the range of difficulties with which families may contend (e.g. Cleaver, Unell and Aldgate 1999) and guidance acknowledges the possibilities of wide variations in parenting style, the law takes the view that objective standards of parenting can be determined, based on the needs of the individual child. This is expressed in the legal notion of 'the reasonable parent' (Guidance 7.1).

GUIDANCE 7.1: THE REASONABLE PARENT

Reasonable parental care is that care which a reasonable parent would provide for the child concerned. (1.34)

. . . the standard of parenting which a child is expected to receive is an objective one. The child's parents are judged by what a reasonable parent would do for the child in question. (3.55) The test is not what can reasonably be expected of the child's parents in their circumstances and given their characteristics. (3.56)

If a parent is not able to provide a reasonable standard of care, *he* is expected to seek the help of others to ensure that such care is provided . . . For example, usually it would be reasonable in the interests of the child to expect a parent who is unable to provide adequate food, shelter or health care and whose child is suffering significant harm to turn to the assistance available from family or friends or from public authorities or voluntary agencies. If the child's parents decline to do so, it could be said that their standard of parenting falls below that which it is reasonable to expect of them. (3.56)

Source: *An Introduction to the Children Act 1989* (HMSO)

As Guidance 7.1 makes clear, there is an element of compulsion whereby parents risk being judged unreasonable if they fail to work together with professionals to avail themselves of services. Compulsion is also mirrored in statutory social work duties to intervene in families whenever the significant harm threshold has been reached.

ENGAGING PARENTS

People who are referred into a 'helping' service can be thought of in one of three ways (Sharry 1999):

- *customers:* recognise they have a problem the service can help with (they refer themselves)
- *complainants:* recognise there is a problem but see it as someone else's fault or responsibility (refer themselves or are referred in)
- *visitors:* do not recognise there is a problem and do not think they need help (generally referred in).

Safeguarding referrals are most likely to fit into the 'visitors' category. Sharry (2001) points out that this is not in itself unhealthy but is part of a developmental stage: the hope is that the majority will start there and mature to becoming customers. Nevertheless, engaging parents is often a difficult task, as the case study in Snapshot 7.1 highlights.

SNAPSHOT 7.1:   A RELUCTANT SERVICE USER

Gina (23 years old, black British of dual heritage) and Alan (29 years old, white British) have been together since Gina was 14 years old. The couple have two two children, daughter Leanne (7 years) and son Ashley (4 years). Gina has left home with the children on a number of occasions because of physical violence, returning after a few days.

Gina is well known to her local social services team through her intermittent phone calls and office visits for practical help in leaving the family home. On these occasions she is often loud and verbally aggressive and has acquired a reputation for being a troublesome client. There is considerable speculation as to the 'real' reasons for her requests for taxi fares to refuges or the point of arranging 'yet another' refuge place when 'she'll be back soon enough'.

Gina has seen a number of different workers over the years, but has strenuously resisted any ongoing social work support and her distrust and dislike of authority figures in general and social workers in particular are evident in her manner. Gina spent some months in residential care at age 14 when she was reported to be 'out of control' by her father.

Gina is accessing services but is ambivalent about many aspects of them: in this sense she is a 'complainant'. Though universal services such as health visiting are positively received by the majority of families, statutory social work services are productive of far more mixed feelings. Of significance are:

- *the nature of the service focus:* Unlike universal services, statutory social work is residual – access is severely rationed and limited to those families where children are identified as in need and/or at risk. Both these categories can tend to threaten parental and family self-esteem.
- *negative connotations:* The combination of a residual service and the requirement to demonstrate an inability to solve one's own problems to acquire services conspire to stigmatise the service for users and would-be users. When parents belong to discriminated groups (e.g. ethnicity or disability), these connotations are likely to be worse.
- *specific social work powers:* There is a prevailing anxiety that any social work involvement may lead to the removal of children. To the extent that this anxiety reflects knowledge of statutory powers vested in social services and their officers it is realistic – social workers can and do on occasion remove children via court orders, although in the majority of cases they do not.
- *the nature of the service:* Social services cannot always deliver what people want. For example, there are difficulties in framing statutory practice in relation to domestic violence that supports women and safeguards children. Research has shown that domestic violence has been found to be a significant factor in many families where child protection concerns emerge (e.g. Ghate 2000, Humphreys 1999, Farmer and Owen 1995) but that agency responses have often failed to address this.
- *professional or expert attitudes:* A traditional professional approach to inter-vention with children and families, particularly in assessment, has been the attitude that the professional 'knows best'. This can make service users feel inadequate or alienated and is never the case – practitioners must learn from mothers, fathers and children how best to help (Parton and O'Byrne 2000).

These impediments to access are accompanied by difficulties for practitioners in working with parents. For example:

- *the need for a mandate:* In the absence of clear evidence of risk or actual significant harm that mandates action under s.47 or a range of court orders, social workers must obtain the mandate of the service user in the form of a self-referral or request for services. The question arises, how far can or should practitioners go in encouraging service users to give their mandate for support services?
- *the difficulty of distinguishing between need, risk and 'no case to answer':* As we saw in Chapter 4, predicting exactly which children in need may become children at risk is by no means simple. Hindsight may be viewed as an exact science and the biographies of adults chronically neglected or maltreated as children make predictable reading, but in the 'here and now' it is often difficult to pinpoint the threshold between in need and at risk. In addition some (approximately one-quarter) of referrals of child maltreatment will be unsubstantiated, but are they the right ones in terms of an individual child's welfare and safety?

- *wariness of undermining family coping skills and opening the gates too wide:* Given that interdependence is a more accurate description than independence of how most people cope, choosing when and how to receive help and from whom, appear to be integral to self-respect; having help thrust upon one is rarely acceptable and may give rise to 'learned helplessness'.
- *recognition of stigma and blame:* Unlike universal services such as health or education, social work remains a residual and stigmatised service and consequently there are social costs which rebound on service users and may understandably make them wary and offset any benefit.

Often, though not always, a solution is to start with what the service user wants. The example in Snapshot 7.2 provides a good illustration and builds on the solution-focused approach we discussed in Chapter 6.

SNAPSHOT 7.2: FINDING OUT WHAT PARENTS WANT

A family centre was set up to service 'families at risk' in a disadvantaged area. Families who had been repeatedly referred for child protection services were identified as those most needing services. The centre began by offering parenting groups and 'drop-in' mornings, but very few people took part.

As a result the workers went out and visited a number of the families to discover what services they thought the family centre should provide. The parents identified a number of needs such as a credit union, IT classes, a toy library and an Internet Café. Acting on this feedback, the centre began to develop and offer these services, which became popular. Other people, not originally identified, began using the centre and new services were developed through further consultation. After a year the parents decided that they would like to set up a 'self-help' parenting group, which the centre supported.

(Source: Sharry 2001: 73)

BUILDING PARTNERSHIP WITH PARENTS

Though a range of practitioners work with adults who happen to be parents, child-care practitioners work with adults *precisely* because they are parents, and the overriding aim of such work is to promote the welfare and safety of the child. This is sometimes referred to as 'working in partnership' with parents. Working in partnership can contribute to engagement and can empower parents and carers. However, 'partnership' is a much-used term and precise definitions are hard to nail down. Calder (1995), for example, identified a number of different models in operation (see Development Activity 7.1).

DEVELOPMENT ACTIVITY 7.1: MODELS OF PARTNERSHIP

Calder (1995: 749–766) identified a number of models of working with parents and families in evidence in child-care work, none of which constitutes an equal partnership between families and practitioners. At different stages in a social work intervention, practitioners may well move between these models. You may find it useful to consider how parents might experience each of the following models and consider the possible implications in terms of best outcomes for the child.

Model	*Possible parental perspectives*
The Expert Model	
• professional in control	e.g. parent's experience 'I have no control'
• professional holds decision-making power	
• low priority accorded to parents' views, wishes, feelings	e.g. outcome for child 'you do what you want with him/her'
• low priority accorded to information sharing	
• low priority accorded to negotiation	
The Transplant (of Expertise) Model	
• professional sees parent as a resource	
• professional may delegate some tasks to parent	
• professional may 'train' parent in some basic skills	
• professional holds decision-making powers	
The Consumer Model	
• assumes parents have rights of decision and selection	
• decision making ultimately in control of parents	
The Social Network/Systems Model	
• perceived network – parents, children and professionals	
• network cast as supportive, developmental and in interests of child/family	
• social worker as facilitator/enabler	
• social worker also arbiter of compliance with statutory requirement	

Given that social workers do have duties, which they cannot abdicate, and powers in relation to the removal of children from home, it is a moot point whether partnership in any egalitarian sense is feasible in child protection cases. What is certain is that practitioners must find effective ways to work together with parents and families and the ability to engage parents' active participation will be critical to outcomes for children.

Research shows that parents and carers expect pretty much what we would all expect: they want to be kept fully informed and to be treated with respect and courtesy (Cleaver and Freeman 1995). Shemmings and Shemmings (1996) propose four conditions of participative practice that should underpin partnership:

- honesty
- answerability
- even-handedness
- sensitivity.

A 'constructive approach' (Parton and O'Byrne 2000) would also add diffidence and the ability not to prioritise professional framing of a problem (problem focus, professional 'knows best'), giving authority to service users to find their own solutions (solution-focused, all knowledge is equally valued).

FLEXIBLE CARE AND CONTROL

The Children Act 1989, in specifying both the duty to promote the welfare of children in need and the duty to take action to protect children at risk reinforced an oppositional tension between the polarities of care versus control in child-care social work. The two poles have become associated with low and high risk, giving rise to the notion that there exists a clearer distinction than is possible to make in practice. This can lead to an overly formulaic approach to engaging parents and families (see Figure 7.1) that can prevent flexible and confident work.

Low risk to child		High risk to child
DUTY TO PROMOTE WELFARE	Children Act, 1989	DUTY TO PROTECT FROM SIGNIFICANT HARM
PARTICIPATORY CONSENSUAL	Style	AUTHORITATIVE DIRECTIVE
SERVICE USER MANDATE PREVAILS	Mandate	LEGAL MANDATE PREVAILS

FIGURE 7.1 A formulaic approach to parental engagement

A flexible approach would merge each of these dimensions drawing on different styles and mandates according to need (see Figure 7.2).

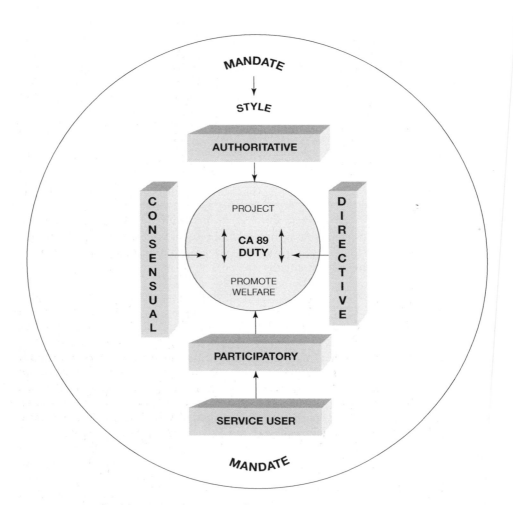

FIGURE 7.2   A flexible approach to parental engagement

Such flexibility could include on occasions:

* adopting a more authoritative or directive approach to ensuring service provision take-up in cases deemed 'low risk'
* adopting a more participatory/consensual approach to some 'high risk' cases.

As control interventions (such as registration and applications for orders) escalate, it can become increasingly difficult to work therapeutically, supportively and in partnership with parents.

SNAPSHOT 7.3: WORKING TO ENGAGE PARENTS 1

Leanne (7 years) and Ashley (4 years) have now been placed on the child protection register as being at risk of physical and emotional maltreatment because of domestic violence between their parents and they need a child protection plan to work to ensure their safety while they remain at home. The decision to conference the children arose from an incident when Ashley presented at hospital with a head injury from an ashtray thrown during a parental argument. No prosecutions have followed the incident and the police indicate that none will follow since there is no evidence as to who threw the ashtray.

Gina reports that Alan is a heavy user of alcohol and occasional user of amphetamine. Alan says they both like a drink but says he has never had time off work. He has worked full-time as a labourer in a local warehouse for the past five years. He controls and manages the family income including the child benefit book.

Alan did not take time off work to attend the conference and Gina left after a final angry outburst when the decision to register was made.

In the first instance, the core group is identified as Annette, social worker, Trisha, health visitor, and Gina.

Overcoming Gina's antagonism will be a crucial determinant of moving this case forward. But the question arises: Where is Alan in all this? Women in violent relationships are frequently held to account for the safety of their children when the risk is posed by fathers and male partners. At the conference, Gina's antagonism to authority, her grievance at the s.47 procedure and her perceived manipulative demands are raised. Her history of returning to the family home is the subject of discussion in terms of her 'failure to protect' and the conference devolves to the core group, who have the task of identifying and promoting Gina's capacity to protect. The question of Alan's responsibility for his behaviour and his capacity to promote and safeguard the welfare of the children and the safety of Gina has not been a feature of the discussion.

The invisibility of men in the child protection system has been a recurrent theme and represents a serious omission and skewing of parental responsibility. Though many factors may contribute to the omission – for example, the gendered profile of social work agencies, prevailing expectations about motherhood and the enduring divisions of child care – agencies and practitioners have yet to devise consistent or satisfactory strategies to overcome this. Current documentation routinely adopts the gender-neutral term 'parenting', thereby subsuming complex differences and tensions which substituting 'mothering' and 'fathering' would highlight.

Staff safety in relation to violent service users is a further issue and highlights additional complexities. All staff have a primary duty of self-care and practitioners are directed to local and national health and safety policies. Where clear evidence of potential violence exists – a previous history of assault on staff or detailed threats made against an individual worker – then clearly steps should be taken to ensure safety before attempts at engagement at made. However, it is equally important that professional action is not paralysed by fear and anxiety. It is also worth considering the contradictions inherent in any situation where children are assumed to be 'safe enough' in households where adults are deemed to pose a serious threat to staff.

SNAPSHOT 7.4   WORKING TO ENGAGE PARENTS 2

The day after the conference, Alan contacted the social services demanding to know 'what was behind putting the children on the child protection register'. Annette used the opportunity to negotiate an appointment to discuss the concerns, the implications of registration and core group working and to initiate the core assessment in line with the *Framework for Assessment*. Alan and Gina kept the appointment, bringing both children, and persistently focused on the question of how long before the children could be de-registered and whether an earlier conference could be convened.

Eventually, Annette was able to wrest an agreement to a session with each of the parents to go through the conference concerns and a session with them together to agree a timetable for the core assessment and ground rules for the core group. Annette confirmed this in writing, with copies for both parents and included proposed times and venues – offering the possibility of early evening meetings to accommodate Alan's employment. At this stage, Annette began to feel optimistic about the prospects for progress.

The time-limited and necessarily investigative nature of s.47 enquiries can be difficult contexts in which to engage parents in a participative endeavour, as can child protection conferences. Even with emphasis on parental attendance at case conferences, as we saw in Chapter 2, the opportunity for parental participation is limited. The primary task of the child protection conference is to decide on the need for registration – based on evidence of maltreatment or likelihood of harm and the need for action in the form of a care plan. A key strategy in taking care plans forward and a means of increasing the meaningful participation of mothers and fathers is the core group.

CONFLICT AND CORE GROUP WORKING

Core groups are responsible to and tasked by the child protection conference with formulating and implementing the detailed plans that will safeguard children registered as at risk. Here there is both the expectation and, in many instances, the scope for developing an active participatory role for parents and children able to benefit.

Who are the core group? As action groups charged with progressing change work, core groups need to be large enough to include the people with hands-on responsibility for effecting change and small enough to ensure they are effective. Membership is drawn from:

- the key social worker
- the resident parent/s
- non-resident parents and significant family members
- other professionals currently working directly with the child or parents
- the registered child or children.

In the case illustrated, the preliminary core group designated by the child protection conference consists of Annette, as key worker; Gina, the children's mother; Alan, the children's father; and Trisha, health visitor for the family. The invisibility of men already alluded to means that particular attention has to be paid to ensure that fathers such as Alan are not precluded by default, and Annette has offered sessions timed to accommodate his employment. However, careful attention will need to be given to Gina's safety.

SNAPSHOT 7.5: WORKING TO ENGAGE PARENTS 3

Leanne and Ashley have now been registered for two months, during which time Annette has been conducting weekly home visits to monitor their welfare and engage the family in the process of the core assessment. When these have failed – on three occasions – Gina has subsequently brought the children into the office and demanded that they be seen by the duty social worker and the fact recorded. To promote the participation of both parents, Annette has made visits in the evening as well as during the day. However, it has proved difficult to arrange individual sessions with either parent and attempts to move discussion onto an examination of concerns and work towards resolving them always flounder on the rock of parental rejection of the need for registration. Annette and Trisha have achieved two joint home visits to kick-start the core group, but attempts to establish and implement a working programme for the group are also floundering. The first review conference is due to take place in four weeks – three months from the initial registration.

Conflict is inevitable in any setting where so many meanings are contested and similar situations give rise to dissimilar judgements about best ways forward. Consequently, conflict can be said to be endemic within child protection. Conflict resolution is a key skill in safeguarding, both in engaging mothers, fathers and children and in direct work that often arises precisely because of violent or ineffective conflict resolution tactics within domestic relationships.

Before work can begin to devise and implement a plan to safeguard children, parents and professionals must usually have a shared understanding of the nature and extent of the significant harm or likelihood of it. Initial work is often geared towards a lengthier examination of areas of concern than is possible in the conference. Mothers and fathers are entitled to receive formal documentation – copies of the social work report and minutes of the child protection conference – in a format accessible to them, taking into account language and literacy. It is good practice, even where parents live together, to provide copies of these documents to both parents. But formal documentation will rarely achieve the level of shared understanding possible during initial core group meetings, which can provide opportunities for parents and professionals to negotiate a shared understanding. The skill in such consensus development is to ensure that the mutual understanding keeps the child in central focus. Subsequent meetings become the forum for sharing information and reviewing progress.

Successful core groups will depend upon achieving working consensus about the following:

- exact nature and extent of harm/likelihood of harm to the child (What are the issues and concerns?)

- Reduction or eradication of the likelihood of significant harm occurring in the future (What needs to be done?)
- What the mother, father and individual family members want (How can different wishes become compatible, e.g. to get off the register (Gina and Alan), to stop Mum and Dad fighting (Leanne and Ashley)?)
- How this can best be achieved (Who should do or supply what?)
- Criteria for evaluation (How exactly will progress be demonstrated?)
- Contingency plans (What happens if the likelihood of harm increases?)

WORKING FOR CHANGE

Though core groups provide the means for identifying the care plan, implementing services and monitoring progress, the core assessment provides the means for identifying factors undermining parental capacity and additional scope for direct work with family members – individually, or with two or more members together. In this way there is scope for workers and families to work creatively. A wide range of tools and techniques can be utilised deriving from the psycho-social tradition in social work (see Table 7.3).

TABLE 7.3 Some therapeutic tools and techniques

Tools and techniques	Brief description
Anger management	Cognitive behavioural therapy that focuses on anger. Recognising and understanding angry behaviour and violent conflict resolution and working to alter the behaviour (see for example Thomas 2001)
Advocacy and empowerment	Building skills to enable mothers and fathers to express themselves and work in partnership with agencies and professionals, including reasoning, vocabulary and alternative methods of communication (see Coulshed and Orme 1998, Chapter 3 and Parton and Byrne 2001)
Family trees (genograms) Life journey work	Diagrams (genograms) to show significant relationships and events in the family history
Counselling	Listening, active empathy, genuineness, identifying and exploring problems, developing coping resources, reviewing problems and solutions (see Chapter 6 and Egan 1981)
Family therapy	Working with the whole family, exploring past or present behaviour and understanding behaviours as contributing to the family as a system (see Coulshed and Orme 1998, Chapter 9)
Eco-mapping	Exploring social networks using diagrams (ecomaps) and looking at where relationships are weak, strong, stressful or supportive. Working on how relationships can change (see Coulshed and Orme 1998, Chapter 11)
Signs of safety	Identifying strengths in the parental/carer relationship and environment and building on these strengths

Behavioural approaches are also applicable and increasingly emphasised, not least because there is a view that they present better opportunities for demonstrating progress. Questionnaires and rating scales can be completed before intervention begins and prior to the next conference to demonstrate change. A number of instruments are available for working with parents and families and practitioners will want to consider incorporating them into their toolbox.

Table 7.4 shows some instruments that are endorsed in the *Framework for Assessment* (Department of Health 1999) and potential uses are highlighted at different points throughout the formal assessment documentation.

TABLE 7.4 Some questionnaires and scales

Instrument	Source	Content/focus	Completed by
Strengths and difficulties questionnaire	Goodman 1997, Goodman *et al.* 1998	Emotional and behavioural problems – children and adolescents	Carers/teachers of children 3–16 Young people 11–16
Parenting daily hassles scale	Crnic and Greenberg 1990, Crnic and Booth 1991	Frequency, intensity and impact of potential 'hassles'	Parents/carers
Adult well-being scale	Snaith *et al.* 1978	Irritability, depression, anxiety – IDA	Self-rating
Recent life events questionnaire	Brugha *et al.* 1985 modified	Frequency/duration/ impact of life events	Individuals/family groups
Family activity scale	Smith 1985 modified child-centredness scale	Activities within family – support/ promote development of children	Carers/parents of children: 2–6 7–12
The alcohol scale	Piccinelli *et al.* 1997	Usage/impact, alcohol disorders, hazardous drinking habits	Adults
Adolescent well-being scale	Birleson 1980	Depression	Self-rating (c. 8–16)
Home conditions scale	Davie *et al.* 1984 The family cleanliness scale	Level of domestic maintenance and repair	Social workers Other professionals

(endorsed in DOH *Framework for Assessment*, 2000)

A further scale that is integral to the solution-focused approach is the signs of safety scale, derived from the work of Turnell *et al.* (1999) and reproduced as an appendix in Parton and O'Byrne (2000). This scale includes physical, cognitive and emotional safety criteria (e.g. I have guards for fires, stairs; I have realistic expectations of my child; I feel able to make changes). Each item is rated between 'not at all' and 'very much'. The benefits of using such instruments can include:

- a concrete focus for assessment work
- establishing grounds for agreement on areas of work
- providing a measure of progress or absence of progress
- therapeutic potential for service users
- promoting inter-professional and inter-parental understanding of issues/evidence.

They should not be used uncritically, however, and practitioners will need to consider, for example:

- cross-cultural applicability and Eurocentric biases
- whether there are implicit assumptions or prejudices such as those related to gender, social class or disability.

As a starting point, practitioners should always have self-administered any instrument before using it with service users.

It can be seen from the forgoing that sustaining or promoting capacity to safeguard children places heavy demands in terms of time management, energy and commitment on both parents and practitioners.

Annette, for example, must manage this work as part of a full case load and alongside the routine administrative tasks such as maintaining case files and preparing reports for review case conferences.

Parents too must manage their time to accommodate assessment sessions, core group meetings, and take-up of any other services identified alongside the ordinary routines of daily life, work and child care. Where parents already have heavy time commitments or have had little opportunity for developing time management skills, merely fulfilling these demands can be a strain. However, the process also demands that parents address personal problems, behaviours, knowledge, skills and even survival strategies that may be long-standing and previously unquestioned, with a view to change. Alan, for example, will need to acknowledge and address his violent behaviour, which is likely to include examining whether and if so how, his use of alcohol is a factor. Gina is likely to have to address her antagonism to social workers and her relationship to and expectations of Alan. If Alan cannot change his behaviours to safeguard his children, then Gina is likely to be obliged by social services to consider the importance to her of attempting to keep the parental relationship going.

Where the assessment process and core group working succeed in the objectives of implementing effective plans and creating change to safeguard children, this will form the evidence for a child protection review conference to take the decision to de-register children.

Where these objectives are not met, de-registration will not be possible and a review conference will need to consider whether a different approach is required. Though the core assessment process and core groups do offer scope for relationship building and creative working, they are not magic bullets.

SNAPSHOT 7.6:
ONGOING WORK AND DECISION MAKING

Annette has completed the core assessment as far as possible given Alan's and Gina's resistance. Information from health and education regarding the children adds very little depth to the picture beyond confirming that both are attending school and their overall development falls within normal limits. Engaging with the children to explore their feelings and views has proved difficult and Annette is concerned that they are being lost sight of in the midst of what increasingly feels like an ongoing struggle between the agencies and the parents. The review conference, attended by both Alan and Gina, commended the couple for their involvement to date, but concluded that registration should continue and urged both parents to engage with professional concerns about the welfare of the children in the context of domestic violence.

In the case of Alan and Gina they have not shown agencies the door, Annette or another practitioner has seen both children on a weekly basis and there has been contact with both parents. Some progress has been made in relation to the core assessment to the extent that Annette has been able to collect information about the health and development of both children, and basic information about Gina and Alan. However, there remains conflict about the issue of child protection registration and both parents minimise the history of domestic violence and the periods when Gina and the children have left the family home. Annette is clear that both parents may have very different reasons for minimising accounts of domestic violence, but is struggling to engage either partner separately on the issue. Many mothers subject to domestic violence are wary of statutory agencies, fearing the removal of their children – a fear that may be crystallised by the child protection process. Research also shows that many women subject to domestic violence seek to manage the risk by placation of violent partners and diffusion of pressure. Perpetrators' motives for minimising violence have been subject to less scrutiny, but potential reasons may include self-preservation where there is a risk of criminal prosecution and entrenched views about the need for and right to control spouses by whatever means, including violence.

Nothing has occurred which warranted the practitioners seeking to remove the children. Equally, there is no evidence that the likelihood of future harm to the children has diminished, and Annette may even begin to wonder whether and to what extent the focused attention of agencies may be contributing to risk to the children and to Gina by such pressure.

If Alan and/or Gina anticipated the first review as an opportunity to achieve de-registration and withdraw from involvement without engaging with concerns, the decision to maintain registration may now trigger a rethink and free one or both of them to acknowledge violence as an issue. The risk here is that, as Annette speculates, the continuing pressure on the family may trigger further incidents of violence.

Another conference might have reached a different conclusion. Though the central issue of violence has not been addressed, no further incidents have come to outside attention and the degree of compliance indicated by staff access to the children and Alan's attendance at the conference may be deemed sufficient evidence of risk reduction.

The risk here is that, for possibly different reasons, the family have battened down the hatches and the children may be subject to harm as a result of future incidents of domestic violence. However, deciding to de-register children may be a compelling option where parents have given evidence of willingness to continue working with professionals voluntarily, and the carrot of de-registration may be a better motivator than the stick of continued registration.

COMPLIANCE VERSUS CO-OPERATION AND COMMITMENT TO CHANGE

Annette's early optimism has abated somewhat and she is grappling with a recurring issue for practitioners: parental compliance – in the sense of going through the motions – is not synonymous with commitment to or co-operation with a change process.

This should not surprise us. Typically, social workers in child protection are seeking to engage the active participation of adults whose circumstances and situation may ill equip them to meet such demands. Sheppard (2002) makes this point in relation to his research with depressed mothers, who constitute a significant group among recipients of child protection services.

> The data indicate that the elements of low self-esteem, vulnerability to criticism, and self blame are key factors in the mother's capacity to work in partnership. Social work practice must take these into account, requiring very high degrees of sensitivity and skill in working with mothers. Indeed, unlocking these pernicious cognitions may frequently require specialist techniques, such as the use of cognitive behaviour therapy. Overall, being 'social worker for the child' means also being 'social worker for the parents (in particular the mother)', who may well require high levels of encouragement.
>
> (Sheppard 2002: 93)

In brief, practitioners must first attend to the capacity of mothers and father to work with them.

FAMILY GROUP CONFERENCING

Individual approaches, as highlighted by Sheppard (2002), may well be valuable in some situations, but they tend to locate the work firmly in Calder's (1995) 'expert model'. Practitioners looking to promote a more participatory style may want to consider family group conferencing (FGC) as a means of progressing stuck cases. This approach may be especially relevant where children may need to be accommodated, as it brings with it the expectation that kinship care will be explored in the first instance.

Family group conferencing (FGC) offers a model with a sound evidence base (Crow 2001, Crow 2000, Marsh and Crow 1998). This model constitutes a significant challenge to professional power and comes close to Calder's (1995) 'consumer model' of partnership.

FGC is a technique for empowering and facilitating families to make their own decisions and plans for meeting the needs of the children. The model developed in New Zealand but is now used in its various forms internationally.

The underlying premises of FGC are that family and kinship bring bonds and obligations and in times of crisis even conflicted families, when given the opportunity, will pick up these obligations. Families have a more intimate and in-depth knowledge of a specific child and their circumstances and are much better able to fulfil their needs precisely because of the obligations they have. Family members have a vested interest in the child, which is hard to replicate in anyone else, however well meaning. Families are immensely resourceful and most families can be empowered to act in the best interests of, and provide the best care plans for, their children. Furthermore, the process is empowering because it promotes the autonomy and capacity of families to resolve problems.

The aim is to involve all people identified by the child and main carers as significant to the family. This can therefore include friends and neighbours. Professionals and agencies are involved to provide information to the family about the range of services and support that will be available if requested and the limits on any actions.

There are three main stages to FGC:

First, the independent family group co-ordinator informs families about the nature and process of family group decision making. The co-ordinator will help the child and carer/s to identify who their family is and who they want to involve. They will encourage the child and carer to recognise the fullest possible range of family, i.e. all those who can be called upon to have the interest at the child at heart. The co-ordinator will also liaise with relevant agencies and professionals with current involvement or responsibilities towards the child and her family.

Agencies can only express 'bottom lines' in relation to their statutory obligations. For example, Social Services could say they would be unable to accept a family plan that included a young child living in a household that includes an uncle with a recent conviction for child sexual abuse.

Second, the independent co-ordinator negotiates and facilitates attendance. This is achieved by contact with all identified members of the family, briefing them about the purpose and process of the event. Attention will also be paid to ensuring that people can get to the venue. Child-care arrangements are considered at this point.

Family group meetings can take place wherever the child and immediate carer would like them to take place. Considerations will include size, comfort, amenities, privacy and availability. Meetings have no predetermined time-scale and once in session, families need to be able to complete their work of planning in their own time. A lot of emphasis is placed on the ritual of the meeting since this serves to emphasise the importance of the event and its potential outcomes. The availability of food, a meal or light refreshments can also be significant – both as a means of bringing members together and on a practical level, since meetings may often last for several hours.

Where the alleged perpetrator is present, thought needs to be given to ensuring that one of the members attending will act as protector or advocate for the child during the meeting. Their role is to ensure that the child's voice and point of view are heard and understood and they will have responsibility for preventing or challenging implicit or explicit threats being made to the child. Where domestic, intergenerational or sibling violence has been a feature among members, the co-ordinator will also need to help the family identify what safeguards and advocacy they will implement during the meeting.

Third, the family meeting takes place. The meeting begins with the co-ordinator reminding the family members who are present about the reason for the meeting – they have come together to write a plan to meet the needs of the child. The co-ordinator will then explain the process and ground rules of the meeting.

Any agencies with resources on offer or concerns about the child are given a brief slot before the start of the meeting at which they identify in clear, jargon-free language the nature of their concerns, the resources they are willing and able to offer and any minimum requirements and outcomes they have for the plan. Once they have done that, the professionals and family group co-ordinator leave the room and the decision-making process within the family then commences. This process is autonomous and the discussion is done without an external/professional chair or leader – allowing the family to come up with its own plan for the care and welfare of the child.

Families are sometimes concerned that 'all hell will break loose' and arguments will erupt, but practice and experience have shown that this is rarely the case. Most families, when given control to resolve the problems, manage it admirably.

The plans are then written down either by the family themselves or by the co-ordinator at the request of the family. Where the plan lacks specific detail, the co-ordinator has a role in encouraging the family to particularise – who will do what, when and what if?

Each plan is unique, reflecting the circumstances and strengths of the family. Once the plan has been written, copies are given to all concerned. This includes the members of the family, the child, any agency with a legitimate interest in the family, and anyone the family wants to have a copy of the plan. The family may decide to review the plan by holding another group meeting, which they can request be facilitated by the co-ordinator. They may, however, decide not to use the co-ordinator or not to review the plan at all.

LENGTH OF TIME SPENT WORKING WITH PARENTS

Whatever models are adopted for working with parents, the overriding consideration needs to be the extent to which they contribute towards change in a time-scale commensurate with the welfare of the children. How long should work continue with parents in stuck cases to bring about change?

- *likelihood of harm:* Where severe and carrying the potential for enduring adverse consequences for children, the time for parental change will necessarily be short. Conversely, where there are protective factors at work (the presence of family members who act as 'buffers' for example) then time-scales will need to reflect this.
- *the age of the child:* The needs of dependent infants and babies cannot be put on hold and there will need to be early and convincing evidence of change in a short time span. However, older children in attached relationships present an argument for longer time-scales.

- *the expressed views of the child:* Where children are of an age and understanding to be able to form views, these must play some part in formulating time-scales.

SUMMARY

Parental responsibility refers to the legal duties and obligations that come with parenthood, and primary responsibility for care and safeguarding of dependent children devolves on parents.

The capacity of parents to fulfil their duties can be undermined in many ways and there is a potential for adversity to be interactive and cumulative. Nevertheless, parents often demonstrate skills and resilience in coping with adversity and assessments must aim to identify and build on such strengths.

Working with parents to safeguard children must aim to achieve meaningful parental participation.

Assessment of parents and provision of services should operate concurrently to promote the upbringing of children by parents or with families.

Core group working is a feature of working in child protection and offers greater scope than conferences and s.47 enquiries for parental participation and creative work to build parental capacity. Core groups are tasked by child protection conferences with devising and implementing detailed child protection plans.

When core group working succeeds in promoting change they will provide the evidence which enables conferences to make sound decisions regarding the de-registration of children.

Change work with parents must take account of time-scales for children. Where parents are unable or unwilling to address concerns, practitioners will need to re-evaluate the risk to children.

Where children cannot be safely retained at home, or returned home in a time-scale appropriate to their needs, practitioners will have to consider alternative placements.

Where this need arises, practitioners will need to examine the potential for kinship care. Family group conferencing is one model for working with families that aims to promote family participation.

FURTHER READING

Cannan, C. and Warren, C. (eds) *Social Action with Children and Families: A community development approach to child and family welfare* London: Routledge

Department of Health (1995a) *The Challenge of Partnership in Child Protection* London: HMSO

Department of Health (1995b) *Child Protection: Messages from research* London: HMSO

Henderson, P. (1997) Community development and children: A contemporary agenda In C. Cannan and C. Warren (eds) *Social Action with Children and Families: A community development approach to child and family welfare* London: Routledge

Jackson, S. and Kilroe, S. (eds) (1995) *Looking After Children: Good parenting, good outcomes* London: HMSO

Jackson, S. and Morris, K. (1999) Family group conferences: User empowerment or family self-reliance? A development from Lupton *British Journal of Social Work* 29: 621–630

Milner, J. (1993) A disappearing act: The differing career paths of fathers and mothers in child protection investigations *Critical Social Policy* 13, 2(38): 48–63

Mullender, A. (1997) Gender. In M. Davies (ed.) *The Blackwell Companion of Social Work* London: Blackwell

Payne, M. (1997) *Modern Social Work Theory*, 2nd edn, Basingstoke: Macmillan

Pennell, J. and Burford, G. (2000) Family group decision making: Protecting children and women *Child Welfare* 79, 2: 131–158

Phillipson, J. (1992) *Practising Equality: Women, men and social work* London: CCETSW

Ryburn, M. (1996) Family group conferences: Partnership in practice *Adoption and Fostering* 20, 1: 16–23

SSI *et al.* (2002) *Safeguarding Children. A joint Chief Inspectors' Report on arrangements to safeguard children* London: The Stationery Office

Thoburn, J., Lewis, A. and Shemmings, D. (1996) Partnership-based practice in child protection work. In M. Hill and J. Aldgate (eds) *Child Welfare Services. Developments in law, policy, practice and research* London: Jessica Kingsley

Williams, M. (1997) *Parents, Children and Social Workers: Working in partnership under the Children Act* Aldershot: Avebury

www.e-parents.org/ (website of the National Family and Parenting Institute)

REFERENCES

Birleson, P. (1980) The validity of depressive order in childhood and the development of a self-rating scale: A research report *Journal of Child Psychology and Psychiatry* 22: 73–88

Brugha, T., Bebington, P., Tennant, C. and Hurry, J. (1985) The list of threatening experiences: A subset of 12 life event categories with considerable long-term contextual threat *Psychological Medicine* 15: 189–194

Calder, M. (1995) Child protection: Balancing paternalism and partnership *British Journal of Social Work* 25: 749–766

CAPCAE (1998) *An Overview of Child Maltreatment Prevention Strategies in Europe: Volume 1* European Commission, Science Research and Development, January, XII/372/97–EN

Cleaver, H. and Freeman, P. (1995) *Parental Perspectives in Cases of Suspected Child Abuse: Studies in child protection* London: HMSO

Cleaver, H., Unell, I. and Aldgate, J. (1999) *Children's Needs – Parental Capacity: The impact of parental mental illness, problem alcohol and drug use and domestic violence on children's development* London: The Stationery Office

Coulshed, V. and Orme, J. (1998) *Social Work Practice: An introduction* Basingstoke: Macmillan/BASW

Crnic, K. A. and Booth, C. L. (1991) Mothers' and fathers' perceptions of daily hassles of parenting across early childhood *Journal of Marriage and the Family* 53: 1043–1050

Crnic, K. A. and Greenberg, M. T. (1990) Minor parenting stresses with young children *Child Development* 61: 1628–1637

Crow, G. (2000) *Hampshire Family Group Conferences in Education: A summary of the research findings on process and early outcomes* Sheffield: University of Sheffield

Crow, G. (2001) *Hampshire Family Group Conferences in Education: Summary of outcomes* Sheffield: University of Sheffield

Egan, G. (1981) *The Skilled Helper: A model for systematic helping and interpersonal relating* California: Brooks Cole

Farmer, E. and Owen, M. (1995) *Child Protection Practice: Private risks and public remedies. Decision making, intervention and outcomes in child protection work* London: HMSO

Ghate, D. (2000) Family violence and violence against children *Children and Society* 14, 5: 395–403

Goodman, R. (1997) The strengths and difficulties questionnaire: A research note *Journal of Child Psychology and Psychiatry* 38: 581–586

Goodman, R., Meltzer, H. and Bailey, V. (1998) The strengths and difficulties questionnaire: A pilot study on the validity of the self-report version *European Child and Adolescent Psychology* 7: 125–130

Hanmer, J. and Statham, D. (1988) *Women and Social Work: Towards a women-centred practice* Basingstoke: Macmillan

Humphreys, C. (1999) Avoidance and confrontation: Social work practice in relation to domestic violence and child abuse *Child and Family Social Work* 4: 77–87

Marsh, P. and Crow, G. (1998) *Family Group Conferences* Oxford: Blackwell

Parton, N. and O'Byrne, P. (2000) *Constructive Social Work* Basingstoke: Macmillan

Piccinelli, M., Tessari, E., Bor, T., Lomasi, M., Piasere, O., Semenzin, M., Garzotto, N. and Tansella, M. (1997) Efficacy of the alcohol use disorders test as a screening tool for hazardous alcohol intake and related disorders in primary care: A validity study *British Medical Journal* 514: 420–424

Sharry, J. (1999) Building solutions in groupwork with parents *Groupwork* 11, 2: 68–89

Sharry, J. (2001) Solution-Focused Groupwork London: Sage

Shemmings, D. and Shemmings, Y. (1996) Building trust with families when making enquiries. In D. Platt and D. Shemmings *Making Enquiries into Child Abuse and Neglect: Partnership with families* London: John Wiley and Sons

Sheppard, M. (2002) Depressed mothers' experience of partnership in child and family care *British Journal of Social Work* 32: 93–112

Smith, M. A. (1985) The effects of low levels of lead on urban children: The relevance of social factors, Ph.D. dissertation, Psychology, University of London

Snaith, R. P., Constantopoulos, A. A., Jardine, M. Y. and McGuffin, P. (1978) A clinical scale for the self-assessment of irritability *British Journal of Psychiatry* 132: 164–171

Thomas, S. P. (2001) Teaching healthy anger management *Perspectives in Psychiatric Care* 37, 2: 41–48

Thorpe, D. (1994) *Evaluating Child Protection* Buckingham: Open University Press

Turnell, A., Edwards, S. and Berg, I. K. (1999) *Signs of Safety: A solution and safety oriented approach to child protection casework* New York: Norton

CHAPTER 8

GOING TO COURT TO SAFEGUARD CHILDREN

LEARNING OBJECTIVES

By the end of this chapter you should be able to:

▢   Distinguish between different types of legal orders and powers and their applications

▢   Describe and operate within the guiding principles of family court proceedings

▢   Describe the role and function of the children's guardian

▢   Make a case for legal proceedings

▢   Operate effectively within a court context.

Working Together, the comprehensive guidance or practice manual of the child protection system, is largely silent about court proceedings and the legal applications. In part, this reflects the emphasis on partnership working and achieving agreement that is seen as central to effective practice. Nevertheless, there will be occasions when agreement is not reached, or breaks down, or the time-scale for that achievement or for changes necessary to meet a child's needs is too lengthy and beyond what can safely be accepted in the child's interest. Similarly, there will be other instances when the circumstances of a child dictate that immediate steps be taken to ensure her safety, either by removing her to a safe place or preventing her removal from a place deemed safe to one where there is risk of significant harm.

In these situations, workers will need to make use of a range of specific legal powers. Working within the framework of the law is at the heart of child care social work – as we have already seen, it sets down the duties and places limits on the powers of those whose work routinely involves intervening in the lives of children and families. In addition to the duties we have already outlined (see Chapter 2) a range of orders are available that can assist in the child protection process. Broadly speaking, we can distinguish two types of order reflecting different stages or levels of intervention (see Table 8.2 later):

- Short-term/emergency orders to cover situations when immediate intervention is necessary. These measures usually amount to removing the child from harm, or harm from the child
- Longer-term orders when issues of long-term planning and child welfare are necessary. These measures are more varied, and though they may involve removing the child or removing the risk permanently, they are also likely to involve working to reduce the risk and remedy the harm.

It should be noted that these do not represent rungs on a ladder, with short-term or emergency orders inevitably giving way to long-term interventions. Indeed, the use of opportunities presented in crisis situations which may typify the use of short-term orders to assess and provide supports to a child and her family may obviate the need for long-term orders.

Though nothing short of an adoption order divests a parent of parental responsibility – those duties in relation to their children as expressed in the Children Act 1989 – legal orders are powerful instruments, having considerable impact on the lives of children and their families. Consequently, their application in relation to each and every specific child and her family must be authorised/granted by application to a court or magistrate. Thus, the powers exist 'in potential' – as instruments that can be brought to bear, but only *after* they are demonstrated to be essential to safeguard a specific child.

GUIDING PRINCIPLES IN FAMILY PROCEEDINGS

In making any of the orders available to them under the Children Act 1989, courts are guided by a number of principles which aim to ensure a balance between action to safeguard children and undue or unwarranted interventions (the welfare balance). Those principles are detailed below.

The child's welfare is paramount – This is easy to say, but in practice it is often a matter of fine judgement for the court. Though the intention is that the chief or overriding consideration for decisions will be the welfare of the child, judgement will be made on the basis of the evidence, which may well be contradictory or contended. In reaching a judgement, the court is also required to have due regard for the wishes and feelings of the child, wherever they are ascertainable. Again this is easy to say but it requires sensitivity and fine judgement since it is also necessary to avoid compromising the child's welfare by placing them in the invidious position of appearing to decide issues where their loyalties, affections and needs are at odds.

The 'no order' principle – Courts should not make an order simply because the grounds for making the order exists. The consideration is whether an order will positively contribute to the welfare of the child. When applications are made or considered, attention will be focused on what the making of an order will achieve, and unless that can be convincingly demonstrated, this principle dictates that no order should be made. Thus, applications for care or supervision orders will need to be accompanied by well-planned and convincing care plans or schedules of supervision.

No undue delay – The emphasis is on ensuring that children and their interests are not drifting, which may constitute a further erosion of their welfare. If court proceedings were allowed to drag on through repeated adjournments, particularly if children are in care, the possibilities of effective rehabilitation are lessened and the 'balance of advantage' is tilted towards continued intervention. Uniform time-tables apply to different orders and must be met. In practice, this does mean that court proceedings must be prioritised and can mean a period of additional stress for practitioners.

In addition to these principles, courts in hearing matters in family proceedings are also granted a wide degree of flexibility in their choice of which orders to make, whatever the original order sought. 'Family proceedings' is the term used to describe hearings under a range of legislation that are held to have in common their actual or potential impact on the lives of children. In broad terms, this covers any issues arising in respect of public and private law relating to domestic family matters. For example:

- private law
    - divorce, marital separation or nullity (under Matrimonial Causes legislation)
    - contact and residence orders (s.8 of CA89)
    - applications for financial relief ('maintenance')
    - domestic violence, occupation of family home and non-molestation orders (part IV of the Family Law Act 1996)
- public law
    - adoption (including step-parent adoption)
    - care proceedings.

In practice this means that courts always consider whether, in addition to or instead of the orders that are sought, other orders are necessary. Thus, in applications for care orders (public law order), courts may consider whether a section 8 residence order (private law order) to a grandparent, perhaps in conjunction with a supervision order (public) and/or a family assistance order (private) might not meet a specific child's needs better. Clearly, the willingness and ability of third parties to fulfil such duties are central to decisions to vary the outcome in this way. Nor can courts impose orders on local authorities. Snapshot 8.1 gives a flavour of instances when courts may act in the broader interests of children.

SNAPSHOT 8.1:
DIRECTIONS TO PURSUE A S.37 ENQUIRY

Brenda and John parted six years ago and the couple's three sons, Ben 7, Liam 8 and Sean 10 have lived with their mother since then with little contact with their father, whose work regularly took him abroad. Two years ago he set up home with his new partner and her 4-year-old daughter and he no longer works abroad. In the course of divorce proceedings, initiated by Brenda, the court has to adjourn when a row breaks out between John and Brenda and allegations are made on both sides of drunkenness and violence. John also alleges that his sons are at risk because Brenda is living with a lesbian partner and both are engaged in prostitution and pornography.

The court issues a section 37 direction to the local authority to investigate the circumstances of the three boys.

SECTION 37 ENQUIRIES

Section 37 of the CA89 requires local authorities to investigate the circumstances of children on the direction of courts, with a view to ascertaining whether their interests require or would be served by the local authority seeking a care or supervision order. These are powerful directions that trigger a thorough assessment. The outcome of the assessment will form the basis for either an application in care proceedings or a plan to support family members seeking a section 8 order, or a report to the court evidencing the satisfactory nature of the children's welfare if no order is sought.

Though the courts cannot impose a full order against the local authority's wishes, it can, in exceptional circumstances, make an interim care or supervision order which the local authority will have to fulfil, pending their assessment and report back to court.

The court's time-scale requires that the local authority present its report within eight weeks, unless an earlier application has been made in care proceedings. You will have noted that this time-scale fits closely with the core assessment of the *Framework for Assessment* schedule. This reflects the nature of the investigation that is required and expected by the court in such matters.

Decisions about such powerful types of intervention do not rest with an individual practitioner and will generally flow from consultation with a line manager, a strategy discussion or meeting, a case conference or a review conference. Nevertheless, practitioners will need to bring their knowledge of law when contributing towards those discussions. Let us look at the issues that arise in more detail through the following snapshots of a case in progress.

SNAPSHOT 8.2: A POLICE PROTECTION ORDER

Police and ambulance officers are called to a flat where they find a man unconscious in the living room with all the signs of a drug overdose. A number of substances, having the appearance of heroin, amphetamines and LSD along with hypodermic syringes, are found. The accommodation is sparsely furnished and there are signs of a recent disturbance in the litter of ripped clothing, broken bottles, ornaments, plates and food cartons over the floor and recent staining on the walls and surfaces. In the kitchen a child, female, of about 18 or 20 months old is sleeping on a jacket on the floor beside a pet litter tray. There are no other adults in the flat and nothing to show whether there are other occupants. The flat may be privately rented but it is not clear from whom or to whom, or it may be squatted. The original call to emergency services came from a man giving only a first name and the few neighbours who can be spoken to can give no information about the child, who is taken to hospital for examination and kept in on a police protection order.

The police then notify the local authority social services department, where the referral is allocated to a social worker, Marc, for action.

POLICE PROTECTION ORDERS

In some instances, the risk to a child is acute in nature and requires urgent action to safeguard her. Unlike social services, the police force is one of the emergency services and by the nature of police work they are routinely faced with people in situations critical to life and limb. Indeed, the law views the police as powerful guardians of public safety and consequently gives them the power (under section 17 of the Police and Criminal Evidence Act 1984) to enter and search premises to 'save life and limb'. In addition to this broad-spectrum power, police officers also have significant powers in relation to safeguarding children. These are set out in section 46 of the Children Act 1989.

The police can take a child into police protection without prior court order where they have reasonable cause to believe that a child may otherwise be suffering or likely to suffer significant harm. Police protection is exercised in one of two ways:

- removing the child from the place where they are deemed at risk, to alternative suitable accommodation
- preventing the removal of a child from a place or accommodation deemed safe.

In this case, the child's situation is critical and demands immediate action. Other situations more routinely encountered by the police are calls to incidents of domestic violence. The Home Office has directed all police forces to be alert to the welfare of children as well as women on such occasions.

These powers reflect the crisis nature of much police work and are not intended to substitute for the more ordinary duties of agencies to safeguard children, but to act as an absolute safety net when need is critical. Police protection is limited to 72 hours during which time they must:

- inform the child, if capable of understanding, of what is being done and why
- elicit the child's wishes and feelings, if practicable
- inform the child's parents or others with parental responsibility of what is being done and why
- inform the local authority of the area in which the child was put under police protection
- inform the child's local authority if that is different
- ensure that the child is accommodated in or on behalf of the local authority.

In the case we are examining, the police have taken the child to hospital, judging this to be the most appropriate safe place since the circumstances indicate a need for a medical examination. They have also contacted the local authority social services, which is duty bound to respond and take up the case. The expectation is that, as soon as possible, the local authority will take over the duties and responsibilities for the child while they are still in police protection and progress actions necessary to ensure the child's safety. But close inter-professional working is still the order of the day as the police must be satisfied with the steps that are taken by the social services. If the police disagree, the law allows for police to pre-empt the local authority by applying on its behalf for an emergency protection order. Furthermore, the social worker will need to work closely with the police, who in any case will be responsible for following up their enquiries as to how the child was placed in such risk with a view to establishing whether criminal charges are to be brought.

At the point at which Marc receives the referral, the child has been temporarily safeguarded, but on the information available to him, it is difficult to see a way forward to her longer-term well-being. Unless a fit person with parental responsibility or a suitable relative can be located in the space of 72 hours, then further short-term measures are indicated. In this case, Marc and his manager, in consultation with the police (a strategy discussion) will be looking to an emergency protection order (EPO).

The Children Act 1989 stipulates a number of circumstances under which an emergency protection order can be sought, any one of which may trigger the application:

(a)   where there is reasonable cause to believe that a child is likely to suffer significant harm if the child is not removed to safe accommodation provided by or on behalf of the applicant or alternatively, if the child is removed from a place or accommodation currently deemed safe (section 44 (1) (a))

(b)   where the local authority is frustrated or impeded in conducting statutory duties in relation to investigating allegations of risk or harm (for example a section 47 enquiry) (Section 44 (1) (b))

(c)   Where the efforts of an NSPCC officer (as a person authorised by the Secretary of State to apply for care and supervision orders) to make their enquiries into the welfare of a child are frustrated or impeded (Section 44 (1) (c)).

By their nature, such powers are often sought in the absence of parents who may hold different views about their necessity. For that reason, the orders are short-term – 8 days with one extension of 7 days if the child's interests require it. Unlike the police powers of protection, an EPO confers a measure of parental responsibility and ensures, in a case such as this, that the local authority can step into the breach of day-to-day decision making and responsibility necessary in respect of all children. Without such an order, this child could be harmed by the inability of anyone to legally take on that responsibility. Table 8.1 summarises the usual range of emergency powers and orders that you will encounter.

Once the decision is taken to apply for an EPO, the procedure is relatively simple. Practitioners represent their authorities in making application for such orders so when they are granted, they are granted to the authority, not to the individual worker. Ordinarily, such orders must specify the child by name, but where, as in this case, the child's name is not known, then she is specified by the location and situation in which she was found.

TABLE 8.1 Emergency powers and orders to safeguard children

Order/Power	Agency	Duration	Effect
Police powers of entry (section 17 Police and Criminal Evidence Act 1984)	Police	Crisis action	Can enter and search premises 'to save life and limb'
Police power of protection (section 46 CA89)	Police – no application to court required	72 hours	Can remove a child to a safe place or prevent a child being removed from a place deemed safe
Emergency protection order (EPO) (section 44 CA89)	Local authority NSPCC (as persons authorised by the Secretary of State) Legally, anyone can apply but in practice, most people contact and rely on the social services, NSPCC or the police (see above) to exercise their powers	8 days (or 9 if 8th day falls on a bank holiday). May be extended once, for 7 days. Once made, the order is unchallengeable for 72 hours. After 72 hours, can be challenged by a parent, other person with parental responsibility or any other person with whom child was living immediately prior to order	Children subject to an EPO cannot be withheld and must be presented ('produced') to the order holder. Confers limited parental authority for duration and authorises holder to: Remove child to a safe place or prevent removal of child from a place deemed safe. If child is removed from family, they must be returned if or as soon as risk can be demonstrated to be past
Additional directions or orders that may be attached to an EPO (section 45 CA89)	Agencies as above	Duration as above	General intent is to enhance effectiveness of EPO
	Holder to be accompanied by registered medical practitioner, registered nurse or registered health visitor		Medical appraisal on the spot allows for authoritative assessment of child's safety and may obviate need to remove. Alternatively, may be helpful if, in addition to concerns about child, there are concerns about mental health of parent or carer

(section 48 CA89)	Requirement of third-party disclosure about whereabouts of the child in question	Useful where a parent or relative has removed a child to frustrate intervention and other family members know or have very good idea where they are
(section 48 CA89)	Authority to enter and search specified premises for named child and can include unnamed children if there is reason to believe there may be others at risk in same place	In practice, rarely sought since the EPO already demands that the child is 'produced'. But there is merit where there is the possibility that other children as yet unknown may also be at risk, since it allows them also to be safeguarded as if they were the subject of named orders, rather than left at risk while a further application is pursued. In the event additional children are safeguarded, the court must be notified as soon as possible afterwards
(section 48 (9) CA89)	Issues a warrant to a police officer to enter premises (by force if necessary) or access the child named in the EPO	Issued where parents or carers have refused access to a social worker or there are good grounds for expecting that they will refuse access
(section 44 CA89)	Restrictions on or requirements of contact between child and named persons	Generally, EPOs (and also police powers of protection) require holders to ensure reasonable contact between parents and child. But if contact with a named person constitutes a risk (from threats of violence or abduction for example) or if insufficient contact with a

TABLE 8.1 continued

Order/Power	Agency	Duration	Effect
(section 44 CA89) (cont)			named person would be harmful (e.g. a non-maltreating parent) then the court may give specific directions
(section 44 CA89)	Medical, psychiatric or psychological (children and adolescent mental health services) examinations or other assessments		Where the court thinks fit, it may direct or specify the type of examination that should be undertaken or not in the interests of the child
(section 38A(1) CA89) (as inserted by s.52 schedule 6 of Family Law Act 1996)	Power to attach an exclusion requirement against a suspected maltreater		Applicable to domestic violence and/or suspected sexual abuse. Requires reasonable cause to believe risk will go with excluded person *and* continued presence of a protective adult (parent or other) who can provide care necessary for child *and* who agrees to exclusion

Practitioners complete standard application forms, which will usually be kept in local offices and present them to the local court (or to a designated magistrate out of hours). Less experienced staff should draw on the skills and support of peers and/or line managers to build confidence until the process becomes familiar. Where social services are following through with action initiated by a police protection order, as here, the application for an EPO is smoothed since the police have the evidence and can apply on behalf of the local authority.

SNAPSHOT 8.3: AN EMERGENCY PROTECTION ORDER

The police protection order gave way to an emergency protection order to the local authority and 'Anna', as the child has been named temporarily, has been placed with foster carers. Paediatric examination during her stay in hospital suggested that Anna was probably nearer 30 months old than the 20 months initially estimated, but in the lowest percentiles for weight and height. Although her hands and face were dirty on admission, her hair and skin do not indicate chronic neglect and her clothing, though grubby, was satisfactory as to fit and quantity. Tests suggest that there may be developmental delay in speech and co-ordination and dexterity.

The man died in hospital five days after admission without having regained consciousness. The police are still unable to establish the identity of the child, her relationship to the dead man or the whereabouts of her mother or other relatives. They are also unable to discover the identity of the man and there is speculation as to whether he may only recently have come to the UK.

Anna's situation focuses our attention by its extremity – a physically dependent child whose closest carers are currently unknown and have abandoned her, whether intentionally or not: steps must be taken to safeguard her. The very extremity paradoxically makes this a relatively straightforward case in which legal action is necessary to formalise the powers of the local authority to look after her. In other situations it may be less clear-cut. Suppose, for example, that the child had been abducted and fit and concerned parents were even now looking for her, or suppose that a suitable relative would take on her care if only she knew her circumstances. In circumstances where the safety of the child could otherwise be met and assured, the existence of an EPO is not sufficient reason for retaining a child for the full duration of the order. Similarly, if an order is granted as a means of allowing a social worker or medical practitioner to see the child, and the child is seen to be safe and well, the existence of the order is not sufficient reason for removal of the child. However, the order runs its course so that if circumstances change again while the order is in force, removal or other action can be taken.

At this stage, Marc will be kept busy with a range of tasks that will include:

* completing necessary paperwork for a looked after child (LAC forms)
* arranging for a family placement, briefing and possibly supporting the foster carers or liaising with the family placement worker who will support them; completing necessary paperwork to ensure that foster carers receive payment

- ensuring that arrangements are made for Anna to have primary health care team cover (a health visitor and GP). In most cases foster carers will routinely take on these tasks, but the arrangements cannot be assumed to take care of themselves
- liaising with police, since identifying Anna and her parents and relatives will be an important step towards progressing her welfare
- checking with colleagues and local authority files and the Child Protection Register in case there may be clues to Anna's identity. Though it is not Marc's job to be a detective, it is possible, for example, that a colleague from the community drugs team has had dealings with the dead man, or knows of other people associated with the flat where Anna was found
- holding a strategy meeting to consider ways forward and/or convening a child protection case conference
- contributing to the decisions that will ensure Anna's safety and welfare beyond the short term of the EPO
- recording his ongoing actions and his initial assessment.

This is a great deal to compress into the eight days of an EPO, alongside a worker's other caseload duties. It requires skills in prioritising, time management and focused working to achieve them. Throughout, Marc will have to draw on his knowledge and understanding of the law and policy in contributing to decision making. Marc, his manager and inter-professional colleagues will need to maintain sufficient flexibility to ensure that contingency plans exist to meet radically different situations. In effect, they must begin planning *as if* Anna's abandonment is total and permanent *and simultaneously, as if* her identity will be established and parents/family located and be able to provide appropriate care imminently.

Following a strategy meeting attended by Marc, his senior, a legal executive from the local authority, police and temporary health visitor, the decision was taken that the local authority would begin care proceedings, by applying for an interim care order. The presence of a legal executive or solicitor ensures that decisions are clearly informed about the merit of any proposed legal order applications and appropriate legal support is available for any such action. It is always sensible to make time to build up working relations with colleagues from the legal department, and beginning practitioners in particular should find them a useful source of information and support.

SNAPSHOT 8.4: AN INTERIM CARE ORDER

The local authority initiates care proceedings and Marc presents a report to the court, which makes an interim care order in respect of Anna and an independent children's guardian, Beth, is appointed to act as her guardian for the duration of the proceedings. The court directs that determined efforts should be made to discover Anna's identity and the whereabouts of her mother and other relatives and issues two specific directions – that DNA testing should be undertaken to determine whether or not Anna was related to the dead man, and that photographs should be taken of Anna and distributed to health authorities throughout the UK and Eire in an attempt to establish her identity.

TABLE 8.2 Possibilities for short- and longer-term legal intervention

	Short-term/Emergency interventions	Longer-term measures
Removal of child from risk	*In absence of parental agreement* Emergency protection order Interim care order	*In absence of parental agreement or significant parental incapacity* Care proceedings, with a view to: Supervision order Care order *and* Placement elsewhere in family or Placement outside the family or Placement for adoption
	With parental agreement Agree to section 20 accommodation for child, arrange alternative brief stay with safe relative or close family friend Negotiate overnight or brief stay on hospital ward (where child has been seen by paediatrician) Assist protective parent and child to a women's refuge (domestic violence) NB: Since the option of an order is a powerful lever, agreement is often possible (often referred to as 'voluntary' arrangements – the importance lies in the agreed action not the level of initial voluntarism)	*With parental and/or family agreement* Provide longer-term accommodation or 'shared parenting' under section 20 CA89 Approve/support a de facto placement within wider family Support a protective parent or relative to seek a section 8 CA89 order Residence order – confers parental responsibility and stipulates where child will live
	Heavily dependent on nature of risk to child In Domestic Violence – Part IV of Family Law Act 1996 allows for removal of offender and non-molestation orders (s.42) and/or for an exclusion order to be attached to an EPO (s.52)	Separation/divorce (research evidences heightened risks to women from domestic violence following separation) Work by/with violent partner on violence

TABLE 8.2 continued

	Short-term/Emergency interventions	Longer-term measures
Removal of child from risk	In sexual abuse by sibling – negotiate removal of offending child to other carers within family where there are no children or accommodate (s.20) with suitable safeguards (e.g. foster carers with no other children in place or residential setting with good oversight)	Work by/with offending child and family to locate sources of behaviour and extinguish
		Separation/divorce/reconfiguring family
		Work by/with parent/s, wider family and child to locate sources of behaviour and support changes
	In physical and sexual abuse (adult offender) – arrest/removal of person believed responsible (police action possible only when evidence available)	In sexual abuse (by adult) – specialist interventions with person believed responsible. Safer strategy for child/ren may be work with/by protective parent and with child
	In neglect – possibilities include negotiating a fit relative or family friend into home to oversee or provide child's care	Longer-term support to family. Enhancing capacity of family to meet child's needs directly (e.g. assisting with poverty/debt reduction, improved accommodation, training in child care, family relationships) or indirectly (e.g. facilitating networks of community supports, resistance to racism)

THE TEST IN CARE PROCEEDINGS

In deciding to initiate care proceedings, the local authority draws on the expertise of a member of the legal department. This is routine good practice, and ensures that the evidence, interventions, services to date, and the proposed plans for future care services are sufficient to do the following:

- meet the threshold test in care proceedings (child's welfare paramount and welfare balance)
- demonstrate that the broader legal duties to the child and her family have been met (child's welfare paramount, welfare balance and no order principle)
- provide a convincing care plan to meet the child's continuing and future needs (child's welfare is paramount)
- show how the order sought will bring positive benefit to the child (no order principle).

All of these need to be met whenever an order is sought in care proceedings if the application is to be successful. Here the application succeeded (again the extreme nature of Anna's situation dictated the outcome). In other cases, other disposals might prevail. For example, parents might successfully oppose an order or present a well thought out alternative to the court, agreeing for a child to move on a residence order to a relative. Previously unco-operative parents might demonstrate a willingness to work alongside the social worker, or the local authority might present a case which fails to convince the court that all necessary efforts to provide supportive services (under sections 17 or 20) have been made.

Though circumstances in families can and sometimes do change dramatically, and agencies should be responsive to these, it is poor service to a child and therefore poor practice to present a case to court where the criteria are not met. The test or threshold in care proceedings is the same whether applying for a care or a supervision order (CO, SO), interim care or supervision order (ICO, ISO).

GUIDANCE 8.1: THE THRESHOLD IN CARE PROCEEDINGS

Section 31 (2) CA 1989: The court may not make an order unless satisfied that:

a) the child concerned is suffering significant harm, or is likely to suffer significant harm;

and

b) the harm or likelihood of harm is attributable to
   (i) the care given to the child, or likely to be given to him if the order were not made, not being what it would be reasonable to expect a parent to give him; *or*
   (ii) the child is beyond parental control.

The terminology can be misleading, giving rise to a view of an interim order as a staging post on the journey to a full care order. This is not so. Both ICOs and COs confer parental responsibility on the local authority, without removing the parental responsibility of the child's mother and father (where the father has parental responsibility). But interim orders are time limited (up to eight weeks in total for an initial interim care order) and may be renewed within that time frame, up to the final time limit. Furthermore, they can have directions attached – for example with regard to medical or other specialist examination, contact and residence. On the other hand, COs cannot be time limited, and will last until the child's eighteenth birthday unless otherwise varied or revoked, and cannot have directions attached. COs and ICOs, while having some similarities, are intended as different types of instrument to meet different circumstances. ICOs represent a powerful but short-term intervention during which time it may be possible to produce change sufficient to continue with family support under section 17 and section 20. The process of applying for and making an ICO may focus the attention and efforts of family and agencies on resolving the issues and planning the means to effectively ensure the child's future welfare. Where matters are not resolved or there is a change for the worse, other orders including a CO can be sought.

COs represent a long-term intervention, recognising that, in some instances, the child's safety and welfare will depend upon the local authority holding and exercising parental responsibility for the foreseeable future and in some cases, until the child attains adult status or until an alternative long-term solution is found, such as adoption or placement under a residency order. Even here, the potential for change to occur within families is covered by the facility to vary or seek revocation of a CO at a later date, unless a child has subsequently been legally adopted. In some instances, applications for COs will be preceded by the making of ICOs – but this is not a required first step and usually reflects either the need for the children's guardian to make their investigations and complete their report or the attempt to try the 'jolt' of an ICO.

CAFCASS: THE ROLE AND POWER OF GUARDIANS

In Anna's case the order is made and a new professional enters her life – Beth the children's guardian, who will act on her behalf throughout the proceedings. Guardians play an important part in such proceedings and one that has developed over the years since the inception of the Children Act. Extensive research between 1992 and 1996 (Brophy *et al.* 1999 cited in Department of Health 2001) identified the following points:

- guardians occupy a central and multidimensional role in proceedings, acting as: 'overseer, mediator, negotiator, broker and, in some cases, gatekeeper to the work of experts'
- most guardians are experienced and skilled social workers
- key features to the guardian's successful case management are: independence and flexibility, an ability to draw on high-level practice-based experience and analytical skills and reasoning backed by academic training.

Beth is employed by CAFCASS, the Children and Family Court Advisory and Support Service. Its creation in 2001 under the Criminal Justice and Court Services Act

2000 (CJ & CSA 2000) represents a significant move forward in integrating children's services by drawing together the services previously supplied by:

- probation (Family Court Welfare)
- local authorities (guardian ad litem and reporting officer services GALRO)
- the office of the Official Solicitor (Children's Branch).

Importantly, too, the creation of CAFCASS further enhances the independence of children's guardians. It is a stand-alone body (non-departmental) answerable to the Lord Chancellor, which indicates the importance accorded to its functions and status as a service.

GUIDANCE 8.2:   CAFCASS

CAFCASS, through its staff, is charged with duties to:

- safeguard and promote the welfare of children subject to family court proceedings
- advise the courts on the needs and interests of children subject to family court proceedings
- make provision for children to be represented in such proceedings
- provide information, advice and other support for children and their families during such proceedings.

(CJ & CSA 2000)

In fulfilling duties to Anna, Beth will arrange for her to be legally represented and will spend time with Anna and her foster carers. In the majority of cases, the child's family would be known and the guardian would spend time with them too. She would also aim to observe the parents and child or children during contact visits. Where it is appropriate (age/functioning) she would spend time alone with the child. Guardians also spend time with the social worker and, where health staff have been involved, will meet with them. Beth will have full access to all the records in the case and would expect to be invited to any case conferences or strategy meetings that are convened. The guardian can request directions from the court about issues that arise as she goes about her investigation. For example, Beth might decide that Anna would benefit from a specialist medical assessment in relation to her developmental level or hearing. In that case she would seek agreement in the form of an additional direction to instruct an appropriate specialist who will provide expert evidence to the court. In some instances, guardians and local authorities jointly instruct such experts – which may have the merit of cost-saving and reducing the number of examinations a child is subject to, but equally may undermine the independent status of the guardian in the eyes of family and child.

In complex or stuck cases, guardians may be received with greater trust from parents because they come from outside the local authority, with whom they may be in conflict.

SNAPSHOT 8.5: ONGOING WORK – CHILD IS SUBJECT TO AN ORDER

The initial interim care order was made for two weeks and renewed for a further two weeks. During this time, Anna was thriving in her foster placement, as evidenced by significant growth and weight gains recorded by the health visitor to whom she was temporarily assigned.

The foster carers described her as showing interest in everything that was going on but found her less demanding than they would expect of a toddler of about 30 months – initially, if put in a play pen, she would sit without expecting any attention.

They reported that she seemed unfamiliar with toys and were pleased that she quickly began to respond to encouragement to play with a range of interactive play materials.

The task of planning for Anna's longer-term care and welfare has to be resolved. Anna's situation demands clarity and focus. In view of her age, she is particularly vulnerable to a drifting situation and plans must be developed to place her permanently with a view to adoption, alongside plans to meet her needs through family placement with a view to assessing rehabilitation if parents are located within a time-scale that has to be decided in line with her age. An older child would have to be actively involved in her own care planning and her wishes and views incorporated, in so far as they are consistent with her welfare. Marc and his manager are now firmly in a stage of dual or parallel planning.

SNAPSHOT 8.6: WORKING WITH A PARENT DURING CARE PROCEEDINGS

Three days before the expiration of the second interim order, Tina, 22 years old, contacted the police and social services looking for her daughter Tanya (Anna's real name). The police indicate that they will be questioning Tina further and will be considering whether or not charges (under schedule 1 of the 1933 CYP Act), perhaps child abandonment or neglect, will be brought. Tina explained that she had taken a summer job in Spain and had arranged for Tanya to stay with a friend for a while until she had checked out how long the job would last and if she could manage to have Tanya with her. According to Tina, the arrangement with Lisa, whom she had known for about a year, was that Lisa would collect Tanya from the coach station where Tina would embark on her overland trip to Spain and Lisa would take Tanya with her to Scotland where Lisa was intending to spend the summer house-sitting for friends. At the coach station Tina received a message that Lisa was delayed but Mickey a mutual friend had agreed to take Tanya to Lisa's sister's and Lisa would collect her from there. Tina put the bag with Tanya's clothing in a left luggage locker and Mickey took the key with him. Tina's phone was stolen shortly after she got to Spain and it had taken her quite some time to locate a telephone number for Lisa, but it was not easy to get to a phone and after several unproductive voicemails Tina said she began to get anxious and decided to come back and sort things out. By Tina's report, Tanya's father was an Australian who had died in an accident after returning to Australia shortly before Tanya's birth. Tina's mother died by suicide when Tina was 11 years old and her father died four years ago in his early 60s. She has no brothers or sisters and knows of no other relatives she might have.

The police were able to locate Lisa in Glasgow and she corroborated Tina's account, but explained that she had been taken aback when she arrived at her sister's next day to be told that Mickey had not been round and that the 'word on the street' was that Mickey was in hospital. Lisa stated that she had tried phoning and texting Tina and when she got no reply concluded that Tina had changed her mind and taken Tanya with her or had made other arrangements.

Neither Tina nor Tanya were previously known to social services and Tina's only previous police involvement was a caution she received aged 15 for underage drinking.

The local authority decide to seek a further interim care order which is made by the court for four weeks. The court also directs a full parenting assessment to be undertaken by the local authority, who are directed to facilitate contact between mother and child.

The child welfare system including courts in family proceedings and children's social services is geared to children in the context of their families. The emergence of Tina has the dual effect of making the social work task more ordinary – that is, assessing a child in the context of her family and the family's circumstances, and the decision making more complex. Similarly for the courts, the presence of Tina places Tanya firmly in her context and tilts the work of the system back into the ordinary. In the continued absence of a parent or established identity for a child, the courts would have little alternative but to make a care order to a local authority to ensure that parental responsibility was exercised in respect of her. Whereas the more usual tasks of courts in family proceedings is establishing findings of fact – e.g. determining if the parents or other adults with parental responsibility have exercised their responsibility effectively/appropriately – and deciding, on the basis of those findings, guided by the welfare balance and no order principle, whether or which legal disposal will best meet the child's paramount welfare needs.

There is a great deal to be accomplished in a short space of time, including:

- fulfilling court directions with regard to contact and assessment
- monitoring Tanya's well-being in her foster care placement
- establishing contact with Tina and arranging an assessment schedule
- inter-professional liaison – the convening of an early child protection conference (or review if an initial conference has already occurred) makes practice sense when there have been, as here, significant developments. In this way, all relevant agencies can be updated and the different strands of the assessment can be co-ordinated under a child protection plan
- production of a court report
- planning and co-ordination.

As Tanya's social worker, Marc has a central role in ensuring that all of this happens, but this is not to say that he must or can do everything himself. An early supervision or briefing session with his line manager and a case conference will provide some scope for a rational distribution of some of the tasks, with Marc co-ordinating the various strands.

ICOS – TIME-SCALES

You will recall from Chapter 2 that 35 days is allowed for a core assessment under the *Framework for Assessment* and that builds on an earlier 7-day initial assessment. Yet the court will certainly expect a sophisticated appraisal, at least comparable to a core assessment, so why the four-week timescale to the next hearing?

Though there is no limit to the number of ICOs that can be made under the CA89, there are set time limits reflecting the principle of no undue delay. Thus, a first order can be made for a period up to eight weeks, and though an element of local practice may evolve, generally the court will be guided by the circumstance of each case in deciding on the exact period. For example, where there is a clear plan for assessment timetable for medical or other specialist examinations, the court may be content to grant the full eight weeks. In fluid situations, as here, where significant parties, e.g. Tanya's family are missing, the court is likely to set a number of shorter periods (which together add up to eight weeks) so that directions can keep abreast of possible developments. Beyond that initial eight-week period, subsequent orders are limited to four weeks, and though there is no legal limit on the number of subsequent orders, again the principle of no undue delay will operate, and courts will need very persuasive evidence to make more than one or two subsequent ICOs.

PARENTAL CONTACT

Only exceptionally will courts deny contact between parents and children in care, and often they will give directions concerning frequency and whether or not such contact is to be supervised. Without such directions, matters are left to the discretion of the authority, which is expected to exercise that discretion with due regard to the interests of the child. Marc is aware that infrequent contact with younger children is prejudicial to a child's relationship with a parent and would therefore be contrary to the spirit of the legislation. Twice a week would be considered the minimum acceptable level and Marc will need to ensure that this is facilitated. If Tina is unhappy with the level of contact, she can seek a further direction from the court. Children who are unhappy with levels of contact can, through the guardian, seek a variation. In the case of children too young or otherwise unable to express a view, like Tanya, the guardian will act on their behalf if more or less contact is deemed appropriate.

SNAPSHOT 8.7: PARENTAL CONTACT – CHILD SUBJECT TO AN ORDER

Tanya continues to thrive and is steadily putting on weight and becoming increasingly active.

Contact arrangements are made and Tina spends several afternoons with Tanya at the foster carers. They report that she brings new clothing for Tanya but shows little initiative as regards holding or playing with her – 'It's more like she's visiting us than her daughter.'

A case conference is held, attended by Tina who expresses her willingness to co-operate fully with all the professionals and who suggests that she would be happy for Tanya to remain in 'voluntary care' (s.20 CA89) when the ICO expires while things are sorted out. The police are not proceeding with any action against Tina. The case conference endorses a care plan based on Tanya remaining with her current foster carers under section 20, and work towards rehabilitation with support services including day care for Tanya.

Tina is currently in temporary accommodation and looking for a suitable place. She has rescheduled two interviews with Marc explaining that she is looking for a flat and has now begun working in the evenings as a waitress to get together a deposit.

The guardian, Beth, was unable to attend the case conference and tells Marc that she is thinking of recommending the making of a full care order, as she sees clear evidence of prior and substantial physical neglect, and in view of Tanya's age is looking to a definite time limit on attempts to rehabilitate. A care order, with a view to placement for adoption if rehabilitation is not successful within 6 months (parallel planning), would in her view best meet Tanya's interests.

MAKING A CASE

It is not a requirement that the social work case be identical to the guardian's, but if there are going to be conflicting recommendations, it is sensible to be alert to them well in advance. Better yet, is to focus efforts on understanding exactly the areas of disagreement and perhaps working to achieve a closer fit. The emphasis in family proceedings is on achieving consensus. However, this will not always be possible, and ultimately, the court will make the decision on the basis of:

• whether conditions for making the order are met
• child's welfare paramount principle
• the welfare balance
• no order principle
• range of evidence before it
• perceived merit of different evidence
• perceived merit of the proposed care plan (if applicable).

Marc must now make the local authority case, in his written submissions (his report) and in person. In doing so, he will need to be certain that he has covered these points in a convincing way. The decision to seek no order and to work in partnership with Tina via use of section 20 accommodation and support services certainly scores in relation to the no order principle and the welfare balance. But whether it is viewed by the court as passing the paramountcy test is less certain. Tanya's rapid growth and weight gain while in care are a worrying feature, as it is a strong indicator of previous neglect. The court will undoubtedly be looking for evidence that this has been scrutinised during assessment and a clear analysis developed which convincingly explains the causes and, more importantly, gives assurance that Tanya will not be put at risk of future neglect.

Giving evidence

Giving evidence in chief (being taken through your report)

This should be straightforward. You should have had the opportunity to discuss with the agency solicitor/barrister beforehand what questions will be asked and what points will be stressed.

- decide in advance if you want to take oath or affirm
- aim to answer clearly and directly
- do not proffer answers outside your knowledge/competence ('I have no direct knowledge of that')
- look at the Bench/Judge
- ask to refer to your report or contemporaneous notes if that would help (any such notes would then be open to the court)
- be open and honest. Do not massage information.

Being cross-examined

Adversarial rules are relaxed in child-care proceedings and many opposition barristers/ solicitors will approach the case in this context. However, there will be exceptions to this. Here are some useful pointers:

- no new news – there should be nothing in your report or any contemporaneous notes that you have not already shared with the family/young person
- be absolutely clear on your facts (rehearse these beforehand)
- ensure that your professional judgement/opinion is well supported (facts *plus* research/practice evidence)
- own your conclusions ('I recommend this because it seemed like everyone else thought it was right' is not a good position to be in)
- do not take questions personally
- answer briefly, *but*
- do not be pushed into a yes/no answer if this is inappropriate (be confident enough to state 'I'm not able to give a yes or no answer to this')
- ask for questions to be repeated if you are unclear about what is wanted.

Going to court – the small practicalities

Going to court, on the day, involves a host of small practicalities that can erupt from the background and create an unwelcome distraction from the 'real' business. Experienced practitioners take steps to cover these practicalities and it is worth doing so to avoid unnecessary distraction from the task in hand (Table 8.3).

TABLE 8.3 Practical considerations at court

Additional documentation	Your report will already be lodged with the court, but you may find it useful to refer to your diary or any contemporaneous notes you made in interviews or assessment	Do I have my diary? Do I have any contemporaneous notes?
Travel and transport	Although court hearings are frequently characterised by lengthy waits, being late for any proceedings is unacceptable professional behaviour	Do I know where exactly I'm going? How travelling? Any arrangements for transporting children or family members? Where is car parking?
Self-care and physical needs	Waiting for proceedings to come on and then draw to a conclusion can be a lengthy process	Have money/small change for refreshments?
Open channel to agency	From time to time proceedings may take an unexpected turn, or unanticipated requests may be made. In those cases, it will be necessary to have easy access to consultation and/or decision making with the agency	Is line manager fully briefed as to stage of proceedings? Do I have a direct dial telephone number to contact line manager if need arises?
Appropriate attire	Formal dress code operates	Is my outfit suitable *and* comfortable?

SUMMARY

The law makes provision for a range of powers that may be brought to bear to safeguard children. These include crisis or emergency measures (e.g. police protection and EPOs), short-term measures (interim care orders or interim supervision orders) and longer-term measures (e.g. care orders).

In considering applications in any family proceedings, the court is guided by a number of principles. The most important of these is that a child's welfare is of paramount consideration. Others include a presumption that orders will only be made where it can be demonstrated that making an order will positively contribute to a child's welfare ('no order principle'), ensuring that interventions in family life are kept to a minimum compatible with promoting and protecting the welfare of children (the welfare balance), and avoiding further harm to children through prolonged court proceedings (no undue delay).

In addition to these principles, courts are also granted a wide degree of flexibility in choice of which orders to make, whatever the original order sought.

Significant harm constitutes the test or threshold in initiating care proceedings.

The children's guardian is appointed by the court to act on the behalf of the child for the duration of family proceedings, to make a full enquiry into the child's circumstances and to report her findings and recommendations to the court. The children's guardian will also appoint a solicitor to represent the child.

Careful planning and a thorough assessment, including the reading of relevant research and a compilation of practice-based evidence, are essential pre-requisites to presenting a case in court.

FURTHER READING

Allen, N. (1998) *Making Sense of the Children Act: A guide for the social and welfare services*, 3rd edn, Chichester: John Wiley

Braye, S. and Preston-Shoot, M. (1997) *Practising Social Work Law*, 2nd edn, Basingstoke: Macmillan

Brayne, H. and Martin, G. (2000) *Law for Social Workers*, 6th edn, London: Blackstone Press

Cull, L. A. and Roche, J. (eds) (2001) *The Law and Social Work: Contemporary issues for practice* Basingstoke: Palgrave/Open University

Hill, M. and Aldgate, J. (eds) (1996) *Child Welfare Services: Developments in law, policy, practice and research* London: Jessica Kingsley

Home Office/Lord Chancellor/Crown Prosecution Service/Department of Health/The National Assembly for Wales (2002) *Achieving Best Evidence in Criminal Proceedings: Guidance for vulnerable or intimidated witnesses, including children* London: The Stationery Office

LASSL (2001) *Local Authority Social Services Letter* 02 The Children and Family Court Advisory and Support Service (CAFCASS) and Complaints about the Functioning of Child Protection Conferences

Lilley, R. C., Lambden, P. and Newdick, C. (2001) *Understanding the Human Rights Act: A tool kit for the health service* Abingdon: Radcliffe Medical

Lyon, C. (1999) The definition of, and legal and management responses to, the problem of child abuse in England and Wales. In M. Freeman (ed.) *Overcoming Child Abuse: A window on a world problem* Aldershot: Ashgate

McDonald, A. (1997) *Challenging Local Authority Decisions* Birmingham: Venture Press.

Vernon, S. (1998) *Social Work and the Law*, 3rd edn, London: Butterworths

Wattam, C. (1992) *Making a Case in Child Protection* Chichester: Wiley/NSPCC

www.carelaw.org.uk (a guide to the law for young people in care – NCH with Solicitor's Family Law Association) This online source for young people is very accessible and user friendly, and equally relevant for providing information to young people, their families and professionals working with them

REFERENCES

Brophy, J. with Bates, P., Brown, L., Cohen, S., Radcliffe, P. and Wale, C. J. (1999) Expert evidence in child protection litigation: Where do we go from here? In Department of Health (2001) *The Children Act Now. Messages from research* London: The Stationery Office

Department of Health (1991) *The Children Act Guidance and Regulations Volume 1 Court Orders* London: HMSO

Department of Health (2001) *The Children Act Now. Messages from research* London: The Stationery Office

CHAPTER 9

STAFF SUPERVISION, SUPPORT AND CONTINUING PROFESSIONAL DEVELOPMENT

LEARNING OBJECTIVES

By the end of this chapter you will be able to describe:

- The role and function of supervision in ensuring effective practice in child protection

- Sources of stress/distress in child protection work and methods for combating them

- The primary importance of self-care

- The benefits of (role and value) peer support

- Whistleblowing and individual responsibilities in relation to professional malpractice

- The role of continuing professional development.

Practitioners will look for a range of supports in delivering their services and developing their practice to safeguard children. These include:

- supervision
- self-care
- peer support
- continuing professional development (CPD).

SUPERVISION IN SAFEGUARDING CHILDREN

The importance of effective supervision to safeguarding children is indicated/evidenced in the many child death inquiries which have highlighted failures in supervision as contributory factors in avoidable deaths (Corby *et al.* 2001).

So, what exactly is supervision and how does it contribute to effective practice?

Supervision has traditionally served two broad functions: the oversight of practitioner work and the promotion and development of practitioner skills. In effect, supervision has sought to meet the administrative needs of the agency and the support and development of the individual worker. These are not of course disconnected; agencies depend upon the skills and knowledge of workers who must in turn have a means of demonstrating their accountability.

Ideal models of supervision typically portray the activity as a working partnership with both parties able to use the space, over and above the administrative 'core business' for more reflexive consideration of practice and policy issues and personal growth. In this jointly owned space, either or both parties would shape the agenda to reflect current needs. The nature of the partnership varies according to levels of practice experience and expertise. Practitioners develop from apprentice through novice to experienced practitioner, when the process is conceived as consultation between peers with the supervisor acting as a prompt to reflective practice. The differences are illustrated in Snapshots 9.1 and 9.2.

SNAPSHOT 9.1: THE BEGINNING PRACTITIONER AND SUPERVISION

Rose is a newly qualified social worker and has begun to work with a single mother of a 3-year-old girl about whom there are suspicions of neglect. Rose is experiencing difficulty in achieving an assessment because of the number of failed appointments, always with plausible explanations. When there is contact, Rose finds herself overwhelmed by the pressing concerns of the mother, whose own childhood was spent partly in care because of physical and sexual maltreatment. She feels like she is floundering and wants some direction and possibly concrete suggestions for how to 'get a grip' on the case.

SNAPSHOT 9.2: THE EXPERIENCED PRACTITIONER AND SUPERVISION

Raheela is a clinical psychologist with a large child-care practice and considerable practice experience. She is currently working with a 9-year-old boy whose emotional and behavioural problems appear resistant to accurate assessment and treatment. Her usual approaches do not

may emerge, such as significant harm. Rachel and her colleagues are to some extent 'boxed' by the title and the ethos of their own team and take pride in their approach to supporting families. In this they are supported by the positive comments of service users and by policy, guidance and research, which is driving a more proactive approach to addressing need. But children and their families are dynamic, situations and circumstances change, needs too can and do change, and the need for protection can emerge from time to time.

The change of gear, the racking up of a case formally identified as child and family support, to one of child protection indicated by the move to a section 47 enquiry, has implications for the relationship between workers, children and families and for the experiences of them as individuals. It may be hard for Rachel to avoid a sense of failure, that an ongoing intervention may be ineffective or is called into question and that she has not been alert to or has failed to make appropriate sense of the children's experiences or the father's capacity or fitness as a parent. For carers, the implications of such enquiries are clear: some if not all aspects of their parenting and the quality of care they provide are being questioned. Furthermore, s.47 enquiries may lead on to conferences and possible registration of children. That this is not an inevitable sequence may do nothing to prevent the spectre of such events.

On the other hand, unless the new information is appraised and previous assessments and plans tested, then there is a danger that opportunities for better protection of the children are missed. At the very least, discussing whether or not a s.47 enquiry is needed has the merit of updating an analysis of the situation. If Rachel can approach the discussion in an open, non-defensive way she has the opportunity to test her understanding and review the current merit of the services being provided. If a plan or a decision is convincing, evidenced by the positive information about the current well-being and safety of the child, then it is also persuasive. The recording of the discussion and the decision, with links in the chain of evidence and reasoning, represents informed and professional action.

The quality of supervision and the capacity of both parties to achieve a good working relationship will depend on a good understanding of the importance and function of supervision in safeguarding children. Supervision in child protection cases must necessarily be intrusive, to the extent that searching questions need to be asked about the nature and basis of decisions, and the performance of required tasks. But the process of intrusive supervision can raise difficulties for both practitioners and supervisors, if the former view it as a personal criticism of their work and the latter view it as denoting a lack of trust in staff. Issues of power can come to the fore in such situations.

POWER AND SUPERVISION

In Rachel's case, the change of supervisor may well be another factor. Supervision can never be merely an instrumental or mechanistic activity. Central to supervision is the relationship between supervisor and supervisee. An effective working relationship in supervision will depend on a number of factors, some of them entirely personal and idiosyncratic (some people get on more easily together), but it remains a professional working relationship for the purpose of ensuring that best practice is attained and maintained in safeguarding children. The onus is on both parties to nurture the professional relationship.

In this connection, it is worth considering the issue of power differentials. In most instances, supervision is provided by line managers, who undeniably have power by virtue of their position in the organisational structure. However, power is a complex feature and rarely best understood in crude polarities of all-powerful or powerless (Fook 2002). Certainly in the context of the supervision relationship, power is perhaps better understood in relation to the different values and legitimacy accorded to different sources of power. In addition to positional power associated with job specification, Plant (1987) identified four other sources, of which 'expert power' from hands-on experience and in-depth knowledge of a situation is a source from which most workers will be able to draw (see Development Activity 9.1). Thus Rachel can contribute to the discussion and analysis from her own prior involvement with and knowledge of the family, but she must also expect her new supervisor to draw on her experience to date of other families and other situations. If Rachel is successful in reframing the purpose and scope of the supervision meeting, then it may well turn out to be an important step in her continuing professional development.

DEVELOPMENT ACTIVITY 9.1: SOURCES OF POWER IN ORGANISATIONS

In thinking about the different sources of power, you may find it helpful to use the second column to audit those that are currently open to you

Source of power	Personal audit
POSITIONAL POWER *Position in hierarchy* Strictly, where you are in the formal pecking order of an organisation But the picture is more complex. Staff in the lowest echelons may have wide contact with staff and service users and may thereby acquire a more complete picture of the organisation than someone higher up. And members of staff who routinely disregard, for example, cleaners and caretakers are likely to discover that such staff have the power to make working conditions uncomfortable **COERCIVE POWER** *'Hire and Fire' capabilities* In most health and social care organisations power does not reside with one individual, but is constrained by disciplinary procedures.	

continued

Membership of a trade union or professional association redresses balance and reduces risk of oppressive use. Professionally qualified staff are a scarce and valuable resource and the option to sell those skills elsewhere is also a counterbalance

REWARD POWER
Ability to award pay increases, honorariums, promotion

Established salary scales, staff appraisal schemes and equal opportunities selection and recruitment policies are constraints

If rewards are taken to include intangibles, such as acknowledging and commending good practice and helpful support, and passing on constructive comments and compliments, then this power is open to all

EXPERT POWER
Derived from professional qualification, experience and role

In some settings, line managers and practitioners may not share the same professional training or discipline. Where they do, very often managers are further from their professional education and their hands-on practice knowledge may be more dated. This may be offset to some extent by length/breadth of experience

Practitioners' 'hands-on' practice and role give them direct experiences and knowledge of a specific child/family

Continuing professional development (CPD) via training courses, post-qualifying awards, practitioner research and reading increase expertise and this source of power/influence is an important element in professional assurance and authority. It is within the control of all to increase this source of power and influence

CONNECTION/ASSOCIATIONAL POWER
Vertical and horizontal

Derived from:

Professional and inter-professional networks and contacts

Regular attendance and participation in staff meetings	
Peer groups	
Membership of working parties and special interest groups and forums, sub-committees of ACPC, professional associations	
This source of power is freely available to those who choose to access it	

(Source: Plant 1987)

It is not possible in practice to separate entirely issues about quality and content of supervision from issues of availability and frequency. Snapshot 9.4 further illustrates potential issues.

SNAPSHOT 9.4:   DIFFICULTIES IN SUPERVISION 2

Sue is two years post-qualified and works in a children and families team whose work is predominantly drawn from 'heavy end' child protection and legal proceedings. The team are carrying one vacancy and one member of staff is on long-term sick leave. The majority of allocated cases involve children registered as at risk, subject to legal orders or subject to ongoing care proceedings. Sue's case load reflects the team's profile and she is key worker to seven registered at risk children from three families, supervising four children subject to care orders and currently working in two sets of care proceedings. In anticipation of an early conclusion to one of the sets of care proceedings, Sue had agreed she would pick up a new child protection case. But complications have emerged and the expected conclusion is now some way off and the further child protection registered case (6-month-old twins with a strong likelihood of care proceedings) is looming.

Sue feels continually under pressure and struggles to find time to meet administrative and recording requirements. She has found herself writing reports at home in order to meet deadlines. She worries that these pressures are affecting her face-to-face contact with children and their families, in terms of both time spent with them and the quality of the interaction. She feels that she often 'runs in, works through her set agenda for action and runs out', and worries that she might be missing critical features or factors about the safety or well-being of the children she is notionally safeguarding.

Sue missed out on her last supervision because she was detained in court and the previous supervision had been cut short because of an emergency. It is proving difficult to schedule her next supervision because of her diary commitments and her line manager has indicated that he will be busy with financial management and administrative returns for the next ten days. Sue is ambivalent about the missed supervisions. She is conscious that her case recordings are not up to date and doesn't welcome her shortcoming being scrutinised as it was in the last supervision, but she dreads another addition to her case load and needs to renegotiate this allocation.

Sue happens to be a social worker in a statutory social work setting, but her experiences and dilemmas are likely to find resonance with practitioners in a range of other settings and from other disciplines. There are a number of issues here:

- failure of supervision to occur
- the nature/purpose of supervision
- Sue's concerns about the quality of her work.

Most agencies will have policies on supervision, often linked to their Quality Assurance frameworks and/or Investors in People status. Supervision policies will generally cover:

- rights and responsibilities of staff in relation to supervision
- frequency of supervision
- recording of supervision
- issues of confidentiality and accountability
- issues of staff development or appraisal.

What such policies lack is the operational detail – how to make it happen, where exactly will it occur when space is at a premium, whether travel is concerned, who will take over supervision in the absence on leave or sick leave of line managers, who will cover for vacant posts or during reorganisations? These fine details can have heightened significance for peripatetic staff or those working remotely from line managers such as outreach workers and many school nurses. In such situations, lack of contact with the supervisor also has the tendency to reduce opportunities for informal supervision.

The increasing preoccupation of many first-line managers with a range of tasks associated with financial management and organisational matters reduces their availability to share elements of practice, for example, making visits with a practitioner as a means of offering support and presenting opportunities to get hands-on knowledge of a particular case. Sue might well feel better about her practice if she had it confirmed by her manager accompanying her and viewing her in operation.

In the case of Sue and her supervisor it appears that legitimate demands are conspiring against them sitting down to supervision. Prioritising is a routine feature of professional activity and staff are always subject to competing demands. However, it should be a matter of concern to both parties when supervision is continually the loser in balancing priorities. Failures in supervision are a recurring theme in child death inquiry reports. Rather than accepting the inevitable, either or both need to consider what steps could be taken to achieve supervision. Possible steps might include:

- both parties arranging to come into the office earlier, or to meet at the end of a day
- having a diary to hand and being assertive in identifying an early date for supervision
- making reference to a supervision contract if one exists or using a staff meeting to table discussion of the team adopting such contracts
- identifying the main points of concern in a memo and email and asking for an early date to discuss these matters.

If such tactics fail, then Sue should contact the next line manager up.

It is worth considering a broader context when examining issues concerning supervision, which may throw light on why sessions are not happening. In these circumstances, supervision for Sue who is only too aware that her recording is not up to date, may be yet another source of pressure and one to be avoided if she feels that it will demonstrate her failings rather than enable her to focus on her anxieties about the quality of practice interactions. Equally, of course, her supervisor may well be experiencing pressure from the knowledge that she is in dereliction of her duties.

To what extent it remains feasible or appropriate for professional social work supervision to be expected to contain aspects of pastoral support alongside administrative control and accountability is questionable. Some agencies have separated the two elements by appointing senior practitioners who, in addition to carrying their own case load, offer consultation and specialist practice support to staff, with managers retaining overall control and accountability.

Many practitioners may feel that they have such a relationship with a line manager supervisor. But it is not without its tensions. Most supervision occurs with line managers whose wider agenda includes staff appraisal and accountability to the organisation for service users and the wider staff group. Under these circumstances, and with the emphasis on demonstrating competence, it requires a deal of trust and respect to voice anxieties or highlight perceived deficiencies. SemBhi and Livingston (2000), for example, surveyed trainee psychiatrists' views about the supervision relationship. Respondents felt it was:

> Impossible to use (the) supervisor as pastoral carer . . . you want the boss to think you're efficient, competent and dedicated . . . (It is) unrealistic to express negative feelings about the job . . . at some point we will ask them for a reference.
>
> (pp. 376–379)

One consequence of this emphasis on administrative functions of supervision may be to increase the sense of pressure or leave staff feeling devalued or helpless. In these circumstances, it is easy for a 'culture of stress' (Thompson *et al.* 1996: 659) to become endemic, affecting both supervisors and supervised. In the case of Sue and her line manager, it seems likely that both are caught up in this culture and resolving it may prove difficult. However, unless the issue is identified, no steps can be taken. Raising matters as items at staff meetings, particularly if accompanied by constructive suggestions for resolution, is one possible way forward.

Where self-esteem and self-efficacy have been eroded by stress, this kind of initiative may be difficult to achieve without smaller steps preceding it. Sue is certainly feeling overwhelmed by work and it may be difficult for her to know to what extent this is legitimate, in the sense that her workload is too high, or whether this reflects her feelings of anxiety and dissatisfaction with how she is conducting her work – on the run and with predetermined agendas. In the absence of supervision or a reflective component in supervision, Sue needs to take responsibility for addressing this issue. If the team operates a workload weighting scheme, she may find it helpful to compare her workload with this. Since the team are two staff down, it may be that work is being spread to cover those gaps. Taking on work in those situations can seem the only way to ensure that vulnerable children and their families receive a service, but it may be ill-conceived if the service is delivered by a harassed professional.

Staff can feel overwhelmed by work for reasons other than sheer volume. As a matter of urgency, Sue needs to take time to identify all the issues and identify her goals. That is, she needs to apply some of the skills she brings to her social work practice to her present predicament. She might begin by reflecting on her ambivalence about missed supervision. In doing this, she should address her self-care and the availability of support.

The child protection system safeguards a substantial number of children and the knowledge that one's work can make a positive contribution to the lives of especially vulnerable and disadvantaged children or their families makes the work worthwhile and rewarding for many practitioners. Others may be deterred from considering this area of practice, perceiving it as highly stressful and potentially dangerous to staff. Though it is important to be alert to potential stresses, and even more important to know how to manage them, it is equally important not to give a distorted picture. Whatever the context or setting, working with vulnerable and disadvantaged service users and the range of associated risks is productive of stress.

NISW SURVEY OF STRESS AND VIOLENCE IN SOCIAL WORK WORKPLACES

The National Institute of Social Work's survey (Balloch et al. 1998) gives the most comprehensive overview to date of social workplace stress and violence and provides a helpful perspective, by highlighting the complexity of the picture. The results of this suggest that the workers at highest risk for both violence and stress were residential workers, especially those with management responsibilities. Managers and staff with responsibilities for elders (excluding home care workers) and also younger members of staff in any area were at above average risk for stress. Male staff were at higher risk of suffering violence.

These findings confirm that social care, as might be expected of any activity which engages with and involves responsibilities for vulnerable service users, is productive of stress and may give rise to violence. Many factors are involved in determining whether or not work will give rise to uncomfortable or dysfunctional levels of stress – organisational, interpersonal, task-specific social and personal factors all operate as mediators of stress. Some areas of practice suit one worker better than another, and though being a volunteer does not guarantee against stress, being a conscript will certainly create stress.

It is also worth noting that stress is an ordinary feature of life, particularly in the context of safeguarding children where parents themselves are often under stress. Problems may arise if we experience stress overload (too many stressors) and our coping mechanisms fail. Though evidence of stress may sometimes be manifest to colleagues and managers who may be able to help, it may not. Ultimately, individual professionals have a primary duty of self-care – how can we help others if we cannot help ourselves?

THE 'BUCKET THEORY'

Practitioners must be alert to and develop ways of managing the emotional wear and tear of close proximity with the pain and distress of children and family members, with its consequent potential implications for professional well-being and effective practice. In terms of Hawkins and Shohet's (1992) bucket theory, it is important that workers know the size of their emotional 'bucket' and that emotional buckets are not overfilled:

> All helping organizations are, by their very nature, importing distress, disturbance, fragmentation and need. This is usually met by individual workers, who, if they are empathically relating to the client's distress, will experience parallel distress and sometimes disturbance and fragmentation within themselves. How much of this they will be able to contain and work through will depend on the size of their emotional container (or bucket), will relate to their personality, their emotional maturity and professional development, the amount of pressure and stress they are currently under at work and at home and, most important, the quality and regularity of the supervision they receive.
>
> (Hawkins and Shohet 1992: 121)

It seems highly likely that Sue's emotional bucket is overfilled and she is rightly concerned about the possible implications for her practice. What are Sue's responsibilities to herself, what are her needs for support, what can she expect in the way of supervision and how can it help her in her predicament?

In Sue's case, she is feeling overwhelmed by the cases she has and concerned that she may be failing the children she is working to safeguard. Though supervision is clearly a critical issue, it may also be queried to what extent Sue's predicament is exacerbated by isolation from, or resistance to, using peer support. Research (Sayers 1991, Thompson *et al.* 1996) reinforces what many practitioners know from experience – the importance and value of support from colleagues. This is not the same as friendship, although friendships may arise in work situations and social functions may be used to promote staff relations. Professional support fulfils a number of functions:

- a sounding-board on which to bounce ideas
- a listening ear to allow for anxieties/tensions to be ventilated
- a source of validation/confirmation ('yes – we have felt like that')
- a resource to draw on in terms of different knowledge and experience
- an alternative perspective – the very best colleague support provides constructive challenges to our practice and reduces the risk of one-dimensional or stuck thinking jeopardising effective work with children and their families.

When teams are short-staffed, or where practitioners operate in isolated situations, this traditional and valuable resource is diminished, to the detriment of professional practice development. In these circumstances, practitioners will need to consider and plan for alternative professional support. Some possibilities include:

- identifying a mentor within the agency
- joining any local or regional forums with a child care or child maltreatment focus
- joining an online discussion group with a similar focus
- joining or setting up informal discussion groups with colleagues from other teams/agencies
- negotiating outside/specialist consultation for particular pieces of stuck or difficult work
- using all opportunities to network.

STRESS IN CHILD PROTECTION WORK

Working with children and their families in the context of concerns about risk of significant harm places heavy demands on practitioners. Holding case responsibility brings not merely the instrumental tasks of monitoring, information gathering and recording, but also the complex task of making sense of the information in a context in which confusion, uncertainty and heightened feelings of the participants will be a factor. Simultaneously, practitioners must retain a close focus on the well-being and safety of the child and endeavour to build or maintain an effective working relationship with a parent or carer who may be causing or contributing harm to that child. Furthermore, practitioners must achieve this in conformity with the current guidance, policy and procedures, which often dictate tight time-scales, while remaining mindful that lapses in those respects may lead to adverse results for children, their families, agencies and practitioners.

In addition, practitioners must be alert to and on guard against potential secondary or vicarious traumatisation, which can lead to failures to act or intervene effectively where violence is a feature in the lives and situations of children and their families. Stanley and Goddard (2002), for example, argue on the basis of research over a fourteen-year period into child death cases that there are links between the violence experienced by the child victims and social work failures in practice interventions.

Development Activity 9.2 summarises different contexts in which stress may arise (sites of stressors) and highlights some of the triggers. You may find it helpful to use the third column to discuss and note down strategies you could use to combat stress in your own working life.

Given the complexity of the demands, practitioners must become skilled in managing the range of stressors and must make use of, and have a right to use, effective support mechanisms. Unmanaged, what is an appropriate focus on 'getting it right' can become a chronic anxiety about getting it wrong. This can lead to defensive practice that fails children and their families rather than safeguarding them. It may also give rise to worker burn-out and/or absence on sick leave. Consequently, it is in the interests of all that stressors be minimised where that is possible and managed effectively where it is not. Supervision is at the heart of those support mechanisms.

DEVELOPMENT ACTIVITY 9.2: MANAGING STRESS IN CHILD PROTECTION WORK

Sites of stressors	Triggers	My strategies for managing potential stress
Organisational constraints	Tight timescales Heavy workloads Scant resources Organisational culture/ethos	
Inter-professional relations	Limited availability/ accessibility of colleague support Limited availability/ accessibility of line manager Nature of inter-professional relations	
Emotional overload (Hawkins and Shoet 1992)	Routine close proximity to pain and distress of children and their families	
Secondary or vicarious trauma (Stanley and Goddard 2002)	Close proximity to children and families where violence is a feature	
Section 8 reviews and public inquiries, public opinion and media portrayals	45+ Inquiries since Maria Colwell Inquiry in 1974 Denigration and demonising of child care social workers	

ACCOUNTABILITY AND WHISTLEBLOWING

Thus far the focus has been on the accountability of an individual worker and individual supervisor. But professional accountability has a dimension beyond the individual (Snapshot 9.5).

SNAPSHOT 9.5:
ACCOUNTABILITY AND WHISTLEBLOWING

Hassiba is recently qualified and new to the long-term children's team. During Richard's absence on holiday, Hassiba is asked to cover his home visits to Leila, 17 years old, and Dannae, her 2-year-old daughter. Dannae was registered before birth arising from concerns about Laila's self-neglect and substance misuse, and was de-registered three months ago, but the case remains open for ongoing family support. When Hassiba made her visit, she had to knock for some time before Leila eventually answered the door, wearing only her knickers. Hassiba was rather taken aback and asked whether there had been some confusion about the time she was to call. Leila laughed and said 'Don't mind me being starkers – Richard never turns a hair.' Dannae is playing with soft toys in a playpen in the sitting room and appears to be alert, adequately clothed, clean and happy. Leila seems very cheerful and happy to chat, but the recurring theme of her conversation is Richard, and Hassiba forms the impression that Leila has a crush on him. As Hassiba comes to leave, she notices a large framed photograph of Leila, 'topless' and evidently posed. Leila tells her that she frequently models for such photos at a local camera club, but she had that one framed because it was a particular favourite of Richard's.

Hassiba feels uneasy and confused as she leaves to keep another appointment elsewhere. Her worries are magnified because she knows from office conversations that Richard is a keen amateur photographer.

It may seem quite demanding enough in the context of child protection to be responsible for one's own practice, without taking on board the issue of colleagues' practice. But, as is evident from accounts of the institutional abuse of children (Corby *et al.* 2001), children may be harmed directly or indirectly by the actions of colleagues or the failure of colleagues to address malpractice or to express concerns.

In the abstract, there are no dilemmas; there is an overriding duty on all professionals to safeguard children and to give paramountcy to their interests. But in practice it may present many difficulties, even where there may be established protocols or procedures. Clearly the details will vary depending on the setting (residential, community, daycare or fieldwork) and the context (health, social care or education professional or shared discipline) but the common elements remain – how to safeguard children when the risk is posed by professionals.

In this instance, Hassiba is grappling with a deep sense of unease that something is amiss and that there are things to be explained and accounted for, but who is to explain and how are they to be accounted for? She has made her visit and seen Dannae, whom Hassiba had thought of as the real client, and who gave her no cause for concern. Nevertheless, she remains uneasy about Leila, who seems to her potentially very vulnerable to exploitation and wonders about the nature of the relationship with Richard. She tries to formulate her concerns as she writes up the visit and struggles to find the balance between reporting and commenting. She would like to discuss her concerns but is not comfortable with raising them with her line manager, with whom Richard appears to have a very friendly relationship, or with colleagues who are very busy and always preoccupied with their own work. Hassiba may well be hampered by her feelings about her status and credibility as a relatively new member of the team and recently qualified. Other factors may include feelings of loyalty to a colleague, reluctance about appearing critical of a colleague, and diffidence about publicly making a fool of herself if her unease is unfounded. All of these factors may be heightened when the context is inter-professional.

The ingredients are there for Hassiba to suppress her unease and do nothing beyond a brief recording showing the date and time of her visit and her observations of Dannae. But, if Hassiba is to exercise accountability, she must find the determination and the strategy for doing so, notwithstanding the tensions and dilemmas this poses. Though Hassiba may perceive Dannae to be the 'real' client, Laila, though a mother, is also entitled, at 17, to the protection of the Children Act 1989. It will be helpful for her to recall that all professional relationships with service users involve issues of power and are required to be transparent.

Both agency and staff need to be aware of anything that may be adverse to vulnerable clients so that appropriate steps can be taken to safeguard the service user or ensure the professional reputation of staff if malpractice is not an issue. In the first instance Hassiba has to reflect on and identify the elements giving rise to her unease – what was said, what was seen and the context – and use this as the basis for an accurate recording which includes her appraisal of any concerns. Once this constitutes part of the official records of the agency, then she can use it as a basis for briefing both Richard and their line manager. The content and outcome of such briefings will also constitute part of the record and ensure accountability and transparency. By recording first, the risks of cover-up by pressure on individuals or massaging information are reduced.

Where risk or harm to children and young people arises from institutional maltreatment, the silencing of individual staff members is a very real problem. In such situations, staff can have recourse to their trade unions or professional associations. Though doing something may be uncomfortable, doing nothing cannot be an option. Taylor, herself a whistleblower over the maltreatment of young people in residential care, asserts:

> Whatever enactments arise, and however much we set standards and parameters of conduct to counteract the downside of human nature, in the final analysis the responsibility for their enforcement and promotion devolves upon us all. The social work profession, charged with the protection of children, must find itself a moral centre, allow its members the right to be responsible for their actions, and face the great dilemma of members policing each other as well as its clients, and of discharging that responsibility in an honourable manner.
>
> (1998: 62)

CONTINUING PROFESSIONAL DEVELOPMENT

The Care Standards Act 2000 has brought about major changes in the regulation and registration of social care workers, bringing them finally in line with colleagues in health. For the first time, social workers and social care workers will be required to conform to a code of conduct setting out standards to be maintained by professionals. In addition, the Training Organisation for the Personal Social Services has drafted National Occupational Standards that will govern the qualification and, subsequently, post-qualification of all staff engaged in personal social services. These occupational standards identify Key Roles associated with different categories of staff, with each Key Role supported by a number of detailed sub-units or practice requirements.

The Key Roles for beginning social workers are as follows:

Key Role 1   Undertake the full range of social work duties, powers and responsibilities with individuals, families and communities
Key Role 2   Manage own social work practice within the organisation
Key Role 3   Develop and maintain professional relationships within and outside the organisation
Key Role 4   Develop self, and be accountable for own practice within the social work role
Key Role 5   Contribute to the development of social work practice and the social work role.

These standards apply across the whole of social work/social care and are seen as a basis for continuing professional development (CPD). But what exactly does CPD mean for busy practitioners, struggling perhaps in teams that are understaffed, and how is it to be achieved?

Lifelong learning and the need to maintain up-to-date skills are frequent themes of current policy. The summary report of the Independent Health Review (2002) of health service provision and the Part 8 process following the death of Lauren Wright highlighted the importance of staff maintaining up-to-date knowledge and skills to ensure best practice in safeguarding children. Traditional views of much social care development have tended to concentrate on specific, often formal training, a kind of ladder that staff have climbed, a rung at a time until they have reached the level considered commensurate with the post they are undertaking. The concept of lifelong learning shifts the emphasis to enabling staff to meet ever-changing challenges presented by new service developments and requirements. Health professionals have always been required to keep their knowledge and skills updated, but the pace of change and the expansion of knowledge and research about safeguarding children represent a continuing challenge.

Both staff and employers have responsibilities in continuing professional development and the post-qualification (PQ) awards and advanced awards (AAPQ) framework in social work constitutes one contributory element. Unless, however, there is recognition by all parties that learning and development are necessary features of professional life, practice and organisations, there is a real danger of a mechanistic approach, with staff trudging along the treadmill and agencies scoring numbers on QA frameworks. There needs in fact to be a culture shift. Increasingly, employers will have to commit to being learning organisations and practitioners will have to be open and pro-active in achieving their learning.

Being alert to learning and development opportunities wherever and whenever they arise is part of the openness to learning that marks the professional who takes responsibility for their own CPD. Central to CPD are:

- personal/professional development and progression
- contributing to the development of the professional knowledge base.

The relationship between the continuing development of the occupation and that of the individual needs to be interconnected, the growth of the individual informed by and informing the profession and both informed by the children and their families who are served by them. There is always an element of fortuity within CPD – the opportunity to participate in a piece of training, or tackle a particular case or undertake a new project – and all good practitioners recognise and acknowledge the important contribution of individual service users to the development of their practice.

Nevertheless, it is important not to depend exclusively on such fortuity. Taking responsibility for your own CPD demands a more methodical approach. A good way of beginning is by an audit of your current knowledge and skills using the table in Development Activity 9.3.

PRACTITIONER RESEARCH AND CPD FOR SAFEGUARDING CHILDREN

The practice knowledge base for safeguarding children is expanding and changing over time, informed by the range of research, large-scale quantitative surveys, or smaller-scale qualitative ones. Though research is a distinct professional activity in its own right, practitioners too have a contribution to make to this expansion and development of the knowledge base. There are many ways in which practitioners can contribute. These include:

- routinely listening to children and ensuring that their voices are heard
- careful evaluation of outcomes of own practice, building up a database of personal professional experience
- dissemination of that experiential database through peer support, special interest groups and professional association membership, mentoring and practice teaching
- writing up practice experiences (with suitable permissions and safeguards for services users) for publication in professional journals
- designing/engaging in specific small-scale research on pressing professional issues.

DEVELOPMENT ACTIVITY 9.3: CPD AUDIT

Current knowledge/ skills	Examples	Strengths	Development needs	How/When to be achieved
Professional/ Educational qualification	Qualifying degree PQ1 PQ child care Advanced awards			
Law/guidance/ policy for practice	CA 1989 HRA Working together			
Working with children	Knowledge of child development Skills in communicating Knowledge/ skills about disability			
Working with conflict	Knowledge of potential conflict triggers Familiarity with conflict tactics scales Skills in defusing tensions			
Resource initiation – locality/ community	Mapping local resources Networking skills			
Locating information – research	Use eLsc and other databases Take professional journals			
Self-awareness	Understand own thresholds for coping Can distinguish stress and distress in self			

KEY LEARNING

Working with maltreated children and their families is demanding work. In addition to high standards of practice, staff may be at risk of direct or indirect violence or 'vicarious trauma'.

Staff must be able to recognise and be alert to indicators of vicarious or secondary trauma in themselves and colleagues and take steps to seek appropriate support/relief. Staff have a primary duty of self-care and will need to be able to distinguish their own distress from ordinary stress.

Peers and inter-disciplinary colleagues are a potential source of expertise and constructive challenge and all staff should be open to such learning opportunities.

Though agencies have a duty to ensure provision for appropriate line management supervision, staff have a responsibility for using supervision or asserting the need for it where organisational provision fails.

Knowledge about safeguarding children is dynamic. Effective practice cannot depend on fading knowledge gained in qualifying courses but depends on keeping up to date with current best practice. Staff and agencies have a joint responsibility for identifying development needs and ensuring that they are met.

Safeguarding children requires all staff to take responsibility for addressing issues of professional malpractice.

Staff have responsibilities for their own CPD and must aim to keep up to date with developments in research and practice and contribute to those developments.

Staff should take a methodical approach to their own CPD.

FURTHER READING

British Association of Social Workers (1995) *Guidance for Social Services on Free Expression of Staff Concerns* Birmingham: British Association of Social Workers

Collings, J. A. and Murray, P. J. (1996) Predictors of stress amongst social workers: An empirical study *British Journal of Social Work* 26: 375–387

Godsby Waters, J. (1992) *The Supervision of Child Protection Work* London: Avebury

Rushton, A. and Nathan, J. (1996) The supervision of child protection work *British Journal of Social Work* 26: 357–374

Sawdon, C. and Sawdon, D. (1995) The supervision partnership. In J. Pritchard (ed.) *Good Practice in Supervision: Statutory and voluntary organisations* London: Jessica Kingsley

REFERENCES

Balloch, S., Pahl, J. and McLean, J. (1998) Working in the social services: Job satisfaction, stress and violence *British Journal of Social Work* 28, 3: 329–350

Corby, B., Doig, A. and Roberts, V. (2001) *Public Inquiries into Abuse of Children in Residential Care* London: Jessica Kingsley Press

Fook, J. (2002) *Social Work: Critical theory and practice* London: Sage

Hawkins, P. and Shohet, R. (1992) *Supervision in the Helping Professions* Buckingham: Open University Press

NISW (1995) *Supervision and the Organisation: A survey of current practice* London: NISW

Plant, R. (1987) *Managing Change and Making It Stick* London: Collins

Sayers, J. (1991) Talking about child protection: stress and supervision *Practice* 5, 2: 1991

SemBhi, S. and Livingstone, G. (2000) What trainees think about supervision *Psychiatric Bulletin* 24, 10: 376–379

Stanley, J. and Goddard, C. (2002) *In the Firing Line: Violence and power in child protection work* Chichester: John Wiley

Taylor, A. (1998) Hostages to fortune: The abuse of children in care. In G. Hunt (ed.) *Whistleblowing in the Social Services: Public accountability and professional practice* London: Arnold

Thompson, N., Stradling, S., Murphy, M. and O'Neill, P. (1996) Stress and organizational culture *British Journal of Social Work* 26: 647–665

Thorpe, D. (1994) *Evaluating Child Protection* Buckingham: Open University Press

Tunstill, J. and Aldgate, J. (2000) *Services for Children in Need: From policy to practice* London: The Stationery Office

INDEX